DIVIDED DYNAMISM

The Diplomacy of Separated Nations

Germany, Korea, China

SECOND EDITION

John J. Metzler

University Press of America,® Inc.
Lanham · Boulder · New York · Toronto · Plymouth, UK

Copyright © 2014 by
University Press of America,® Inc.
4501 Forbes Boulevard
Suite 200
Lanham, Maryland 20706
UPA Acquisitions Department (301) 459-3366

10 Thornbury Road
Plymouth PL6 7PP
United Kingdom

Library of Congress Control Number: 2014930806
ISBN: 978-0-7618-6345-8 (clothbound : alk. paper)
ISBN: 978-0-7618-6346-5 (paperback : alk. paper)
eISBN: 978-0-7618-6347-2

To my Mother

Contents

List of Figures and Tables

Acknowledgements

Confucius once opined, "The Longest Journey begins with the first step." My writing odyssey had its inception as a longtime United Nations correspondent--watching and chronicling the political postures of divided nations. This books genesis came amid popping champagne corks celebrating the collapse of the Berlin Wall. Its continuing passion ensued from visiting Hong Kong during the heady days of the Hong Kong handover.

Thanks again go to the United Nations Dag Hammarskjold Library in New York where the staff courteously and expeditiously helped me wade thorough both the Official Documents Collections as well as the Periodical Room. My perennial visits to Periodicals, a virtual treasure trove of publications from around the world, was made doubly rewarding by the tireless and able staff who made my trips both professionally rewarding and personally pleasurable.

So too at the National Archives in Washington D.C. where there never seems sufficient time to unearth historic gems in the State Department files collection, or to the National Library in Paris, one of Europe's premier collections. Equally the University of Texas at Austin has allowed use of maps from their Perry-Castaneda Library Collection which have enhanced the volume.

Naturally there are scores of off-the-record briefings and discussions by officials, diplomats, and scholars from the states involved; due to the often sensitive nature of many discussions, their names cannot be listed here. They know who they are.

To my manuscript readers, such as Dr. Frederick W. Marks III who exhibited unflappable perseverance in deciphering my editorial foibles and then making positive suggestions, I owe special gratitude.

A particular vote of thanks and confidence goes to Louise McKenzie and the St. John's University E Studio & Instructional Technology division who tirelessly helped with the formatting revision and the technical foibles of the book.

Of course assistance from one's own University is paramount to success; I thank my department; Government and Politics as well as the Institute of Asian Studies for providing me the lectern from which to teach and the atmosphere in which to work.

Heartfelt thanks go to my own family who not only ceaselessly supported my efforts but also endured the seemingly endless editorial trek to the fruition of this account.

Introduction

The cultural vitality, economic prosperity, and political dynamism of a Nation, is best expressed through national unity in peace and freedom. Partition thus divides the peoples and refocuses many valuable national talents and capital towards both State survival and international justification. By dividing an historic nation through geographic separation, the best talents and philosophical aspirations are often separated into two politically competing states. Those nations have thus seen their intrinsic dynamism divided.

For divided nations, unification policy has thus emerged as a central political philosophy, an *ethos*, of the State. Yet in its practical application, this philosophy has often been molded and formed to fit political objectives; namely, advancing the agenda of the ruling party or oligarchy of the respective governments.

This account proceeds from the traditional view, espoused by the late French President Charles de Gaulle, "The State may change, but the Nation remains the same." Clearly de Gaulle's classic paradigm cogently and brilliantly illustrates the dilemma of six separate States representing three distinct Nations. Despite often amazing changes in political regimes and philosophies, the *ethnos*, nature of the peoples and their historic nation, has in each of the countries, remained constant and generally intact.

In Germany's case, unification became a *sine qua non* of all major political parties. Yet, while keeping the goal of Unification in a near Olympian chimera, the practical political realities reflected the priorities of the ruling party. Konrad Adenauer spoke memorably about "no unity before freedom." Willy Brandt brought the discussion onto the humanitarian level of bringing socio/economic improvements to the lives of individual GDR citizens. Making Germany's division more livable was the leitmotif of a 1984 *Bundestag* multiparty resolution "To make the consequences of partition more bearable."

Chancellor Helmut Schmidt perhaps best summed up Bonn's policies vis-a-vis the GDR: *Prudence, Persistence, and Predictability.*

In inverse order the GDR policies evolved from "German unity in socialism," through an enforcement of the *status quo*; namely, a firm and guaranteed niche for the "socialist state on German soil" alongside other European states including the Federal Republic.

For the FRG, the State view of unification was translated into practical action by the Party in power; CDU, SPD, or CDU/CSU/FDP. In the GDR, the view of unification reflected a Party/State approach; namely, the SED's unquestioned ideological interpretation of Unity.

Bonn's *Deutschlandpolitik* while carefully calibrated, nonetheless reflected both domestic political concerns and the international climate. While unity of the nation was an unquestioned political nostrum by all of the players, in practical application it reflected the political policies. Nonetheless, Bonn achieved a remarkable *modus vivendi* with East Berlin through values integration. Political changes in the East/West power structure combined with the sweeping 1989 revolutions, allowed the political window for unity.

For Koreans, the unity of the divided peninsula was claimed by both the ROK and the DPRK albeit through fundamentally different formulas. Rhetoric was turned into reality in 1950 when North Korea attacked the South in a bellicose bid for unification. Piercing memories of the war and Pyongyang's refusal to renounce the military option to reunify Korea, had long poisoned relations between two Korean governments. Equally, though the peninsula was divided by foreign hands, the regime that attacked the ROK in 1950 is still led by the same Kim family *power clique.*

Tepid reconciliation in the once glacial inter-Korean relations has emerged as a direct result of a meltdown in the Cold War in East Asia. The once frozen logjam is broken and there is some localized movement. Nonetheless, Korean unity, as in the German case, will emerge in parallel with events stemming from the geopolitical shifts of the major neighboring powers.

Unity, although a political mantra of both Seoul and Pyongyang, reflects the individual formulae of the ROK and DPRK. During the days of Syngman Rhee, South Korea enunciated a militant reunification policy. This was ironically tempered by the military regimes of Park Chung Hee and later Chun Doo Hwan who while speaking about unity, favored building an economic power base in South Korea. Roh Tae Woo, encouraged by international events, encouraged official contacts but failed to make appreciable changes in humanitarian contacts, travel, and trade.

For the ROK, a Military/State approach kept the issue of unification in unquestioned lockstep out of party politics until Roh's rule. With the civilian governments and increasing democratization of society, Seoul began to reflect a fractious political approach to unity.

For the DPRK, Party/State, unification polity reflects the gospel according to Kim. What changes have emerged result not from political party pressures inside the DPRK but rather a recalibration of Pyongyang's tactics. This movement results from geopolitical shifts in the East Asian balance of power.

Importantly, despite the initial euphoria after German unity, Koreans soon surmised that peninsular unification was not a political given but a comprehensive challenge. Despite polite calls for Korean unification, regional states fear its emergence. Equally regional powers may write the political script.

Will a war precede unity? How economically strong would a Korea of seventy million people be? Given South Korea's global standing, one assumes that reunification with the North would, adding the resources and population to a unified Korea, create a new East Asian power. This is not necessarily the case. Unity may eventually usher in a new age of prosperity but may cause medium term disequilibrium.

In China's case, the unification discussion rests on the premise of a country divided as a result of Chinese hands. Present political positions are the result of the outcome of the civil war which ended in 1949. The two Chinese states see themselves as historic and constitutional heirs to the nation. And contrary to North Korea or East Germany where the communist State was an appendage of larger power interests, the PRC in itself is the power player.

Interestingly, while the two Korea's have managed relations in a hierarchical structure mode with little perceptible humanitarian or economic movement between them, the two Chinas manage relations through a two-tier structure. While high profile ties and formal concessions across the Taiwan Straits are few, on a practical *de facto* side, business and tourist links are booming. Thus while Taipei has carefully managed ties with the Mainland, the private sector, with official acquiescence, has opened a plethora of contacts with fellow Chinese promoting values integration.

Official ROC policy retains the mode of State/Rightful Heir. Contrary to Korea, the ROC's government until 2000, remained religiously committed to the unification of China, a totality which it ruled until 1949. The KMT viewed themselves as "rightful heir" the nationalist government has espoused an evolutionary unification policy which evolved from the militant "re-conquering of the Mainland" to a more conciliatory "One China, two political entities."

Taiwan's democratic multiparty politics have drastically challenged the orthodoxy of this State/Rightful Heir Party policy.

Official PRC policy has evolved from an equally militant stance to bring "Taiwan back to the Motherland" to a seemingly conciliatory offer; "One Country, Two Systems." Ominously, Beijing has *never renounced* the use of force against Taiwan. Yet since the PRC state has never ruled Taiwan province, its claim rests on the political goal to unify all China under the Beijing center.

Here, too, flexibility has emerged; PRC unification policy rests on the dictums of the Party/State approach. In other words, the formula rests with the Chinese Communist Party, the sole legal political entity and decision making apparatus.

Chinese unity will be much more a direct consequence of intra-Chinese concurrence between the ROC and PRC. While the great powers have an abiding interest in its outcome, its stimulus will be based on a domestic national reconciliation rather than accord among regional allies.

China's unity in freedom would represent the apotheosis of democracy in the world's most populous country. In the shorter run, Chinese unity would mean combining some of the world's biggest markets with some of the world's most talented people.

Chinese unification would usher in a new East Asian dynamic and quite possibly open a new global vortex of both economic and political power.

In the grand scheme, unification policies of the six states considered reflect less of a national *ethos* than a changing political and ideological policy of the respective governments. Dynamic competition between the opposing state players vying for the mantle of national legitimacy remains pronounced and potentially destabilizing. This volume attempts to view the merits of the individual state players and then attempt to synthesize the case for *national unity* to overcome the despair of national division.

A prudent historical view teaches that the grand goal of unity can be postponed but not precluded. History has a way of correcting itself.

The still divided *nations,* see their social, cultural, economic and political personalities split by division. Thus the *dynamism* of the Korean and Chinese *nations*, still politically *divided*, is yet to be realized.

Chapter 1

Federal Republic of Germany/The West

First Divided, First United—An Introduction

The geopolitical and moral *Gotterdammerung* of the Third Reich in 1945, saw Germany as a decimated and shattered nation. Military defeat was compounded by the psychological context of occupation and partition by the victorious allies—Britain, France, the U.S. and USSR.

Division was envisaged by the London Protocol, outlined at the Yalta Conference and codified by the Potsdam Declaration, in which the Allies became the administrators of Germany—the British in the North; French in the Southwest; U.S. in the Central/South, and the Soviets in the East. This compendium provided a practical military solution to neutralizing the Reich, but as importantly, created a new political cartography on German soil.

The commonly cited West/East divide in which the Allies controlled the Western Zone and the Soviets the Eastern Zone, with each of the Four Powers sharing equal responsibilities in the capital city Berlin, became an indelible socio/political landmark which was to affect Germany for a generation until unification in 1990. As a historical note, even following the cessation of the formal Zonal partition in 1949 and the creation of the pluralistic Federal Republic of Germany (FRG) in the West, and the totalitarian German Democratic Republic (GDR) in the East, the Zones represented a *de jure* military occupation which was to evolve into a *de facto* protectorate for the respective governments in both Bonn and East Berlin.

In the German model, division thus emerged from military defeat, subsequent occupation, and later integration of each of the German states into the respective framework of East/West political/security alliances. Importantly, Germany's partition resulted from external forces crushing Hitler's totalitarian regime; the divide was not the result of a civil war, a religious conflict, or a social revolution. In this context, the German nation a people sharing a common history, territory, language, ethnic homogeneity was nonetheless divided into two separate states.

Yet in the early Cold War years, both German states became the cutting edge of diplomatic and defense policies of their respective alliances and thus realistically lost unification policy flexibility short of what Chancellor Konrad Adenauer, *DerAlter*, called "a great and unexpected political event." That event, nearly a quarter century after Adenauer died, was the collapse of communism and an acquiescence of the Soviet Union to permit the once unthinkable; a Germany joined in freedom, peace and unity.

From Zonal Rule to Sovereignty/1945-55

The unconditional surrender of the German military in May 1945 did not nullify the status of Germany in international law. The victorious powers assumed governmental authority in Germany, but under the Hague convention of 1907, the victors had rights as well as responsibilities in the occupied country.[1]

The Yalta Conference outlined plans for "complete disarmament, demilitarization, and dismemberment of Germany." In June 1945 the Allies issued three declarations in which they assumed supreme authority with respect to Germany, including all government powers, the establishment of an Allied Control Council, and the physical division of Germany into four occupation zones, with Berlin into four sectors. Later in Potsdam, outside Berlin, the allied leaders set forth specific policies. In the splendid neo-Tudor setting of the *Cecilienhof*, President Harry Truman, Marshall Josef Stalin, and Prime Minister Winston Churchill and later Clement Atlee, framed the postwar policy parameters; political organization, reparations, and border questions were outlined.

"What is meant by Germany?" queried Churchill rhetorically. "What she has become after the war," said Stalin sardonically, "the country no longer exists, it is merely four occupied zones." Yet, President Truman pressed for Germany's borders of 1937. The discussion ironically echoed Metternich's jibe at the Congress of Vienna, "the German people" and "Germany" were abstract concepts.[2]

Significantly while the Potsdam declaration stressed the need for economic decentralization for the purpose of eliminating the present excessive concentration of economic power, the settlement divided Germany, as reduced by the war, into four zones under the Allied occupation.[3]

Even before the end of the war, the U.S. State Department argued against the partition of Germany, not least of all for its Europe-wide economic consequences. State stressed that "the disruption of German economic unity would carry with it grave dangers for the economic stability of Europe as a whole and not merely Germany." In place of partition, State recommended a federal system of government in the entire territory."[4]

Despite the continuing socio/economic privations from the World War throughout Europe, the American initiated Marshall Plan would prove to be a significant step towards creating economic equilibrium. So, too, would the currency reforms in which the *Deutsche Mark* (DM) was introduced in the three western zones and sectors of Berlin. As importantly, constitutional reforms were added to the new political landscape.

The absence of a central German administration envisaged in the Potsdam Declaration saw Allied authorities take the initiative in drafting and adopting state constitutions in the U.S., Soviet and French zones. American influence in the constitutions is reflected in the emphasis upon individual rights and an independent judiciary. Indeed the decision to establish a federal west German state with strong *Lander* and a weak central government reflected the views of many European countries. According to Dr. Heinrich Winkler, "France in particular, insisted on a strongly federalized state, not because it corresponded to French ideas of political organization, but because Paris wanted to prevent any future concentration of power east of the Rhine."[5]

A constituent Assembly was thus authorized and duly convened. By July 1948, the Minister Presidents of the West German federated states withdrew their earlier objections to a separate entity and agreed to proceed with the *creation of a new political state*. The Basic Law was later promulgated on 23 May 1949.

FRG unification policy was rooted *de jure* in the *Grundgesetz* (Basic Law) the foundation on which the Bonn government was built. The Preamble states: "The entire German people are called upon to achieve in free self-determination the unity and freedom of Germany." Yet the jurisdiction of the Basic Law extended only to the *Laender* (federal states) controlled by West Germany. Article 23, however, adds that for the other *Laender*, "In other parts of Germany it shall be put into force on their accession."

Thus through Article 23, the FRG's constitutional order extended eastwards upon unification. The Basic Law was to remain in effect only until reunification (article 146) and adoption of a nationwide constitution; thus the lexicon Basic Law rather than Constitution.[6]

Following free elections in the western zone, the formal creation of the Federal Republic in September 1949 ushered in a new era in German history. Germany was slowly shedding the control of the Allied occupation and emerging as a state reborn. Importantly, in the early Adenauer era, policy goals rested as much on rebuilding the rubble of Germany's international reputation as on restoring her cities and factories. As Adenauer so eloquently described the postwar political situation, "Germany is situated in the very heart of Europe...geographically we found ourselves between two power blocs whose political concepts were radically opposed. We had to choose either one or the other lest we be crushed between them." He continued, "There was only one direction for us if we were to preserve our political freedom, our individual liberty, our security which was a way of life that has been ours for centuries. We had to oppose steadfastly and with resolve any pressure from the East."[7]

Rejecting the poisoned chalice of German *unification in neutralism* offered by Stalin in 1952, *Der Alter* chose instead to firmly anchor the nascent FRG to the West, the noted *Westbindungs* policy. Consolidation of the democracy, sovereignty, defense deterrence, and above all confidence building with the Western occupiers/allies, became political cornerstones for Adenauer's policy in the early 1950's.

The common aim of a reunited Germany enjoying a liberal democratic constitution was agreed on by both Bonn and the Western allies. As importantly, the allies offered Bonn a unique political benediction—"the three governments consider the Government of the Federal Republic as the only German Government freely and legitimately constituted and therefore entitled to speak for Germany as the representative of the German people in international affairs."[8]

In 1952, in Article 2 of the Treaty on Germany between Bonn and the three Allied powers, Germany gained the "full power of a sovereign state." With the subsequent softening of the occupation, Bonn's Foreign Ministry shifted towards a Euro/Atlantic policy in which integration, trust, and regained respectability became the order of the day. Membership in the European Council (June 1950), the European Steel and Coal Community (April 1951), the Treaty on Germany (May 1952), and the Paris Treaty (October 1954), were all part of a growing reintegration of the FRG into democratic Europe. Clearly, the 1954 Paris Agreements among the Western powers and Germany set the stage for true sovereignty. Ending of the Occupation statutes and abolishing the Allied High Commission opened the way for the Federal Republic to have full authority of a sovereign state over its internal and external affairs."[9]

NATO membership (May 1955), admission to the European Economic Community (EEC), and EUROATOM (March 1957), are among the major policy milestones of the Adenauer era. Gaining Observer Status to the United Nations in 1952 and admittance to the World Bank and International Monetary Fund (IMF) were significant multilateral policy successes.

Military statutes hindering full German sovereignty were amended to the point where on 5 May 1955, Adenauer proudly proclaimed, "The Occupation is over. The Federal Republic of Germany is truly sovereign." A hierarchy of philosophical values, freedom, peace, and unity (*Freiheit, Friedens, Einigheit*) became the FRG's foundations. Adenauer prioritized the linkage of West Germany with the democratic West. European integration and *Westbindung*, especially integration into NATO, were seen as crucial to FRG security concerns.[10]

Adenauer wrote prophetically, "Only through the fast integration of the Federal Republic into the Western alliance system can we obtain active support for our unification policy. Only through confidence in our reliability as an alliance partner, can we make our Western allies agree to a contractual commitment to strive jointly for the unification of Germany in peace and freedom." He added, "It is our task to dispel the distrust toward the German people that has prevailed throughout the Western world. The basic prerequisite for that was an unequivocal, unwavering, pro-Western position."[11]

Chancellor Adenauer took his party and the Federal Republic down the path of Western European cooperation. Centerpiece in this policy was his *Frankreichpolitik*, a model of reconciliation with his neighbor France, which served as the model of his successors' *Deutschland* and *Ostpolitik* after 1969.

This model had three components relates Dr. Edwina Campbell: pursuit of bilateral relations within a multi-lateral framework; second, confronting the implications of recent German history through an implementation of confidence building measures; and finally, a major component of the strategy of reconciliation going beyond formal ties between Bonn and Paris encouraging private groups and local governments to establish people-to-people relations. As Adenauer's policies began to take shape, Paris came gradually to believe that the economic and political strength of the Federal Republic did not detract from, but enhanced its own security.[12]

A landmark Franco/German Treaty was signed in 1963 between President Charles de Gaulle and Chancellor Konrad Adenauer.

From the Hallstein Doctrine to *Ostpolitik*

Adenauer's prudent policies began to rebuild the tarnished trust between a discredited Germany and the Allies. "American concentration on the integration of Western Germany in the Western European community rests on cogent political and military considerations," opined a Brookings report in 1954, adding, ...Militarily the objective has been to complete the defense structure of Western Europe by the inclusion of the manpower and resources of Western Germany; by creating a bastion in the heart of Europe, and above all, by securing an indispensable base for the continued stationing of American and British forces on the Continent."[13]

Consequently, a policy of non-recognition of the GDR, became a *sine que non* for FRG policy. In December 1955, West German Foreign Minister Heinrich von Brentano proclaimed the Hallstein Doctrine in effect, an enforcement clause of the One Germany policy. Named after the noted legal scholar and Rector of Frankfurt University, Walter Hallstein who was serving as Adenauer's State Secretary in the Foreign Ministry, the Doctrine initiated a policy of diplomatic isolation of the GDR, insuring that Bonn would sever diplomatic and economic ties with countries recognizing the GDR. In 1957, for example, Bonn broke ties with Yugoslavia over Belgrade's recognition of East Berlin; in 1963 ties were severed with Cuba over Castro's recognition of the East Berlin communists.

The Hallstein Doctrine was singularly successful. Between 1950 and 1969 only two countries, Yugoslavia and Cuba, had recognized the East Berlin communists. Bonn's tripartite policy of One Germany, non-recognition of the GDR, and the international isolation of the GDR, put the East Berlin authorities in diplomatic checkmate. Given West Germany's growing economic power, the policy offered Bonn an unparalleled diplomatic advantage and a corresponding obstacle to East Berlin.

In the context of the 1950's bipolar confrontation in Central Europe, and with the support of the conservative pro-West Christian Democratic (CDU) government in Bonn, the "One Germany" policies and their effective enforcement through the Hallstein Doctrine proved sustainable. Moreover, events in Eastern Europe in the wake of Stalin's death and especially the communist crackdown on workers in East Berlin on 17 June 1953 demanding German Unity, along with the brutal Soviet smashing of the Hungarian revolution in November 1956, conclusively proved, at least in the perception of many policymakers, that Moscow's East German comrades were unstable and perhaps short lived.

For two decades between 1949-1969, the Christian Democratic Union (CDU) governed Germany. Until 1963, Konrad Adenauer had a firm hand on the helm of the new democratic ship of state exerting a major influence on the foreign policy of the Federal Republic. In the face of stubborn opposition from the Social Democrats (SPD), he forged systematic and lasting ties with the West whether in NATO membership, close links with the U.S., or a pledge to European unity.

As President Dwight D Eisenhower wrote in his Memoirs *Waging Peace*, "Chancellor Konrad Adenauer, the man who more than any other, had been responsible for the rapid rehabilitation of West Germany and for her solid, courageous alignment with Western philosophy." Eisenhower added of Adenauer, "he had staked his political career on West German individual sovereignty, association with the West, and eventual reunification of Germany. Even the slightest kind of recognition of East Germany's government "was anathema to him."[14]

As Karl Kaiser, Director of the German Society for Foreign Affairs stated, "For Adenauer and the majority of Germans, freedom, not unity, was the priority of national policy. Germany could have had unity without freedom in the post-war period, but that course was rejected."[15]

The building of the Berlin Wall commencing on 13 August 1961, harshly reinforced the riveting realities of Konrad Adenauer's *Westbindung* policy. While West Germany was isolating its Eastern neighbor politically, the communists in the German Democratic Republic were physically sealing off East Berlin from the West. The graphic Cold War confrontations at Checkpoint Charlie, the crossing-point on *Friedrichstrasse* from the American Sector in West Berlin to the socialist side of the city, witnessed tense face-offs between U.S. forces and the Soviets.

The Berlin Wall, while hardly a result of Adenauer's policies, was in effect their ironic vindication. The "free" sectors of Germany, in this case Berlin, were what the Chancellor liked to call "a magnet" for the Germans in the East. So effective was the pull that the communists had to bar exit from the Worker's Republic. Above all the profound psychological shock of this physical barrier illustrated the painful reality that Germany was not only divided but was the nexus of overlapping East/West security concerns in the heart of Europe. The Berlin crisis illustrated the danger of the FRG being in the crosshairs of U.S./Soviet geopolitical confrontation.

Not since the Berlin Blockade in 1949 had the German capital been in the forefront of East/West tensions. During June of 1963 President John F. Kennedy, addressing 300,000 cheering free citizens at *Rathaus Schoneberg*, made the case for a closer Atlantic Partnership of the U.S. and Europe. Historian Frederick Kempe states, "His speech outside West Berlin's City Hall would be the most emotional and powerful he would ever deliver abroad." In the company of Adenauer and Brandt, Kennedy proclaimed in solidarity, "Ich bin ein Berliner."[16]

It was during the tenure of Willy Brandt, the feisty former Berlin Mayor and new Social Democratic Chancellor (SPD), that the historic rapprochement, *Ostpolitik,* began with Eastern Europe and the USSR. On his election in October 1969, Brandt announced a "departure for completely new shores." *Deutschlandpolitik*, the policy towards the GDR, was likewise invigorated. As Brandt wrote while Foreign Minister in the previous Grand Coalition government, "It is our task to work for better neighborliness between the two parts of Germany. We want to lessen the tragedy of the division, under which many Germans are suffering bitterly. We want to maintain and strengthen the feeling of belonging together."[17]

Lessening East/West tensions and Bonn's consummate desire to rebuild trust and respect with Eastern Europe comprised the general framework for *Ostpolitik*. Eastern Policy was based on two key premises—that only on the basis of the FRG membership in NATO and European Community could the policy be pursued and secondly that since the federal government is committed to human rights, detente cannot blur the contrasts between the FRG and the socialist states.

Specifically Brandt signed landmark treaties with the Soviet Union and Poland in 1970. After heated debate, the Bonn *Bundestag* ratified both treaties in 1972. The Treaty of Moscow required the FRG to "respect without any reservation the territorial integrity of all states in Europe in their present borders." The Polish Treaty acknowledged the *Oder/Neisse Line*, established by the Potsdam Conference, as Poland's Western boundary.[18]

While Willy Brandt conceded to the existence of two *de facto* German states, he insisted that his government would never accept the GDR as a foreign country. He advanced the thesis that two German states existed within the single German nation. In a reversal of the Hallstein Doctrine, Brandt announced that the FRG would no longer oppose recognition of the GDR by third states.[19]

The *demarche* on the Doctrine was soon evident. Bonn soon established diplomatic relations with Bulgaria, Czechoslovakia, Hungary, People's China, and restored them with Cuba. Regarding the GDR, the Brandt policies did not offer *de jure* diplomatic relations but rather a workable *modus vivendi* between two parts of the German nation. The Four Power Agreement on Berlin (1971), the Transit Treaty (1971), and the Traffic Treaty (1972), brought a human dimension to the closed and hermetically sealed frontier.

Egon Bahr, the Chancellor's confidant and an architect of *Ostpolitik* spoke of "a change through rapprochement" with East Germany. In December 1972, the Basic Treaty of Relations between the FRG/GDR outlined a workable coexistence between two parts of the estranged German family. It likewise offered the GDR rulers a level of legitimacy never achieved since 1949. In short the Treaty enumerated the following points:

> Article 1 agrees that the two states would develop "normal good neighborly relations based on equality."
> Article 2 affirms the U.N. Charter as the basis of their conduct.
> Article 3 agrees to settle differences without the threat or use of force.
> Article 4 affirms that neither German state would represent the other abroad.
> Article 5 outlines that the states would respect each other's independence in domestic and external affairs.
> Article 6 stresses that jurisdiction of each of the two states is confined to its own territory.
> Article 7 offers cooperation in fields of economics, science, traffic, post and telecommunications.
> Article 8 agrees that the two states would exchange permanent Representatives.[20]

The Basic Treaty gave the GDR's Socialist Unity Party (SED) what it had sought since 1949 and what Bonn had always denied it; recognition of its separate existence and of its full equality with Federal Republic. Bonn still refused to recognize the GDR as a state under international law but the Treaty made it respectable for all the Western states, both in and outside NATO, to open ties with the GDR. A rush towards recognition commenced.[21]

The Basic Treaty outlined a series of concessions between "two states of the German nation." The GDR opened diplomatic relations with twenty new states in December 1972. "Thirteen more followed in January 1973 including NATO members Italy and the Netherlands. The USA formally recognized the GDR in 1974. By 1978 East Germany maintained official relations with 123 countries," states Winkler. As Germany's dual statehood was now recognized internationally, both states were free to join the United Nations.[22]

Despite the Basic Treaty, the FRG Federal Constitutional Court ruled that "While there is no alternative to the Treaty...the Treaty does not abandon the continued existence of Germany as a legal entity; it avoids characterization of the German Democratic Republic as a foreign state; it upholds the unity of the German Nation and German nationality; it does not recognize the German Democratic Republic...it does not legally or practically obstruct a reunification."[23]

The era of detente between Germany and the East, while shadowed by the Soviets crushing of the Prague Spring in Czechoslovakia in August 1968, was brightened by Brandt's boundless optimism that emerging U.S./USSR detente offered Germany the opportunity and the obligation to open lines of communication and commerce long closed. The Brandt era, ending in an espionage scandal in 1974, nonetheless codified a legal regime between both German governments. The *de facto* West/East division, had assumed an evolving *de jure* character.

NATO/ Anchor of Security

German diplomacy, much less defense policy, would not have maintained a credible level of deterrence in the absence of strong treaty ties with the West. In the bitterest days of the Cold War and Berlin Blockade, one must recall that the Allied Powers themselves (Britain, France and the U.S.) provided the shield against any Soviet intimidation of or aggression into West Germany.

In July 1949, when the French National Assembly was debating ratification of the North Atlantic Treaty, Robert Schuman, Minister of Foreign Affairs declared, "As regards Germany I have been asked, can she become a member of the Atlantic Pact? This is a question which does not arise in the present or the future...it is unthinkable either from France's viewpoint or that of her allies, that Germany should be allowed to join the Atlantic Pact for the purpose of defending herself or helping to defend other nations."

By October 1950, French policy had made a *volte face*. Premier Rene Plevan stated to the Assembly, "Germany although not a party to the Atlantic treaty is nonetheless a beneficiary of the security system for which it provides. It is therefore right that she should make a contribution to the defense of Western Europe."[24]

The catalyst for the constitutional changes allowing German defense forces, the *Bundeswehr,* and subsequent NATO membership was the Korean war. Much as the defeated and occupied Japan had been rehabilitated as a necessary and strategically placed ally, so too had Germany profited politically by events in Korea.

Adenauer feared that Stalin would attempt the same tactics in Germany as he did in Korea; namely, to encourage one part of a disunited nation to "liberate" the other. "The Federal Republic was in a very dangerous situation indeed," he warned, "We were totally unarmed and we had no defense forces of our own. If the Russian zone army were to attack with tanks, the consequences of their advance were easy to foresee. The population of West Germany would stay neutral in the face of this advancing army, first and foremost for psychological reasons, because the troops would be Germans."[25]

Marshall Stalin tried to neutralize Germany and went so far as to offer unification in exchange for neutralization. German unity within neutralism, was spurned by the Allies and the Adenauer government. "The neutralization of Germany would mean not only the loss of its potential, but a significant weakening of the present defensive organization of Western Europe," reflected Washington's views.[26]

Stalin was in his last days but at the *zenith* of his power. Shortly thereafter, amid feverish behind the scenes diplomacy, Britain, France and U.S. offered Bonn a favorable Treaty which was signed in Paris on 23 October 1954, expanding German sovereignty and opening the door to full NATO membership. Here too external forces, in this case the Moscow's March 1954 move granting the GDR *sovereignty* and "calling for intra German elections, rapprochement and the conclusion of a peace treaty," became the catalyst. The USSR proposal buffeting the U.S., Britain, and France, went so far as to say the occupation was "incompatible with the national right of the German people," and was "one of the main obstacles on the road to national reunion of Germany." From a domestic view, the point was equally fraught with friction; Gustav Heinemann, in an open letter to Adenauer in early 1954 advised, "The Soviet Union will not pull out of its Zone and simply give up to a government determined to integrate itself into the Western bloc."[27]

Leading up to the Paris Conference, U.S. Secretary of State John Foster Dulles negotiated the plan for the integration of German forces into NATO just as he inspired enough confidence in Adenauer to win support for a German army. Intricate and sensitive agreements had to be approved by Bonn, as well as Paris, in view of the recent World War.[28]

When the allies met in Paris in October of 1954, the way was clear for FRG's accession to the NATO alliance. The Paris Agreement stated in Article 1, "The government of the United States of America shall on behalf of all the Parties communicate to the Government of the Federal Republic of Germany an invitation to accede to the North Atlantic Treaty."[29]

As Chancellor Adenauer advised, "We were threatened; we were the object of the foreign policy of others; we were unable to defend ourselves. This state of affairs would change fundamentally and rapidly after the ratification of the treaties." Two days before Bonn joined NATO he said, "We will now be a member of the strongest alliance in history. It will bring us reunification."[30]

U.S. Secretary of State John Foster Dulles had adroitly managed Germany's acceptance into NATO thus assuring the Atlantic Alliance a firm continental anchor. From Adenauer's view, admission to NATO in May 1955, just a decade after the German defeat in WWII, was both a major political victory for Bonn and, as importantly but often overlooked, a reinforcement of the fledgling Atlantic Alliance with a geographically crucial and militarily significant component. If one views the Soviet political pressures to keep Germany out of NATO in inverse proportion to Western goals achieved by Bonn's accession, one sees the brilliant stroke achieved by German membership. The Austrian State Treaty concluded shortly thereafter in provided an extraordinary *encore.*

Politically Dulles stressed German unity "should be a major objective of the West" adding that the "attitude of the West towards the Soviet Union should be determined by the endeavor to promote the unification of Germany in freedom."[31]

As crucial was the extraordinary rapprochement between Chancellor Adenauer and French President Charles de Gaulle. Despite wartime animosity de Gaulle spoke of both France and Germany being ancient nations, "the Gauls and Germania" as having a common destiny in a united Europe. The General spoke of the permanence of peoples and the character of the nation. De Gaulle's s classic dictum, "The State may change but the Nation remains the same," illustrated this point splendidly. Franco/German ties, exemplified by the 1963 Treaty of Friendship, proved this exceedingly well.[32]

For the *Bundeswehr*, defense planning was firmly based on membership in the Atlantic Alliance, specifically the geopolitical integration of Germany with North American and European partners. The Harmel Report emerging from a 1967 NATO Ministerial meeting stated the political context of Germany's situation, "A final and stable settlement in Europe is not possible without a solution to the German Question, which is the nucleus of current tension in Europe."

Defense Minister Hans Apel, writing in Bonn's 1979 *White Paper*, clearly stated, "To our country, security is achievable only if it is founded on the broad firm bedrock of Western unity of purpose. The North Atlantic Alliance has been guaranteeing the security of Europe for thirty years." Integration inside NATO became *sine qua non* for the security of the Federal Republic, facing off massive Warsaw Pact armies based on the GDR/CSSR territory. The German share of NATO forces in the Central Front was an impressive 50 percent of land forces, 30 percent of the combat aircraft, and 100 percent of Baltic Naval forces. In fact, the *Bundeswehr* provided the largest contingent of conventional forces in NATO Europe.[33]

Total *Bundeswehr* strength stood at 490,000 in 1980 and 545,000 at unification in 1990. Defense expenditures as a percent of GDP stood at 4.1 % in 1980 and 3.6% at unification. On the Central Front, only France allocated similar resources for defense. U.S. defense spending in the same period averaged 5.8%. By 1998, the *Bundeswehr* totalled 333,000 troops with spending slashed to 1.5% of GDP.[34]

During the tenure of Chancellor Helmut Schmidt, Bonn's role in the Alliance grew militarily while at the same time balancing the need for realistic and prudent detente between Bonn and the East. Nonetheless, NATO's 1979 Dual Track Decision to deploy U.S. nuclear Cruise and Pershing missiles in Europe to counter Soviet mobile SS-20 missiles already in place, while at the same time pursuing arms negotiations with Moscow, set the stage for conflict. The Dual Track brought a severe political strain on the Alliance and Helmut Schmidt in particular; the decision induced a severe split in the SPD thus causing a collapse of Chancellor Schmidt's government in 1982.

Though the plan was initiated by the Europeans, a vociferous peace movement in Germany primarily blamed the U.S. for the defense decision. Only after the end of the Cold War was the wisdom of this policy fully realized.

There has been a significant evolution in Germany's security policy since 1990. Military spending and status of forces clearly reflects a post-Unification and post-Cold War policy. By 2012 the *Bundeswehr* strength has slipped to 251,465. Defense spending had fallen to 1.34% of GDP as compared to the

NATO average of 1.6% or the United States average of 4.77%. The government has formally phased out military conscription.

The Atlantic Alliance and the European Union remain the foundations of German security. Thus the Berlin government has played an active role in the Afghanistan deployment with over 5,000 troops as well as with 1,500 deployed in Kosovo.[35] The crucial triad of an American defense umbrella, NATO membership, and Bonn's own formidable military stature, safeguarded the FRG's economic growth and prosperity throughout the Cold War and reunification.

EEC Integration/ The *Wirtsshaftswunder* and Prosperity

The other pillar of the Federal Republic's policy has been that of the European Community/Union. Having been a signatory of the 1957 Treaty of Rome, the FRG had joined Western Europe's economic bloc, and as a result, been further integrated into continental unity. By the time Bonn joined the Europe of the Six, Germany' post war miracle was moving apace guided by the able hand of Dr. Ludwig Erhard. The West German economy relied on market forces instead of controls to accomplish recovery from the wartime devastation. Erhard, a disciple of the economist Wilhelm Roepke, knew that the controversial cure of introducing a new currency, and as importantly, lifting constricting wage and price controls, would reinvigorate Germany's production and potential.

The guiding concept was *Soziale Marktwirtschaft*, social market economy, the principles of which were translated into practice by Erhard who became Adenauer's Minister of Economics. One fundamental principle of the market economy was the creation of a stable currency. In 1948, the reform took place with the *Deutsche* Mark (DM) issued at a rate of one tenth of the old currency. Besides the remarkable success of monetary reform, the Marshall Plan, and Germany's membership in the Organization for European Economic Cooperation facilitated foreign trade. Postwar monetary and fiscal policies were oriented towards production.[36]

The Marshall Plan, aimed at European recovery, offered significant benefits for Germany. "In politico-psychological terms the Marshall Plan helped to stabilize confidence in the Deutsche Mark and the new economic order that was emerging," advised Alan Kramer, adding "It was moreover of fundamental importance for West Germany's growth from the beginning of the 1950's that the Marshall Plan helped West Germany in its return to foreign trade." Of a cumulative total of $14 billion in aid between 1948-1952, Germany received $1.4 billion or ten percent. Britain was the largest recipient at $3.4 billion and France at $2.8 billion. Importantly *only* the Western Zone received aid.[37]

Foreign economic assistance, a focused recovery plan, and unfaltering hard work became the secret of the FRG's *aufbau*, the rebuilding. Fiscal responsibility was its midwife.

Export driven growth saw the FRG's real GNP surpass pre-war levels in the aggregate by 1950. West Germany's auto manufacturing soon regained its place in the world. In 1938, some 357,000 motor vehicles were manufactured in Germany of which 22 percent were exported. By 1955 the level of exports stood as five times higher than 1938. Equally GNP growth was 10.4 percent in 1955. Per capita incomes rose significantly over pre-war levels.[38]

The 1950's emerged as a period of high economic growth and marked a return to normalcy in West Germany. The time of reconstruction was over; the economy entered a period of consolidation. GNP growth in the 1950's averaged 8 percent and during the 1960's 4.4 percent. Industrial growth rates averaged 10 percent in the 1950's and 5.2 percent in the 1960's; the highest in Europe. By the early 1960's the FRG was one of the world's economic powers.[39]

By the early 1970's with a population of 60 million people and a GNP of $260 billion, the FRG had become Europe's largest national market. Still the Brandt era saw a rise in social market expectations, higher inflation from the petroleum crisis, and growing state intervention in the traditionally free market.

As the economy matured, the traditionally high growth rates fell from the four percent a year between 1967-1977, to only 1.5 percent over the next decade. By the time of unification, growth had been steady but strong at an average of 1.9 percent between 1985-1993. Germany's 1993 GNP stood at $ 1.9 trillion.[40]

Regarding the GDR, the Treaty of Rome contains a Protocol relating to German "internal trade and connected problems," or less cryptically, East Germany. Called the "part of Germany which the Basic Law does not apply," the clause allowed the GDR to gain *de facto* membership in the Common Market. As Alfred Grosser related, the European Community did not have an eastern frontier because the dividing line between the two Germanies was a frontier only in the eyes of the GDR.[41]

After the rapprochement between Bonn and East Berlin during the Brandt era, intra-German trade flourished. Quietly, trade between other EEC members and the GDR also expanded under the *de jure* framework of the Treaty of Rome. Intra-German trade was never banned; equally it was tariff-free. In 1955, two-way trade amounted to more than DM 1 billion; in 1960 the trade reached DM 2 billion, in 1970 DM 4.5 billion, in 1980 DM 11.7 billion, in 1985 DM 16.7 billion, and in 1989 DM 15.3 billion. [42]

Intra-German commerce was a small fraction of the FRG's total trade. Yet, the FRG was the GDR's second largest trading partner after the Soviet Union. Bonn's trade with the GDR was a mere two percent of the FRG's global trade. Trade with the Federal Republic made up ten percent of GDR total trade. Bonn never viewed this exchange as foreign commerce, thus intra-German trade was tariff-free. Importantly the GDR could sell agricultural produce through the FRG avoiding steep EEC levies. Much of the GDR trade westward was in effect un-tariffed "exports" to such EEC members as France.[43]

During the 1980's consistent economic growth and an expansion of the social state brought the FRG unprecedented prosperity but signaled looming competitiveness problems. Direct wages and benefits for workers in West Germany were almost double those in the United States or Britain. Yet, trying to harmonize such a social system with the reunified eastern *laender* posed serious structural hurdles both internally and *vis-a-vis* Germany's global standing.

Unification proved a mixed economic blessing. The level of subsidy to the East, which accounts for a near albatross to the overall German GDP, has barely fallen since 1990. Yet wages remained high and Germany enjoyed the status of being one of the global economy's major exporters. The German economy grew by 3% in 2000, its best performance since the post-reunification boom at the start of the 1990's. Yet, by 2002 growth was flat at 0.0% only to rise to 0.8% in 2005 and 2.5% in 2007 on the verge of the global recession.[44]

United Nations Admission/A Forum for Competition

The Federal Republic of Germany and the German Democratic Republic, two separate *states* representing the German *nation*, were concurrently admitted into the United Nations in 1973. Both Bonn and East Berlin had the backing of their respective allies and the assurance of non-use of Security Council vetoes. Germany's path towards United Nations membership was highly complicated, representing a tripartite legal problem.

First it had to bypass the U.N. Charter's "Enemy States clause" precluding German membership as well as that of Finland, Hungary, Italy and Japan. Article 53, the "Enemy States clause" applies to any state which during the Second World War has been an enemy of any signatory of the present Charter."[45]

The *second* issue arose from the nature of Bonn's juridical claim to represent the *entire* German nation. In order to isolate the communist controlled East German regime, and to avoid international recognition of Germany's division, Bonn used the Hallstein Doctrine through which the Federal Republic would break relations with states who recognized East Germany. Curiously, Bonn had maintained diplomatic relations with Moscow since 1955, stemming from Adenauer's landmark visit in which he negotiated the return of thousands of German POW's from the Second World War.

Revision of the Hallstein Doctrine in the mid-1960's led to Bonn's recognition of Eastern European countries and the emergence of *Ostpolitik*. If the Federal Republic was open to diplomatic ties with communist countries concurrently recognized by East Berlin, then by implication, Bonn's assertion to represent all Germany was in doubt. Soon there would be momentum towards intra-German relations.[46]

Not until the December 1972 Basic Treaty between the two German governments regulating their coexistence, could an application for U.N. membership be considered.

Thirdly the Allied powers, Britain, France, the U.S. and USSR as the former occupying powers, held incumbent rights which infringed on full German sovereignty, especially over the divided capital of Berlin.[47]

Curiously Stalin's famous Diplomatic Note on Germany in March 1952 allowing unity in neutralism contained an oft-forgotten passage concerning the

U.N. The Note, addressed to the Three Western Powers, said that "the government concluding a peace treaty with Germany will support an application of Germany as a member of the United Nations."[48]

In view of this complicated juridical situation, both German states maintained U.N. Observer status. They keenly participated in the work of the organization via its specialized agencies. At U.N. Headquarters in New York, the FRG established an Observer Mission in 1952; the GDR opened its New York Observer Mission in 1972. As importantly, Bonn established a Mission in Geneva to facilitate contact with specialized agencies. The FRG became a member of the World Health Organization (WHO), the United Nations Educational, Scientific and Cultural Organization (UNESCO) and the International Labor Organization (ILO) in 1951, International Civil Aviation Organization (ICAO) in 1956, and the International Atomic Energy Agency (IAEA) in 1957.[49]

On the eve of full membership, the inevitable question hung like a diplomatic Damocles sword. Would one of the Security Council's Permanent members veto the admission of one of the German states?

While Bonn was protected by the diplomatic and defense support of three permanent members (Britain, France, U.S.), East Berlin was supported by the Soviet Union. Significantly, neither German state had applied for formal admission until 1973 and thus had not faced the barrages of membership vetoes as had South Korea and South Vietnam. In June, the representatives of Britain, France, the U.S., and USSR, transmitted a letter to the Security Council acknowledging both German governments' request for membership and signaling acceptance by the Four Powers, which "support the applications for membership," but which, "shall in no way affect the rights and responsibilities of the Four Powers" in Germany.[50]

On 22 June 1973, the Security Council approved separately the requests for admission by the FRG and the GDR. On 18 September 1973, the General Assembly voted to extend U.N. membership to the two German states. Both the FRG and GDR subsequently pursued an active but separate political agenda until unification in October 1990.[51]

Interestingly, the FRG's Ambassador Rudigar von Wechmar was elected as President of the 35th U.N. General Assembly in 1980. The GDR's Ambassador Peter Florin held the same honor for the 42nd General Assembly in 1987. No other divided nation's representative has ever held such a prestigious U.N. post until South Korea did so in 2001.

The 1970's witnessed a surge of Third World radicalism and its corresponding reverberations in the United Nations. The General Assembly agenda became embroiled with issues primarily concerning Israel, South Africa, and increasingly the U.S. The PLO had gained legitimacy through Observer status, and was actively using its position to radicalize the Middle East debate. For both Germanys, admission into this political *maelstrom* nonetheless proved a political blessing. For Bonn, UN membership was a cherished policy goal. Likewise, having achieved a new level of diplomatic legitimacy, East Germany profited disproportionately by embracing radical causes and countries in a politically rarefied setting which was uniquely able to grandstand GDR policies.

For the FRG, no longer trying to isolate the GDR diplomatically but rather confront it with a system of values, and increasingly a package of foreign aid disbursements, the policies were decidedly different. Both bilateral and multilateral development assistance to Third World states emerged as a key component of Bonn's foreign policy before and after U.N. admission. Although Bonn's official development assistance (ODA) was originally viewed as a political instrument to counter both Soviet and GDR inroads in the Third World, from the Brandt era the sums reflected a social priority to battle poverty; namely, a "basic needs" approach to rural development.

While never reaching the ODA target of 0.7 percent of GNP, the FRG nonetheless became a major global donor. ODA flows rose from $223 million in 1960, to $602 million in 1970, to $3.56 billion in 1980. By 1988, the figure had reached $4.73 billion. Unification did not drastically cut Germany's global generosity.[52]

In 2011 Germany's ODA reached $14.5 billion. Germany has a policy of giving two-thirds of its ODA as bilateral and one third as multilateral. The Berlin government ODA/GNI target reached 0.4% in 2011. Major recipient countries include China, India, Afghanistan and Brazil.[53]

U.N. budget assessments for member states are calculated by a complex formula involving GNP, commercial balance, and national reserves, the so-called "sacred triangle." In 1973, when both German states joined the world body, the Committee on Contributions assessed the FRG 7.1 percent ($18.6 million) and the GDR 1.2 percent ($3.2 million). In 1989, the last full year in which both states held separate seats, the FRG was assessed 8.08 percent ($60 million) and GDR 1.28 percent ($13 million). Total regular and voluntary contributions for Bonn reached $407 million and for East Berlin, $35 million. By 2012, Germany's share of the assessed U.N. budget stood at 7.14 percent or $201 million.[54]

Commensurate with its financial contributions to the United Nations system, the government's of Kohl, Schroeder, and Merkel have continued to press for a permanent seat on the Security Council as to have equal status in the political arena.

Unification: Bonn's View

While the Basic Law's Preamble called on the German people to "achieve in free self-determination the unity and freedom of Germany," thus setting the legal framework of the Bonn government's unification strategy, the ebb and flow of East/West political tensions constituted the realistic agenda for unity.

Chancellor Adenauer had always stressed, "One of the supreme goals of the policy of the Federal Republic was to bring about unification in freedom." The Federal Ministry for Inner-German Relations was established with his government and later renamed the Federal Ministry for the Total German Question. Its central mandate was to work for the *unity of the Nation.* "The German question is open; Freedom is the core of the German question," was Adenauer's *modus* in dealing with the division.[55]

Deutschlandpolitik, Bonn's policy towards East Berlin, mandated by the Basic Law, was predicated on peacefully solving of the *German Question* through self-determination. Former Inner-German Relations Minister Heinrich Windelen stated, "A *Deutschlandpolitik* that gave absolute priority to unity at the expense of freedom and self-determination would run counter to the reunification commitment embodied in the Basic Law."[56]

Thus, starting with the Grand Coalition 1966-69 and gaining speed with Willy Brandt's *Ostpolitik* in the early 1970's, the locus of *Deutschlandpolitik* changed. While the 1972 Inner/German Basic Treaty created the framework for socio/economic developments between Bonn and East Berlin, both SPD and CDU governments confronted the intransigent political nature of Moscow's East German ally.

At that time, Chancellor Helmut Schmidt argued that narrowing the rift between the Germanies was not possible if both states "adhered to maximalist claims and arguments." He said that the people on both sides want "practical solutions that would permit the nation to live together more easily." He added, "We think it useless to continue pretending there is no GDR; not that we approve of this regime or of its social system...but neither do we call its existence in question any longer." Schmidt stressed, "There is one thing which we refuse to do: recognize the other part of Germany as a foreign country. The Germans are one nation and will remain so."[57]

The accession of Chancellor Helmut Kohl's government rekindled a more focused discussion on the future of the nation and the Bonn government's aspirations for its unity. "Germany is divided, but the will of the German people for unity is undivided," Kohl told the Bundestag in 1985. He added, "Our country is divided but our nation lives on. We Germans cannot change this division by our own efforts. We must however make the division more bearable and less dangerous. It remains our task to work for a state of peace in Europe in which the German nation will regain its unity through free self-determination."[58]

"The division of Germany resulting from the military and ideological confrontation of East and West cannot be overcome in the short term. As long as the situation continues, we shall have to make the consequence of separation *more bearable* for the people in both states in Germany," stated Dr. Dorothee Wilms, Bonn's Minister for Inner-German relations. She added significantly, "We realize that we cannot pursue a policy of reunification in cooperation with SED. The political systems of the two states in Germany are diametrically opposed to one another." Still, "We have a duty to seek practical cooperation whenever possible without submitting to outright extortion."[59]

In other words, Bonn would openly work with the *de facto* authorities in East Berlin to make GDR life more bearable. Annual payments to the GDR for transit fees to Berlin, postal payments and road tolls totaled DM 1.2 billion. To this was added the *ransom* of political prisoners by Bonn. "Between 1963 and 1989, West Germany paid DM 5 billion (U.S. $3 billion), to the communist regime for the release of 34,000 political prisoners," stated John Koehler.[60]

Both physical and postal contacts were encouraged. Trips by West Germans to the GDR rose from 2.8 million in 1967 to 7.7 million in 1977, but fell to 5.5 million in 1987. Telephone calls between West Germany to the East rose from 821 thousand in 1977 to 1.5 million in 1987. Letters in both directions rose marginally from 160 million in 1977 to 165 million in 1987. By 1989 over fifty towns had become sister cities.[61]

Within Germany the forty years of separation had long since become the norm. Although a high percentage of West Germans declaring their support for the constitutional aim of reunification remained constant at 70 percent, the population had begun to accept partition as a given. One third of West Germans regarded the GDR as a "foreign country." When Willy Brandt declared in 1988 that the "hope of reunification" had become the "living lie of the German second republic," he expressed a widely held, if politically awkward view.[62]

Less than six months before the collapse of the GDR regime, FRG President Richard von Weizsacker cautiously pondered the issue of unification. Dr. Winkler stated, "By the 1980's, the pan-German national idea no longer played much of a role in West German political thinking." The FRG was seen as a "post-national democracy."[63]

Unimaginable changes in the geopolitical constellation of East/West forces, most especially in Moscow itself, prompted the *German Question* to regain the historical limelight. The Soviet socio/economic inability to sustain its Empire, the brittle nature of the East Bloc regimes, and Moscow's political paralysis, opened a floodgate of socio/political changes which surged over the Berlin Wall and opened the gates to German unity. In the wake of the collapse of the Wall and an unwillingness of its ideological mentors in Moscow to come to its military assistance, the GDR regime could not sustain itself, reinvent its *raison d'etre*, or regain more than a smidgen of political legitimacy without the help of its fearsome Stasi. Tumultuous throngs throughout the GDR chanting "*We are the People*," changed their political call to "*We are One People!*"

Faced with this historic if mercurial political situation, the Bonn government had to choose between two paths offered in the Basic Law. Under Article 146 "all German" elections would be held to choose delegates to a national constituent assembly. But the other option, Article 23, offered a second possibility. Article 23 permitted "other parts of Germany" to simply join the Federal Republic. This article had been used for the incorporation of the Saarland in 1957. Dr. Rice recalled, "This was a provision for a takeover. The GDR would *become part* of the existing Federal Republic. The constitution, form of government, rights and responsibilities in the international system of the FRG would remain intact."[64]

Chancellor Kohl's bold decisiveness and clear political vision, brought the dream to political fruition on 3 October 1990. Yet, the physical and psychological unification of the two politically estranged cousins would be more complicated. While the goals of freedom and democracy were clear, what of the economic and social costs to merge the two political polar opposites?

Clearly the global situation favored unity. Importantly the United States and western allies were willing to settle one of the last loose ends of WWII. The political paralysis in Moscow moreover, allowed a window of opportunity, given that General Secretary Gorbachev could be persuaded, albeit grudgingly, to permit the process to move forward. Germany had earned respect in western capitals and sullen acquiescence from the Soviets.

Dr. Condoleezza Rice who was a key player on the American negotiating team leading to the historic moment said, "One thing is certain. German unification took place with uncommon speed and as amicably as any major negotiation in recent memory....No one understood the issues of timing better than Helmut Kohl. He has reaped both the praise and the blame appropriate to the momentous role that he played in his country's rush to unity."

"Kohl was reelected with a comfortable margin of victory in December 1990. Although the difficult period of adjustment to the unification of East and West continued to prompt questions about his leadership, Kohl was narrowly reelected again in October 1994, a victory that made him the longest serving and influential Chancellor since Konrad Adenauer."[65]

Kohl's long-serving CDU/CSU/FDP coalition lost elections to the SPD in September 1998. Sadly thereafter Kohl's personal reputation suffered from a series of party finance scandals tarnishing both his own as well as the CDU's standing. At the time of unification in 1990, West Germany stood as a model democracy and a successful socio/economic paragon in Europe. Indeed the FRG state was at the apex of its standing before the challenges of reunification.

Chancellor Kohl stressed, "As Konrad Adenauer never tired of saying, there is only one place in the world for us Germans and that is shoulder to shoulder with the free nations. This fundamental rejection of a neutralist or go it alone stance is reflected in our membership of the Euro/Atlantic community. That membership proved to be one of the key factors enabling Germany to achieve unity in peace and freedom and with the consent of all its neighbors."[66]

While the Soviets were seemingly intransigent, the British and French were less than enthusiastic concerning German reunification, especially in the anxious months following the collapse of the Berlin Wall. Very real possibilities existed for chaos, or more likely, an expensive Western subsidy to the continuing socialist *status quo* of a *reinvented* GDR regime. Such a solution would have allowed tarnished GDR institutions to remain intact while an *"enlightened"* communist government still ruled, albeit with strong financial support from Bonn. Such a compromise would have called for murky military arrangements, and a possible dilution of the NATO commitment thus creating a nebulous security context in the center of Europe. Despite his electoral loss and political fall from grace, Helmut Kohl will be chiefly remembered for the singularly significant achievement of German Unity.

ENDNOTES

1. Konrad Adenauer, *Memoirs 1945-53*, Translated by Beate Ruhm von Oppen, (Chicago: Henry Regnery, 1966), 68.

2. Winston Churchill, *Triumph and Tragedy*, (Boston: Houghton Mifflin, 1953), 651.

3. *Major Problems of United States Foreign Policy 1954*, (Washington DC: Brookings Institution, 1954), 221.

4. Cordell Hull, *Memoirs of Cordell Hull*, (New York: Macmillan, 1948), 1606-1607.

5. *U.S. Department of State, Documents on Germany 1944-1985*, (Washington DC: GPO, 1985), 147-149, and Heinrich August Winkler, *Germany:The Long Road West* Volume 2, (New York: Oxford University Press, 2007), 122.

6. *Basic Law of the Federal Republic of Germany*, (Bonn: Press and Information Office/BPA, 1981), 13, 24.

7. Adenauer, 78-79.

8. U.S. Department of State, *American Foreign Policy 1950-1955 Basic Documents*; Volume 2 (Washington DC: GPO, 1957), 1711.

9. Documents on International Affairs, 1957, (London: Royal Institute of International Affairs, 1957).

10. Tiemo Kracht, "German Unification Policies Since 1949: Implications for China," *Issues & Studies* 27 (December 1991): 27; 36.

11. Heck 1987, 4.

12. Edwina Campbell, *Germany's Past and Europe's Future: The Challenge of West German Foreign Policy*, (New York: Pergamon-Brassey, 1989), 12-15.

13. *Major Problems of U.S. Foreign Policy*, 225.

14. Dwight D. Eisenhower, *The White House Years: Waging Peace 1956-1961*, (New York: Doubleday, 1965), 331, 351.

15. Karl Kaiser, "Forty Years of German Membership in NATO," *NATO Review* 43 (July 1995), 3-8.

16. Frederick Kempe, *Berlin 1961*, (New York: G.P. Putnam's Sons, 2011), 499-500.

17. Willy Brandt, *A Peace Policy for Europe*, (New York: Holt, Reinhart, and Winston, 1969), 148.

18. *Mandate for Democracy*: Three Decades of the Federal Republic of Germany, (Bonn: Press and Information Office/BPA), 160.

19. Lawrence Whetten, *Germany's Ostpolitik: Relations between the Federal Republic and the Warsaw Pact Countries*, (London: Oxford University Press, 1971), 116.

20. *Dokumente zur Aussenpolitik der Deutschen Demokratische Republik*, (Berlin : Staatsverlag der DDR, 1972), 891-894.

21. David Childs, *The GDR: Moscow's German Ally*, (London: Allen & Unwin, 1983), 86.

22. Winkler, *Germany The Long Road West 1933-1990*, 286-287.

23. Dieter Blumenwitz, *What is Germany? Exploring Germany's Status After WWII*, (Bonn: Kulturstiftung Der Deutschen Vetribenen, 1989), 130.

24. Alfred Grosser, *Germany in Our Time: A Political History of the Postwar Years*, Translated by Paul Stevenson, (New York: Praeger, 1971), 306.

25. Adenauer, 436.

26. *Major Problems* 1954, 227.

27. *Documents on International Affairs*, (London: Royal Institute of International Affairs, 1954), 101-102.

28. Frederick W. Marks, *Power and Peace; The Diplomacy of John Foster Dulles*, (Westport, CT: Praeger, 1993), 59-60.

29. Documents 1954, 102.

30. Kaiser 1995, 3.

31. *U.S. Department of State Bulletin*, Washington D.C. 1956, 485.

32. Pierre Maillard, *De Gaulle et L'Allemagne: Le Reve Inacheve*, (Paris: Plon, 1990), 208-215.

33. *White Paper/Security of the Federal Republic of Germany and the Development of the Federal Armed Forces*, (Bonn: Ministry of Defense, 1979), 4

34. *NATO Review 1999*, 32-33.

35. *Military Balance 2012*, International Institute for Strategic Studies London; 2012), 118, 120, 467.

36. Martin Schnitzer, *East and West Germany; A Comparative Economic Analysis*, (New York: Praeger, 1972), 8-11.

37. Alan Kramer, *The West German Economy 1945-1955*, (New York, Oxford: Berg, 1991), 151-156.

38. Ibid, 185-188.

39. Eric Owen Smith, *The German Economy*, (London: Routledge, 1994), 9.

40. L.H. Gann and Peter Duignan, *Germany: Key to a Continent*, (Stanford: Hoover Institute, 1992), 4.

41. Grosser, 316.

42. Joachim Nawrocki, *Relations Between the Two States in Germany: Trends, Prospects, and Limitations*, (Bonn: Press and Information Office/BPA, 1988), 137.

43. Ibid, 77.

44. *UNECE Countries in Figures 2009*, (Geneva: United Nations, 2009), 39.

45. *Charter of the United Nations and Statute of the International Court of Justice*, (New York: United Nations, 1991), 29.

46. Karl Kaiser, *German Foreign Policy in Transition; Bonn Between East and West*, (London: Oxford University Press, 1968), 89.

47. R.G. Sybesma-Knol, *Status of Observers in the United Nations*, (Brussels: Free University, 1981), 55-59.

48. *Documents on International Affairs 1955*, 88.

49. Sybesma-Knol, 58-59.

50. *United Nations Security Council/ S* 10955 June 1973, 2.

51. *United Nations General Assembly/ A* 9080 1973.

52. Siegfried Shultz, "Trends and Issues of German Aid Policy," *Konjunkturpolitik* 1989, 361-381.

53. *Development and Cooperation Report 2012*, (Paris: OECD, 2012), 210-211.

54. United Nations General Assembly/Committee on Contributions 1991, 7-8; UN ST/ADM 28 February 2001, p. 7; UN ST/ADM 24 December 2012, 3.

55. Adenauer, 437.

56. Heinrich Windelen, "The Two States in Germany," *Aussenpolitik*, 3/1984, 227-229.

57. Helmut Schmidt, "Germany in the Era of Negotiations," *Foreign Affairs*, October 1970, 47-48.

58. USDS/Documents on Germany, 1384-1396.

59. Dorothee Wilms, Konrad Adenauer Institute/Position Paper, 1987, 2-3.

Divided Dynamism

60. John Kohler, *STASI; The Untold Story of the East German Secret Police,* (Boulder, CO: Westview, 1999), 17.

61. Nawrocki, 129-137.

62. Stephen Eisel, "The Politics of a United Germany," *Daedalus* Winter 1994, 150-151.

63. Winkler, Germany The Long Road West, 583-584.

64. Philip Zelikow and Condoleeza Rice, *Germany United and Europe Transformed; A Study in Statecraft,* (Cambridge: Harvard University Press, 1995), 201-202.

65. Ibid, 366.

66. Helmut Kohl, "German Security Policy on the Threshold of the 21st Century," *Aussenpolitik* 1/1998, 5.

Chapter 2

German Democratic Republic/The East

Socialism on German Soil/History Rewritten

Emerging from the Soviet occupation Zone, the German Democratic Republic was formally founded in 1949, as the "socialist state on German soil." From the onset, the GDR sought to establish itself as both the antithesis of the disgraced Third Reich and, as importantly, the historical heir to all progressive trends throughout German history.

Just prior to the Third Reich's capitulation in May 1945, the Soviets brought the *Gruppe* Ulbricht back to the land of their fathers, wrote John Dornberg. Walter Ulbricht and his entourage were German communists who had spent the Hitler years in exile in the USSR; now they were returning to Germany to form a new regime. Ulbricht's mission in the early days was starkly simple, to revive municipal services in Berlin's twenty boroughs. The objective was not to put communists in the forefront but on the contrary to fill the posts with non-communist political figures. "It had to look democratic," he warned, "yet the real power had to remain in our hands." The motive was to avoid looking anything like a communist coup. As Stalin's designated *pro-consul* Ulbricht went so far as to have democratic politicians in important posts but communists were directly behind them in making key decisions.

Yet for the SBZ, political control soon came under a united front of antifascist parties, notably among them the Communist Party (KPD) and the Social Democrats (SPD) as well as other smaller allied parties such as the Christian Democrats advised Dornberg. The GDR regime claimed to be a synthesis of many political groups working alongside the ruling communists. "Through most of 1945 and the early months of 1946, the Social Democrats were clamoring for the socialization of all basic industries while the KPD ironically took a more careful approach. Even more ironic: the Social Democrats were the first to propose formation of a socialist unity party…a tactic the communists originally rejected but soon seeing the possibilities, became its staunchest champions by January 1946."[1]

The merger between the SPD and KPD was both a voluntary act and a result of coercion. Dr. David Childs adds, pressure from the Soviet occupiers was strong, and the SPD rank and file was not consulted. Still the SPD leadership, with the notable exception of Kurt Schumacher, went along with a party merger in April 1946. Set to the music of Beethoven, Offenbach and Strauss, and enacted in the Admiralpalast, the political fusion of the KPD and SPD was conducted with elaborate ceremony. William Pieck of the KPD and Otto Grotewohl of the SPD became co-chairmen of the Socialist Unity Party of Germany. "The KPD aided by the Soviet authorities was coaxing, cajoling, menacing and maneuvering the SPD all the way to the altar for a hasty wedding," no wonder Childs adds, "some Social Democrats questioned the bride's state of health and future intentions."[2]

By January 1949, the SED adorned with Leninist garb, became a vanguard party. SPD members were soon forced from the Central Committee and after January 1951, a drastic purge took place expelling 300,000 social democrats from the Party, relates Alfred Grosser.[3]

On 15 October 1949, the Soviets recognized the GDR. Soon the other "fraternal socialist states" were quick to follow; Bulgaria, Poland, Czechoslovakia, Hungary, Romania and the People's Republic of China. Before long North Korea, Albania and North Vietnam would follow. Still, any meaningful breakthrough with the Western states was blocked by Bonn's deft diplomacy, and later by the Hallstein Doctrine. However, states Dr. Haftendorn, "Since the West generally viewed the GDR as a protectorate of the Soviet Union, international recognition was limited to states from the socialist camp." The West German government reacted to the founding of the GDR with a statement in which it proclaimed the sole right to represent German interests."[4]

"The unity of the German working class was achieved by uniting the KPD and the SPD," according to GDR historians. Through the Socialist Unity Party (SED), the communists retained tight political control over the GDR through a "united front" *Einheitsfront* regime in which the "bourgeois parties" were allowed superficial rights and limited roles to legitimize the state. French historian Dr. Grosser recalls, unlike the USSR's Supreme Soviet, the GDR *Volkskammer* maintained the *facade* of being a multiparty parliament. The political structure having been formalized, the GDR soon set upon its socialist economic course. In 1950, private enterprise accounted for 43 percent of total economic production; by 1968 this figure had fallen to 6.3 percent. In 1950, 94 percent of the land was in private hands but by 1968, 94 percent belonged to "socialist enterprises."[5]

Yet the worker's state faced its own glaring contradictions. In the wake of Stalin's death and in the midst of internal bickering inside the Party, a "New Course" was announced by the SED on 9 June 1953. Discrimination against farmers would cease, political prisoners would be released, and price increases would be withdrawn. Days later workers in Berlin's *Stalinallee* struck;

stoppages took place throughout the GDR. The 17 June movement's high-point came when workers marched through the Brandenberg Gate into West Berlin demanding freedom. The Soviets cracked down brutally on the revolt imposing martial law, killing 21 demonstrators, and arresting more than 1,000. The 17 June became the first popular uprising in the Soviet controlled East Bloc. The workers "revolting against the workers and peasant state," politically and psychologically jolted the GDR leadership and poignantly highlighted the severe social and political cleavages in East Germany which could be bound together only through force.

The "East Zone" or the "other Germany," was both a smaller geographical and population entity than was the West. Despite the initial demographic gain of 3 million Germans from the Eastern territories in Poland, the GDR population which stood at 19 million in 1948, had slipped to 17 million by 1961. Remarkably, this figure, due to emigration and negative growth birth rates, remained the population at the time of unity in 1990!

From the establishment of the GDR in 1949 to the building of the Berlin Wall in 1961, more than 2.5 million citizens had fled to the West. The Wall made it possible for the GDR to develop its economy to a remarkable extent. It stabilized the State through *coercion* and the use of force.[6]

In a vainglorious attempt to seal East Berlin from the West, the GDR authorities had begun the construction of the infamous Wall on Sunday morning, 13 August 1961. Erich Honecker, then Secretary of the National Defense Council recalled in a 20th anniversary issue of *Horizont* commemorating the event, "Within a few hours our state border around West Berlin was reliably protected...It had become clear to all adventurers who still did not want to realize that the GDR is a sovereign state which acts on its own soil without restriction, that the independence of the German socialist state, also the inviolability of its borders, were also borne by the power of the socialist defense coalition."[7]

Over the years, the Berlin Wall and the increasingly sophisticated intra-German frontier fortifications, became brutal barriers to free movement but not to free ideas. The GDR imbibed a socialist flavor to German history even if it meant a historical reappraisal of such militarist figures as Prussian King Frederick the Great. National People's Army (NVA) military tradition was replete with torchlight marches, goose-stepping troops, and military regalia often evocative of the *Third Reich*.

On the more pastoral side, the GDR seized the 500th anniversary of Martin Luther's birth as a cause to rally both local Christians and many Protestant congregations worldwide to the progressive message of the Reformer; an agenda cleverly rewritten by the SED's propaganda *apparat*. "The 1983 Lutheryear afforded the GDR a unique political legitimacy among progressive Christians. In what amounted to a Marxist synod reducing religion to a political statement within the trappings of a festival, East Germany paid homage to Martin Luther...the 15th century churchman was elevated into the pantheon of GDR proletarian heroes."[8]

GDR Diplomacy/Third World Largesse

East Berlin's diplomacy reflected both a desire by the SED leadership to achieve a political legitimacy in parallel to Bonn and, as importantly, to advance the Soviet Union's geopolitical agenda. Thus after having broken from the isolation imposed by Bonn's Hallstein Doctrine, the GDR strove to gain diplomatic recognition not only from the Third World but likewise the developed countries.

While communist countries had recognized East Berlin out of solidarity with the SED regime, Western European states, while readily trading with the GDR, withheld *de jure* ties until after the Intra/German Basic Treaty on 21 December 1972. Neutral Switzerland accorded diplomatic recognition on 20 December, while Sweden and Austria recognized East Berlin on the 21st. Belgium was the first NATO country to afford recognition on 27 December; the Netherlands, Luxembourg, Finland, Spain, Ireland, Denmark, Norway, Italy followed suit in January. The Basic Treaty produced a seismic jolt diplomatically. Between October 1949 and November 1972 only 32 states, mostly communist and third world socialist had recognized the GDR. From December 1972 to January 1973, 34 countries opened ties with East Berlin. Britain and France waited until February 1973; the United States and Canada were among the last Western states to open relations in September 1974 and August 1975 respectively.[9]

Significantly when Washington opened diplomatic ties with East Berlin, the move emerged as the first and only instance when the United States had simultaneously recognized both *de facto* governments of a divided nation.[10]

East Berlin focused its attention, and both economic and military largesse, on the developing world. Furthermore, the GDR's political/ ideological relationship with the USSR remained the main determinant of East Berlin's foreign policies. The relationship was enshrined in Article 6 of the 1968 constitution, in which the GDR "develops in the spirit of socialist internationalism, comprehensive cooperation, and friendship with the USSR and other socialist states." Further, Article 7 codified the military cooperation among the GDR, USSR and other socialist states. The 1974 Constitution revised Article 6 to state that in foreign policy matters the GDR is "forever and irrevocably allied with the Soviet Union."[11]

In this context East Berlin's role was set for playing an active Marxist mission in the Third World. As early as the epic Soviet 20th Party Congress in 1956, Nikita Khrushchev declared, "The present disintegration of the imperialist colonial system is a postwar development of worldwide historical significance." During the 1966 Afro/Asian Solidarity Conference in Havana, the GDR played a notable role in mobilizing support for North Vietnam. Despite Soviet prodding, East Berlin was still significantly constrained even in the Third World by the Hallstein Doctrine as much as by an attempt of some leaders such as Egypt's Nasser to successfully play the GDR off against the FRG. Only after a long and costly courtship between 1959 and 1969 did East Berlin finally make a breakthrough in the Arab world. Actually as a reaction to Bonn's close ties to

Israel, Iraq became the first Arab state to recognize the GDR in 1969. Syria and Egypt soon followed suit.[12]

The GDR pursued two fundamental goals in its Third World policies; achieving coveted diplomatic recognition and thus legitimacy as well as providing the Soviets support functions of a military/security nature. Ideologically stated, the GDR role was defined in the messianic terms of Marxism with the cutting edge of Leninism. Writing in *Deutsche Aussenpolitik* on "Africa's Liberation Struggle Analyzed," SED Central Committee members Trappen and Weishaupt stated, "The struggle of the peoples of Africa for national independence and social progress and against colonialism represents a significant stage in the global class struggle....it is part of the struggle between the forces of socialism and Imperialism." During the Ninth SED Party Congress, Erich Honecker stated, "Our party has always regarded peace and anti-imperialist solidarity as interconnected objectives of our foreign policy."[13]

GDR foreign policy was thus moored to the twin pillars of active techno/economic support to socialist states, and militant military assistance to national liberation forces. Beyond its tightly integrated military and economic structure within the Warsaw Pact and COMECON, the GDR had likewise concluded a series of political/military arrangements with both communist and Third World states.

In 1955 East Berlin signed a cooperation treaty with People's China. A myriad of friendship and cooperation treaties were drawn up in the late 1970's with Vietnam, Kampuchea, Afghanistan, and Angola. Inter-party agreements between the SED and communist parties were numerous. The tendency of bloc formation, based on proletarian internationalism, worked in league with the Brezhnev Doctrine. According to policy specialist Boris Meissner, no other Soviet satellite had adopted these aims more clearly than the GDR. By de-Germanizing its constitution and entering into bloc treaties, the SED leadership had assumed a vanguard role for the Soviets.[14]

Between 1970 and 1979 the GDR built 650 factories and sent 15,000 specialists overseas. Foreign Minister Oskar Fischer told *Berliner Rundfunk* that the GDR "had concluded 150 agreements on scientific, technical and industrial cooperation...a crucial foundation for genuine independence in newly liberated states."[15]

General Secretary Honecker addressing the 10th SED Party Congress in Berlin revealed that treaties of Friendship exist between GDR and Vietnam, Cuba, Angola, Ethiopia, and Mozambique and Yemen. He stated that since the 9th Congress in 1976, a total of 8,500 young Third World citizens have been trained in the GDR. Friendship brigades of the FDJ youth organization have trained 2,750 apprentices in African and Arab Countries. From the rostrum of the Party Congress he boasted, "We hail all fighters for national and social liberation in Africa, Asia and Latin America, assuring them they can always count fully on our party and people in the GDR in the struggle for national liberation."[16]

The character of the GDR's foreign policy from the first days of its existence was to support the liberation struggles. Such relations were based on proletarian internationalism and stressed solidarity and support to the liberation movements.[17]

Such ties were unambiguously serving the GDR's global quest for legitimacy, reaffirming the *status quo*, and vainly stressing its militant socialist identity as a separate State of the divided German nation.

The Foreign Ministry outlined aid policies. In 1982 GDR assistance to developing states and national liberation movements totaled 1.58 billion marks which was 0.79 percent of the national income. By 1983, 29,249 persons from such countries were undergoing trades training in the GDR; since 1970, some 54,000 people from developing lands had received training in the GDR. Furthermore in 1982, some 814 GDR technical experts were working in developing countries; since 1970, the number had exceeded 20,000.[18].

The Solidarity Committee furthermore allocated large sums towards the Third World. In 1983, 200 million marks went towards vocational training for liberation movement cadres. For example, the Solidarity School at Stassfurt was attended by 900 Mozambiquans and 240 Nicaraguans. Teachers, craftsmen and nineteen paramilitary Free German Youth (FDJ) Friendship teams operated in ten countries.[19]

Development cooperation did not have its own budget; for the most part it was financed by other budgets. Of the total expenditures on aid between 1986 and 1989, 89 percent was financed from the state budget and the remainder from the Solidarity committee. The GDR's financial contributions reflected artificial exchange rates based on the *Ost* Mark; the actual value of such contributions at the beginning of the 1980's stood at $245 million which declined to $184 million during 1987-88.[20]

The 11th SED Party Congress in 1986 again set the stage for "active anti-imperialist solidarity." Assistance to Angola, Mozambique, Nicaragua, and southern African liberation movements, emerged as a clear focus for action. Aid in 1986 reached 224 million Marks or 0.89 percent of the nation's budget.[21]

Clearly East Berlin's socio/economic "solidarity" aid to the Third World was carefully integrated into the SED's policy objectives of foreign influence building, isolation of Bonn, and at least tacitly serving Soviet foreign policy objectives.

While East Germany had no formal ministry comparable with Bonn's Federal Ministry for Economic Development (BMZ), the overall coordination of such action was the Berlin based Solidarity Committee of the GDR, founded in 1960. Although formally autonomous, the Solidarity Committee was directly answerable to the SED Central Committee. While viewed from the standpoint of international East/West rivalry, the scope of East Germany's involvement was nonetheless impressive; some 0.82 percent of the national income was disbursed in the 1980's for developing countries. On average through the 1980's, some 6,500 places for vocational education and 250 places in higher education were made available annually.[22]

Kurt Seibt, President of the GDR Solidarity Committee explained the mission of the organization's actions which were aimed "first and foremost to the peoples of Angola, Mozambique, to the Namibian people, the African National Congress (ANC) of South Africa, and to our friends in Nicaragua." In 1989, annual assistance of 200 million Marks, supported about 6,000 students and 2,000 technical trainees from Africa, Asia and Latin America. Key to this effort was the Solidarity school at Stassfurt.[23]

Significantly with the collapse of the GDR and subsequent unification some 106 projects in fifteen countries remained operational. Based on an assessment by Bonn, a decision was made to continue 65 projects with funds provided by the Federal Ministry for Economic Cooperation. While military agreements were canceled, most of projects concerned education, health and agriculture. A total of DM 120 million was provided for continued assistance in 1991 and DM 110 for 1992. At the time of unity the FRG maintained diplomatic ties with 160 states while the GDR had relations with 130.[24]

Following reunification, the Federal Foreign Ministry *did not integrate any former GDR diplomats* into Bonn's foreign service. Such was a prudent political and indeed security decision reflecting the credentials and professional qualifications of the overwhelming majority of GDR diplomats.

Military Aid to Liberation Movements

A Declaration by the Warsaw Pact in 1978 proclaimed, "The fraternal states will continue to support the national liberation forces and the peoples of the liberated countries...they again affirm their firm intention to continue their efforts to develop diverse forms of collaboration and comradely cooperation with the young socialist oriented states."[25]

Such solidarity became enshrined in the GDR's 1974 Constitution in which Article 6 stated unambiguously, "The GDR supports the nations and peoples in their fight against imperialism and its colonial regimes for national liberation and independence, in their struggles for social progress."[26]

The SED party line was equally evident; "The support of the African peoples' struggles for national and social liberation, the establishment of close and trustful political relations has at all times been one of the principal thrusts of the foreign policy of our Party and State...on the basis of anti-imperialist struggle, solidarity and political and moral and material assistance for the liberation movements, FRELIMO in Mozambique and MPLA in Angola, have been developing since the formation of these movements."

GDR success in former Portuguese Africa resulted from closely cultivated ties it had developed with the liberation movements before independence. Samora Machel who led the armed struggle against the Portuguese in Mozambique stated that between 1964-1974, FRELIMO was an early beneficiary of GDR military and political largesse. Even before Mozambique's independence, Machel was an honored guest at the 8th SED Party Congress in

1971. He stated, "Since the founding of FRELIMO, almost ten years ago, we have been supported through the solidarity of the GDR." He also praised FRELIMO's party-to-party relations with the SED. Once the East African country achieved independence in 1975, the GDR reaped political benefits.[27]

GDR military aid to national liberation movements likewise stoked resistance to South African rule in Namibia. In this case, aid to the South West African People's Organization (SWAPO) was aimed at ousting Pretoria's presence from German speaking South West Africa/Namibia. The GDR maintained particularly close political, party and military ties to SWAPO. Sam Nujoma, SWAPO's General Secretary was a regular guest in East Berlin. Likewise GDR luminaries such as Erich Honecker visited with Nujoma in SWAPO's Angolan headquarters to express comradely ties between the central committees of SWAPO and the SED. The SWAPO chief unreservedly praised his GDR patrons for support to the liberation struggle.[28]

Assistance to the ANC in South Africa was so extensive that beyond terrorist training to militant cadres even the ANC's magazine *Sechaba* was printed at the Erich Wienert press in Neubrandenberg.

"Erich Mielke's Ministry for State Security (STASI) was the closest ally of the Soviet KGB in the communists attempt to establish a foothold in the Third World," advises Koehler, adding, "The two services areas of responsibility were clearly delineated: the Soviets supplied military hardware, money, military advisers, and other support of an ideological and propagandistic nature. The Stasi organized and trained secret police forces and intelligence departments." Indeed East Germany was notably active in supporting Nicaragua and assisting liberation movements throughout sub-Saharan Africa. GDR units were active in military/security related operations in places as diverse as Angola, Mozambique, Namibia, Rhodesia and South Africa. In 1988 East Berlin's military/security/training assistance in the Third World reached an amazing $444 million.[29]

As was typical of the hazy demarcation between GDR solidarity aid and military assistance, proclamations from East Berlin proudly spoke of its internationalist mission, "The GDR will continue its friendly cooperation with the Front Line states and liberation movements in southern Africa."[30]

The GDR had emerged as a pivotal socio/military force serving the Soviet Union's geopolitical agenda in Africa.

War By Other Means—The Olympics

Parallel with its political efforts to achieve diplomatic and social success against the Federal Republic, the GDR stressed sporting prowess, especially in the pantheon of the Olympic Games. Not surprisingly in the 1950's, the Bonn government tried to sidetrack a separate GDR team identity. Thus until 1964, its athletes were members of a joint German Olympic Team. In fact in the Tokyo Summer Games, both German teams marched into the stadium under the

Olympic banner, not their respective national flags. After that time East Berlin moved its competitors on the fast track to worldwide sporting success which brought political glory for the socialist state on German soil.

The hagiography of East Berlin's Olympic movement actually paralleled political moves. In the early 1950's following Stalin's *dictat* formula for German unification, the GDR favored an all-German team. The mood soon changed with demands for a separate GDR team. Nonetheless, at Melbourne (1956), Rome (1960), and Tokyo (1964), the GDR athletes were compelled to compete on a unified national team. By the Mexico Olympiad in 1968, the GDR was permitted to participate individually. In Munich 1972, during the Brandt era, the GDR gained the ultimate recognition, a separate team, the use of its flag, and its national anthem.[31]

The advent of a more "East Friendly" government in Bonn "had a huge impact on the Munich Olympics, effectively putting an end to the possibility of a boycott by the East European nations. Yet precisely because of *Ostpolitik* implied a softening of the boundary between the two Germanys, it encouraged East Berlin to sharpen its separate identity as a socialist nation," opines David Large. This "tendency would be visible at the Munich Games."[32]

While most communist regimes stressed sporting success and Olympic glory, in the GDR case, the hurdle surmounted by East German victories brought an isolated regime out of the shadow of the wall and into the mainstream of athletic recognition. The spectacular results achieved in the Olympic movement were tarnished by the state-sanctioned use of steroid drugs to enhance athletic performance. The aim was unambiguously simple, to lead the world in Olympic medals. Equally by 1976, the GDR fielded a high-profile winning team in Montreal.

The documented use of drugs in East German sport dates to the 1960's when the state began to compete separately from West Germany. Steroids were not formally forbidden in Mexico in 1968 or Munich 1972 for that matter, and it was not until 1973 that German athletes were well prepared with a special regimen to ensure that drug taking would not be detected. Documents relating to the doping program were uncovered following reunification.

As in all GDR endeavors, political goals, that of legitimacy and acceptance of the socialist state on German soil were paramount. GDR athletes were cast as internationalist warriors representing both the conflict between the two German state's political systems as much as an high profile mark of international image and identity, through sport, for the GDR. Their sporting prowess would equally serve to motivate the citizens of the socialist state.

The Prosperous Prussians; the GDR Economy

Supporting vigorous solidarity with the socialist states and serving as a leading edge in technological/scientific achievement for the Soviet sphere, the GDR economy was the jewel in the Kremlin's crown. While serious economic comparison with West Germany showed the socialist state on German soil to be the poor cousin, the fact remains that by COMECON and indeed Third World comparisons, East Germany was at least inheritor to Prussia's disciplined past.

The USSR *forbade* the GDR to accept Marshall Plan assistance. Moreover the Soviet occupiers, in the tradition of conquerors, physically stripped Eastern Germany of its undamaged industries, carted off rolling stock, and used prisoner of war labor long after 1945.

Prior to 1939, eastern Germany was primarily agricultural with a strong service sector while western Germany combined a strong industrial base along with agriculture. Both East and West Germany suffered heavily during the war, but the damages inflicted by the Red Army far exceeded anything comparable to those in the West. Besides dismantling of the infrastructure, high reparations to the USSR were extracted from the East until 1953. For the first eight years these exceeded 25 percent of the GDR's total industrial production. Direct exploitation of the German Democratic Republic by the fraternal Soviet Union exceeded $19 billion.[33]

The East's economic sluggishness resulted in a net emigration prior to 1961, partly resulting from an over centralized Soviet-style economic plan. Only in 1963 when Ulbricht unveiled the New Economic System was there a dose of harmony between central planning and economic realities. The New Economic System was intended to counter the appeal of the Western *Wirtschaftswunder* by setting attractive material goals, not production for its own sake. Sparked by the plan, production rose 25 percent between 1962-1966.[34]

The year 1960 is significant because it marks the final drive for socialization of resources in East Germany. In fact the private sector of the Eastern economy was eliminated in degrees as in other socialist states. And while the Soviets broke up the large *Junker* estates in parts of Prussia, the land was at first given to peasants. In 1950, state ownership of land was just over five percent, in 1953 the figure climbed to 26 percent, but by 1962 the total reached a stifling 93 percent.[35]

Despite its initial disadvantages, the GDR command economy diverted resources into production of capital goods rather than consumer goods. Furthermore, wages were much lower than those in the West. Naturally the system could only be enforced through political control the most heinous example of which was the Wall built in 1961.

During the period 1945-1960, East German growth lagged behind that of West Germany. It was not until 1959, that the East German economy reached the 1939 level of economic development, while the West had achieved this rebounding goal by the early 1950's. GDR per capita income ran about 75 percent of the West in the post-war era; production was two thirds of the Western level in 1960. Given the diligence and resourcefulness of the Germans in both parts of the nation, the FRG reached number four of the world industrial powers while the GDR stood at ninth as of 1970.[36]

By the early 1970's the GDR despite its political pedigree, had become a notable economic force. Nonetheless inflated statistics and *faux* facts emerged part of the GDR's economic achievements; typically such statistics were enthusiastically reflected in sources such as the *New York Times* and other Western newspapers who presented these fanciful statistics illustrating the myth of prosperity.

The GDR played a significant role in Soviet Space science through the *Interkosmos* program. The most notable contributions were the MKF6 six channel multi-spectral camera for space satellites produced by the Carl Zeiss facility in Jena, the Potsdam geodesic laser station, and the Robotron digital picture processing system.[37]

Perhaps the high point in the GDR/USSR space cooperation came when Sigmund Jahn flew on a Soviet *Soyuz* spacecraft in 1978. Yet most GDR residents were faced with more earthly concerns. The SED's high production goals forced a higher adult working population to work long and disorienting hours. Norman Naimark recalls, women played a large role in the workforce. Combined with scarce housing and intense competition for consumer goods, the GDR birthrate dropped to dangerously low levels, seeing the 1977 population actually fall below 17 million.[38]

For those comrades falling afoul of the GDR regime or those whose senior years made them less "valuable" to the proletarian state, there was a quiet but operative formula to go to West Germany; cash buy-outs. From its inception in releasing some Protestant church workers in 1962, the formula evolved into a formal dissident exchange scheme. British historian Timothy Garton Ash relates that Willy Brandt, after signing the Basic Treaty, suggested to the GDR that in the twentieth century states would not normally expect to pay *ransom* as in the Middle Ages. The remark deeply affronted the East Germans!

"By the early 1970's, the price for a 'normal' *Freikauf* buy-out was set at DM 40,000. In 1977 the price per head was increased to DM 95,847," cites Ash. Originally the figure was DM 96,000 but then 'one of the participants said we must make the figure uneven, so it doesn't look like a price per head.' Over the period from 1963 to 1989 nearly 34,000 political prisoners were bought free by the Bonn government, and more than 250,000 cases of family reunification 'regulated' through this system. "For these humanitarian services," adds Ash, "Bonn paid to East Berlin, in cash or kind, a round total of DM 3.5 billion."[39]

Bonn similarly underwrote part of the GDR financial debt, estimated at $20.6 billion at the end of 1989. Liabilities in hard currency stood at a staggering $9.5 billion. Beyond this, the FRG granted a so-called swing credit for the purchase of West German goods. After unification, a Credit Fund, *Kreditabwicklungsfonds*, assumed East Germany's external debt.[40]

Alas, from the 1950's to the 1980's, the FRG/GDR relationship had evolved from political hobgoblinization to a socio-economic acquiescence, some would say political acceptance, of the workers and peasants state on German soil. Such a political accommodation by Bonn was rooted both in the genuine fear not to provoke any military confrontation with the Warsaw Pact as much as a willingness to stoically accept and indeed subsidize, a socialist *status quo* for the eastern Germans.

Unification: East Berlin's View

The German Democratic Republic seemed cursed with a split constitutional personality. The dynamic was complicated by the parallel creation of the Federal Republic in September 1949. The GDR came into being on 7 October, and was founded as a transitional state to last only until all Germany could be reunited under the socialist banner.

The Stalin Note of March 1952 added a new quality into Moscow's *Deutschlandpolitik,* writes Helga Haftendorn, "it proposed that the three Western powers enter into negotiations on the reunification of Germany as a democratic state within the borders defined at the Potsdam Conference. The pivotal condition was that this unified Germany agree not to be part of any military alliance." Both the government in Bonn and the Western powers saw the Soviet note as a tactical maneuver.

In fact as Dr. Haftendorn adds, "After the archives of the USSR and the GDR were opened, it became possible to ascertain that at the same time the Soviet leadership had absolutely no intention of sacrificing the GDR in order to establish a reunified Germany, even if it was nonaligned."[41]

The Soviets ostensibly granted the GDR full sovereignty in May 1954; Moscow insisted that reunification was a matter for the two German states. When West Germany entered NATO in May 1955, the Soviets revised their policy emphasizing that the *German question* could no longer be solved by a unified federal state but a pan-German confederation of two autonomous states. At the end of 1956 SED Chairman Ulbricht proposed a confederation and elections to a common National Assembly; the GDR's concept of accommodation consisted primarily of forcing social policy changes in the Federal Republic.[42]

Article 1 of the 1949 Constitution states, "Germany is an indivisible democratic Republic...there is only one German citizenship." Clearly the article stresses unity. Article 2 added, "the colors of the GDR are black, red, gold...the capital of the Republic is Berlin."[43]

While this earlier document did not make a specific appeal to Unity as did the FRG's Basic Law, Article 1 unambiguously stressed unity by calling the Republic indivisible and enumerating a single German citizenship. The case of the flag is interesting too. Both states flew the same banner until 1959 when the GDR adopted its characteristic worker template compass in the center.

In 1968 matters changed dramatically when the GDR became a state in its own right. The purpose of a new constitution seemed to purge the notion of "Germany" from GDR life. The 1968 document still acknowledged the German *nation,* yet the GDR became the *socialist state* of that *nation.* Reference to the "German people" had been dropped in Article 6. Article 8 no longer enumerated efforts to strive for unity.[44]

Specifically the revised Article 1 stated, "The GDR is a socialist state of workers and peasants It is the political organization of the urban and rural working population under the leadership of the working class and its Marxist

Leninist Party." Article 1 continues "the flag of black, red, gold bears in the center the state insignia of the GDR," and exclaims that the GDR remains "part of the nation, freed from capitalism," the way of the future for the *entire* German nation. Marxist Leninist rule under the Socialist Unity Party (SED) was affirmed as the guardian of Socialist state power.[45]

Significantly, Article 8.2 called for "the establishment and cultivation of cooperation between the two German states on the basis of equality...and support the step by step rapprochement of the two German states until the time of their unification on the basis of democracy and socialism."[46]

A new dynamic emerged during the Chancellorship of Willy Brandt. Two concepts defined the unity debate. *Abgrenzung* (demarcation) and *Annaherung* (coming closer) honed the new lexicon. As Norman Naimark stated, "*Abgrenzung* describes the official East German policy of sharply delineating the GDR's self-image, history, politics and social life from that of the *Bundesrepublik. Annaherung* is the official West German stance towards the GDR; increasing contact and concessions (governmental, diplomatic and economic) in order to broaden the interaction between the German peoples of the GDR and the Federal Republic."[47]

Despite Party boss Walter Ulbricht's continued calls for unity, the Iron Saxon's inability or unwillingness to accommodate himself to Soviet *detente* policy, along with his challenge to Soviet views, and his attempt to present the GDR as a model for the "developed system of socialism" contributed to his forced unexpected retirement in May 1971 and his replacement by former protege Erich Honecker.[48]

"Ulbricht's dream of a united Germany under SED leadership having been abandoned by his successors, the party was forced to develop new goals and for the future, new concepts of the GDR's role in the communist bloc, the European Community, and the world at large," states Naimark, adding, "This role was solidified in 1972-73 with Honecker's repeated vows of SED loyalty to Moscow." A series of dramatic diplomatic moves; the FRG/Soviet Treaty of 1970, the Warsaw Treaty of 1970 and the Four Power Agreement on Berlin 1971, left the SED with no other option. Either the party would follow the policies of its Moscow mentor or face politically disastrous isolation.[49]

Clearly a new constitution would hone the Marxist Leninist edge of political power and SED control. In 1974, a revised document, nearly grafted the GDR into the political superstructure of the Soviet state. Orwellian *newspeak* reached new levels of "no sing" concerning the GDR's anthem *Risen from the Ruins* which would no longer be sung as to avoid the politically incorrect line "Let us serve you for the good Germany, united fatherland."

Article 6 of the 1974 Constitution went so far as to stress that the "GDR has entered into a permanent and irrevocable alliance with the USSR. This close and fraternal alliance guarantees the people of the GDR further progress on the road to socialism and peace. The GDR is an inseparable part of the socialist community of states."[50]

Even the oath for military recruits into the National People's Army (NVA) stated, "I swear, to loyally serve the German Democratic Republic, my fatherland...on the side of the Soviet army and the armed forces of the socialist states." Significantly the GDR's identity had thus evolved from a *progressive* German Republic, to a *socialist state* on German soil, to a German *scion* of the Soviet Union. In the later years, the GDR stressed its own unique identity, thus downplaying any desire for reunification.

When both German states joined the United Nations in 1973, East Berlin officials stressed that the dual admission brought international recognition to the territorial *status quo* in Europe, including the existence of two German states independent of each other. Foreign Minister Otto Winzer told the General Assembly, "In the GDR there is developing a socialist German nation, closely associated with the peoples of the socialist community...it follows conclusively that between the German Democratic Republic and the Federal Republic of Germany, unification will never be possible. But what is possible, and necessary, are good-neighborly relations of peaceful coexistence."[51]

"The German Democratic Republic moved away from the idea of one German nation in the early 1950's replacing it with the theory of two German nations, the old capitalist and the new socialist one," opines Dr. Winckler. He adds, "The GDR was the ideological state *par excellence* among the members of the Warsaw Pact: a state without a national identity and therefore more dependent than all the others on 'proletarian internationalism' as a surrogate."[52]

General Secretary Honecker coined a new policy, "Citizenship: GDR, Nationality: German." The new tact was codified in the Constitution. Similarly the SED's program for 1976 dropped the formerly unequivocal commitments to national unity. Honecker told the Party newspaper *Neues Deutschland*, "There were Germans of the FRG, and Germans of the GDR, but there was no longer a Germany. The FRG was a foreign country."[53]

It was not the GDR's aim to overcome the *status quo* in Europe. Instead the SED strove for a GDR identity within that *status quo*. The SED's *status quo* orientation focused on allowing the regime both political legitimacy and existence as a legal entity of the German nation. Honecker would later boast, "Two independent states with different social systems have arisen on German soil, the *socialist* GDR and the *capitalist* FRG. One can unite them just as little as one can unite fire and water."[54]

ENDNOTES

1. John Dornberg, *The Other Germany; Europe's Emerging Nation Behind the Berlin Wall,* (Garden City, NY: Doubleday, 1968), 29-40.

2. David Childs, *The GDR: Moscow's German Ally,* (London: Allen & Unwin, 1983), 16.

3. Alfred Grosser, *Germany in Our Time: A Political History of the Postwar Years,* Translated by Paul Stevenson, (New York: Praeger, 1971), 268-269.

4. Helga Haftendorn, *Coming of Age: German Foreign Policy Since 1945,* (Lanham, MD: Rowman & Littlefield, 2006), 124-126.

5. Grosser, "Germany in Our Time," 272-273.

6. Grosser, "Germany in Our Time," 261.

7. *Horizont*/East Berlin, 1981, 8, 32-33.

8. John J. Metzler, "East Germany's Lutheryear," *Freedom at Issue,* No. 77, March/April 1984, 7.

9. *Dokumente zur Aussenpolitik der Deutschen Demokratische Republik,* Berlin: Staatsverlag der DDR, annual 1986, 782-783.

10. *Aussenpolitik der DDR,* 1974, 912-913.

11. William B. Simons, /Editor, *The Constitutions of the Communist World,* (Alphen an den Rijn: Sijthoff & Noordhoff, 1980), 164-165.

12. *Aussenpolitik der DDR,* 1969, 417-419.

13. Freidel Trappen and Ulrich Weishaupt, "Aktuelle Fragen des Kampfes um Nationale und Soziale Befreiung im Subsaharischen Afrika," *Deutsche Aussenpolitik* February 1979, 27-39.

14. Boris Meissner, "The GDR's Position in the Soviet Alliance System," *Aussenpolitik* 35, 1984, 377-387.

15. *GDR Press*/United Nations, 60/1980.

16. *GDR Press*/United Nations, 20/1981.

17. Helmut Mardek and Renate Wunsche, "Die Beziehungen der DDR mit der Nationalen Befreiungsbewegung und den Staaten Asiens, Afrikas und Latinamerikas," *Deutsche Aussenpolitik* 24 May 1979, 54-55.

18. *United Nations General Assembly,* A 38, 7 October 1983, 1-3.

19. *GDR Press*/United Nations, 1/1984.

20. Siegfried Schultz, "Characteristics of East Germany's Third World Policy: Aid and Trade," *Konjunkturpolitik* 36 1990, 310-314.

21. *Horizont*/East Berlin, 1987, 16-17.

22. Hendrik Sebastian, "Aid Under the Banner of Ideology: Development Policy in East Germany," *Development + Cooperation* 1990, 7-8.

23. *Foreign Affairs Bulletin*/GDR, August 1989, 187-188.

24. Memo/*Entwicklung* 1991, 1.

25. *Neues Deutschland,* 24 November 1978.

26. Simons, 166.

27. Trappen and Weishaupt 1979, 37-39.

28. *Neues Deutschland* 19 February 1979; Mardek and Wunsche 1979, 57-58.

29. John Koehler, *STASI The Untold Story of the East German Secret Police,* (Boulder, CO: Westview, 1999), 297, 316-317.

30. *GDR Press*/United Nations, 54/1988.

31. Childs, 184.

32. David Clay Large, *Munich 1972: Tragedy, Terror and Triumph at the Olympic Games*, (Lanham, MD: Rowman & Littlefield, 2012), 94.

33. Jean Edward Smith, *Germany Beyond the Wall: People, Politics, Prosperity.* (Boston: Little Brown, 1967), 84-85.

34. Ibid, 96-97, 107.

35. Martin Schnitzer, *East and West Germany: A Comparative Economic Analysis*, (New York: Praeger, 1972), 18-19.

36. Ibid, 21-22, 386.

37. *United Nations General Assembly*/AC 10 5 January 1983, 2-5.

38. Norman Naimark, "Is it True What They're Saying About East Germany?" *Orbis*, Fall 1979, 560.

39. Timothy Garton Ash, *In Europe's Name: Germany and the Divided Continent*, (New York: Random House, 1993), 144-146.

40. Eric Owen Smith, *The German Economy*, (London: Routeledge, 1994), 130-131; Ash, 654.

41. Haftendorn, "Coming of Age," 128-129.

42. Joachim Nawrocki, *Relations Between the Two States in Germany: Trends, Prospects and Limitations*, (Bonn: Press and Information Office/BPA, 1988), 37.

43. *GDR Constitution*, (Dresden: Staatsverlag der DDR, 1949), 17.

44. *GDR Constitution*, (Dresden, Staatsverlag der DDR, 1968), 9-13.

45. *Verfassung der Deutschen Demokratischen Republik/Dokumente*, (Berlin: Staatsverlag der DDR, 1969), 216-220.

46. *GDR Constitution*, 1968, 9-13.

47. Naimark, 554.

48. Ronald Asmus, "The GDR and the German Nation: Sole Heir or Socialist Sibling?" *International Affairs* 60 (Summer 1984), 408.

49. Naimark, 556-557.

50. Simons, 166.

51. *White Paper/The German Democratic Republic: Member of the United Nations*, (Berlin: Ministry of Foreign Affairs, 1974), 87.

52. Winkler *Germany the Long Road West*, 584.

53. Asmus, 410.

54. Bernard von Plate, "Scope and Interest of the GDR's Foreign Policy," *Aussenpolitik* 35, 3/1984, 159-160; Asmus, 403.

Germany

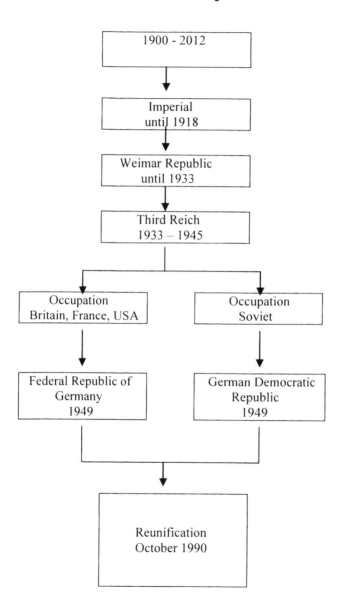

1900 - 2012

Imperial
until 1918

Weimar Republic
until 1933

Third Reich
1933 – 1945

Occupation
Britain, France, USA

Occupation
Soviet

Federal Republic of
Germany
1949

German Democratic
Republic
1949

Reunification
October 1990

Chapter 3

German Unification/The Road Ahead

Otto von Bismarck, the Chancellor who forged German unity in 1871 once advised; "Political changes are as slow as geological changes." Alas, German unity in 1990 disputed the Iron Chancellor with a seismic jolt.

Like a political fairy tale come true, German unification emerged from the near magical and violence free disappearance of the GDR goblins, a crashing of the Berlin Wall, blissfully reuniting the divided national family.

The Germans had gotten what they wished for but their brooding national character was soon beset by at least some selfish remorse as the cost for unity became appallingly clearer. Yet as in any fairy tale, witches and goblins abound, whether in the form of the lurking Stasi, whose still potent files haunt nearly the entire political class in the East and a fair number of politicos in the West, or the staggering socio/economic cost of transforming the moribund socialist state on German soil into the Federal Republic's prosperous equal.

While historians will debate the political and financial wisdom of Chancellor Kohl's *schnellbahn* unification process, which was truly revolutionary in its heady idealism, the simple fact remains that an evolutionary and plodding process would have achieved the same result at a possibly greater cost with many GDR institutions intact.

The SED state lacked legitimacy argued Drs. Gann and Duignan. It was therefore unrealistic for West German politicians to call for a transition period before completing the amalgamation of the two German states. However desirable such a solution may have been in theory, the mass of East Germans would not wait, and the organs of East German authority lost all authority when the Wall opened.[1]

"The State Treaty abolished 'socialism' and reconstructed the DDR as a 'social market economy.' Wrote Lange and Pugh, "The Treaty involved no compromise between the BRD and the DDR but rather, the abolition of central planning and the assimilation of the Eastern economy into the economic structures of the West." Indeed in the rapid move to Unification, "politics was in command. Overriding political priorities drove the process and the decisions were taken without regard to their economic consequences."[2]

It was often opined that Uniting the Germanies meant westernizing the East, not ossifying the West. Kohl envisaged the goal that a smoothly united nation "with the landscape of the *new Laender* in bloom" would come forth. On 3 October 1990, Germany was peacefully united amid unbridled enthusiasm but far underestimated socio/economic costs. Given that through the 19th century until Bismarck's 1871 Prussian unification, Germany had consisted of hundreds of independent political units held together in a loose confederation, the democratic 1990 unification of two separate states would seem almost simple.

The task of renovation would prove daunting. Most Western experts had *underestimated* the East German communist incompetence. In fact, the favorable impression of the GDR rested on fabricated statistics. Falsified data found credence among Western professors, statisticians and intelligence agents.[3]

Interregnum Germania

To recall the oft forgotten setting, unification came amid extraordinary historical circumstances. Political paralysis of the GDR politburo, the peaceful uprising by the masses, military hesitation of the Soviet Union, all guaranteed the internal setting. Positive concurrence of the British, French, and especially the U.S. facilitated the external environment for Chancellor Kohl's decisive political gambit.

Indeed the dramatic implosion of the GDR regime was as much the failure of the SED's socio/economic mismanagement as it was the Party's vainglorious wish to cling to power through the rubric of "renovation and renewal." On the day the Berlin Wall was breached by a flood tide of freedom seekers, Egon Krenz, the newly appointed SED Chairman replacing Honecker, met with Minister President Johannes Rau of North Rhine Westfalia. Krenz still ironically insisted "the sensible relationship between the two German states presupposes respect for the society of each other...the FRG's insistence on claiming custodianship for all Germans was at variance with the people's right to freely choose its social system." That night in Berlin, the *Joshua trumpet* sounded and the masses began to make their historic free choice to the chagrin of Krenz and the communists.[4]

Few observers envisaged the inevitable even on the very eve of the dramatic events which reshaped Europe. Vernon Walters, U.S. Ambassador in Bonn foresaw the collapse of the East German regime, but two months before the fall of the Wall, Secretary of State James Baker seriously questioned the envoy's judgement, labeling such thoughts "quixotic or muddled." Walters recalls that his prediction that unity would soon occur was contrary to the Secretary of State's view that it would not happen before the end of the century. The former diplomat recalls that he twice threatened to resign after Secretary Baker excluded him from unification meetings with the West Germans and sent his own State Department aides secretly to Bonn to negotiate.[5]

The brief and uninspiring tenure of Egon Krenz as SED General Secretary, reflected the GDR's political bankruptcy. A new but multiparty government led by SED Premier Hans Modrow wishfully promised to "renew our socialist society and its state." Still the formal collapse of the GDR regime did not *ipso facto* bring Bonn to the gates of East Berlin demanding immediate unity.

Rather Chancellor Kohl and Foreign Minister Genscher, having been given the go ahead by Gorbachev to proceed with the "internal unification" of Germany, soon proposed a confederation plan. Kohl's Ten Point Program called for "confederative structures" leading to, at the most distant point, full state unity. Yet the vocal demands of East Germans, a flood of Westward emigration, and the collapse of GDR authority caused Kohl to speed up the timetable. Events soon outpaced plans. Premier Modrow at long last conceded the obvious, and proposed his moribund "Germany-united fatherland" plan.[6]

Political euphoria, however, ruled the day and neither scenario was ever enacted. For Modrow who strove to revamp the *old order with a new face* bringing "a better kind of socialism," the changes were indeed irreversible. Free elections in the GDR swept aside the SED, voting in a Christian Democratic government. Premier Lothar de Maiziere was unequivocal in his support for unity; "Our future lies in Germany's unity in an undivided Europe...unification will add substance to the process whereby the confrontation between two power blocs will be abolished."[7]

As Drs. Rice and Zelikow, part of the American diplomatic team working on the historic event opine, "The story of Helmut Kohl and German Unity is not about the chancellor's vision but about his extraordinary feel for the pulse of the German people. It is fitting that it was Kohl who sensed the latest urge for unity in the East German people, and drawn to unity himself, found a way to shape that longing into a force that could not be denied. Always conscious of history, throughout his career Kohl had an unfailing instinct for the politics of the street. If the recalcitrant Honecker had reacted sooner, had Krentz been more skillful, or had Modrow not arrived on the scene too late, Kohl might not have had the chance to channel the hopes of the East German people."[8]

Yet stark reality shadowed Germany on the eve of unity. Issues such as the status of nearly 339,000 Soviet forces in the GDR would only be resolved after Bonn agreed to substantial financial incentives to the economically bankrupt Soviet Union. Phased withdrawals commenced in 1991-93; all Soviet forces left the former GDR ahead of schedule at the end of August 1994.

The "Two Plus Four" Formula (FRG/GDR Plus France, U.K. U.S., USSR), proposed by U.S. Secretary of State James Baker, called for a two track negotiation, an informal division of labor between Bonn and Washington. One track would be between the two Germanies on their future internal political and economic arrangements leaving Kohl responsible to manage this process. The other track that President George Bush and Secretary Baker would orchestrate involved the two Germanies and the Four Powers to settle the external aspects of unity, recalls Robert Blackwill, the White House's chief officer on German unity.

The "Two Plus Four" talks, led to a formal Settlement Treaty which codified German unification as a "significant contribution to peace and stability in Europe." Soviet troop pullouts were outlined in Article 4. Article 6 codified that Germany's membership in NATO would not be affected. Equally, as Article 7 of the Treaty affirmed, the former allied powers "hereby terminate their rights and responsibilities relating to Berlin and Germany as a whole...the united Germany shall have full sovereignty over its internal and external affairs."[9]

The question of Soviet troops on German soil was decreed by the 12 September "Two Plus Four Treaty." A new accord of 12 October regulated individual details of the withdrawal process, and the Soviets would respect German sovereignty and observe German law, including civil and criminal liability. Bonn would make substantial financial contributions to repatriate to Russia an army which in early 1991 numbered 338,000 soldiers and 207,000 family members, spread over an area of 240 sq. kms, almost the size of the Saarland. Since the end of WWII, more than 6 million soldiers from the former Soviet Union had served in Germany. Their status however, was entirely different from that of the Americans, being until German unification, confined to their barracks and bases.[10]

"The German people have exercised at long last their right to self-determination. Germany has overcome its painful, unnatural division," stated NATO Secretary General Manfred Worner. "We now include the whole of Germany in our Alliance as we reassess our strategy and out force posture." Manfred Worner, himself German, proudly added, "The unification of Germany in conditions of peace, freedom and prosperity is a vindication of our perseverance: and also of our values which have proved infinitely more powerful than military force."[11]

The largest peacetime withdrawal of the Soviet occupation army was in itself an extraordinary testament to diplomatic tenacity. Indeed the changes were equally stunning for the GDR armed forces, the National People's Army (NVA). The *Bundeswehr* found itself in a historically unique position, the peaceful termination of the erstwhile enemy. While not defeated in the field of battle, the NVA was sacrificed on the green felt tables of diplomacy as the July 1990 Kohl/Gorbachev Summit sealed its fate as a potentially independent military player. Beyond a change into the *Bundeswehr* uniforms, the real differences were deeper; no former NVA personnel could hold command positions.

Heinz Schulte recounts, the GDR a "formidable member of the Warsaw Pact and integral part of the Pact's first strategic echelon poised to take Western Europe by storm," saw its military totally disbanded in less than a year. By September 1990 the NVA had shrunk from 170,000 to 109,000.[12]

By the time of reunification in October 1990, there were 90,000 NVA soldiers remaining. Of these the *Bundeswehr* retained 6,000 mostly junior officers and 10,000 Nco's. Following unification six NVA divisions were disbanded...moreover to effect a clean break with the ex-GDR, the *Bundeswehr* decided against using NVA weapons and equipment due to safety reasons and the lack of NATO compatibility. Interestingly, one element of the NVA arsenal adopted was a squadron of Mig-29 *Fulcrums* the top-flight Soviet interceptor.[13]

The Road Ahead

To those who glibly opine that unification places an unfair and insurmountable burden on the West to "rebuild" the East, one should recall the painful postwar experience in which a totally devastated country suffering from moral and psychological defeat was able to revive and evolve into the proud *wirtshaftswunder*. Today, nobody can seriously say that the task of rebuilding the former GDR, through the assistance of the wealthy FRG, begins to impose the burden or evoke the trauma of the brick by brick *aufbau* of the late 1940's.

To be sure, the economic cost is immense and social hurdles equally difficult. Both were economically underestimated and politically understated. Yet one of the primary and rarely stated problems rests in the very nature of bourgeois Western society which has embraced well earned creature comforts and good living to near narcissistic degrees, and quite plainly, does not want to share the wealth with its wayward cousins.

The West German economy ended the 1980's with strong economic growth, low inflation and unemployment and a manageable budget deficit. The combined invariables of a growing world recession and the collapse of East German communism, opened an historic window of opportunity for long sought unification. The successful, if controversial, implementation of the currency union in July 1990 in which the near worthless GDR *Ostmarks* were exchanged in near parity with the FRG's financially formidable *Deutschmarks* at an average rate of 1.8 was one such move.

Addressing the *Bundestag* concerning the Treaty on Monetary Union, Chancellor Kohl stressed, "Only if monetary economic and social union are speedily achieved will it be possible that Meckelenburg, Saxony/Anhalt, Brandenburg, Saxony and Thuringia will soon become flourishing areas again...only the prospect of monetary, economic and social union has raised the hopes of many of our fellow countrymen."

The Treaty of Monetary Union emphatically outlined the principles of the social market economy as the foundation for economic union. The accord specified that the Deutsche Mark would be the sole legal tender from 1 July 1990. Equally the treaty established the foundations of monetary, economic, social security, trade union, and pension insurance within the parameters of the rule of law. Likewise the pact went so far as to establish the FRG's strict environmental and building code standards for the former GDR.[14]

Significantly while the Treaty outlined the socio/political order and juridical agenda of the nation about to be reborn, on the practical side the Treuhand trusteeship agency focused on East German firms slated to be privatized.

Beyond the commercial logic of firms freshly on the market, the companies status was hampered by unclear property ownership rights.

Facilitating the static social structure of GDR economic infrastructure required selling off overstaffed and unproductive state firms. Painful workforce layoffs ensued from the Treuhand trusteeship as privatizing and restructuring cut deeply into the 4 million jobs represented by the agency. Treuhand regularly advertised a myriad of business privatization opportunities in publications such as the *Economist* of London.

Never before in history had an organization been tasked with privatizing an entire economy in such a short time. Lange and Pugh state, "The scale and scope of privatization were enormous. State-owned enterprises accounted for 88 percent of net output in 1988 with cooperatives accounting for a further 8.4 percent." Thus Treuhand gained charge of almost 90 percent of East Germany's productive capacity. As the authors advise, "privatization by the governments of Mrs. Thatcher amounted to marginal adjustment: two terms in office (1979-87) reduced the proportion of the GDP accounted for in state enterprises from 11.5 percent to 7.5 percent."[15]

The Treuhand agency sold 10,669 of its 12,515 companies in the first two years following unification. By late 1992 it still held 3,189 firms employing 549,000 people. Privatization had attracted 523 foreign firms investing $9 billion in the former GDR. The U.S. and France led the list with $ 1.6 billion each. Foreign holdings saved 120,000 jobs out of 800,000 contractually secured.[16]

In 1990 Treuhand was the world's largest holding company. Yet "with 90 percent of industrial workers in loss making enterprises, continued employment on any significant scale depended on subsidy," stated Lange. In Autumn 1992 almost 4,500 enterprises had been fully privatized and about 5,200 remained officially on the books; by January 1993, Treuhand stated 4,998 enterprises had been fully privatized. During the same period there were 1.3 million job guarantees and investment commitments amounting to DM 155 billion.[17]

Moreover as Smith asserts, "East German impatience for West German prosperity was enhanced by an entitlement mentality which survived the communist economic system that fostered it. Similarly, the post-war Western disposition of treating east Germans as western citizens fuelled unrealistic expectations."[18]

Through its efforts, by the end of 1994 when the trust was phased out Treuhand had concluded 42,000 privatization contracts. Foreign investors, especially from the USA, Austria, and the Netherlands became major investors. Observers say that the agency's virtue was its relative independence from political interference but its bane was an obsession with privatizing as quickly as possible. Amongst the financial assets which were not sold were the KoKo firms, a curious GDR collection of 221 companies which earned foreign currency outside the official socialist economic plan. Located both in East Berlin and in places from Panama to Lebanon and Switzerland, KoKo would trade with the "non-socialist economic zone," to earn hard currency to purchase both luxury products for the SED elite as well as fund covert operations. Many such KoKo companies were close to the former Ministry of State Security. All these businesses were liquidated.[19]

The combined assault of the 1990-1993 world recession and the downsizing of the Eastern companies, caused a large, and for Germany, a politically volatile unemployment problem. Likewise a collapse of the GDR's traditional trading ties with COMECON saw East German exports plummet. As Lange and Pugh opine, "The DDR was a command economy, meaning the resources were allocated by centralized administration, in accord with political priorities, rather than by markets and the price mechanism." Thus, "in addition to an essential bias against innovation and change" the GDR products lost ground because of non-competitiveness and relatively lower quality and the inability of state firms to switch to competitive exports.[20]

The Labor Ministry reported that nationwide unemployment three years after unification set a postwar record reaching 3.5 million in October 1993. This reflected a rate of 7.6 percent in the West and a destabilizing rate of 15.3 percent in the East. As a point of comparison in 1972 unemployment stood at an amazingly low 103,000 and in 1982 reached only 2 million.[21]

The situation failed to improve markedly over time; in December 1998, there were 4.5 million jobless; by January 2002, a key election year, the rate slipped only to 4.3 million.[22]

Reconstruction of the East necessitated an unprecedented transfer of wealth from the West. "The integration of a much less competitive economy of Eastern Germany proved to be economically costly and had a long lasting influence on economic developments," states an IMF working paper.[23]

In the first few years after 1990, the East's economy surged at an average of 8 % annually in the first half of the 1990's; by 1997, the situation trended down drastically. In the first decade after unification the view of analysts and politicians has shifted according to Dr. Michael Burda of Humboldt University, Berlin. 'At the beginning of the 1990's attention focused on the introduction of institutions of parliamentary democracy and the privatization of state-owned assets by the Treuhand. Today public interest is directed at the promised convergence of the East German economy and the achievement of similar standards of living throughout Germany."

Dr. Burda stresses, that "since 1990 more than DM 1.5 trillion flowed to the east in the form of equipment and infrastructure investment. This is more than triple the East German GDP."[24]

"By the end of the 1990's, Germany was dubbed 'the sick man of Europe.' Growth came to a standstill and the economy underperformed for much of the early 2000's,"according to the IMF, adding,"Despite high unemployment, the institutional responses of the previous decades had raised wages to unsustainably high levels, and for the first time in decades Germany lost a competitive edge...pessimism about economic prospects became widespread.[25]

Naturally the cost of unity has impacted on the living standards in both West and East. Nonetheless for the eastern states, enormous strides have been made since reunification not only in civil and political rights but in material terms as well.

Wages, pensions and GDP per person have almost doubled. Yet as renown economist Hans-Werner Sinn opined, that shortly after reunification West German employers and trade unions set up new wage bargaining associations in eastern Germany" they worked out new collective bargaining agreements in spring 1991 which were aimed at raising wages in the east to western German levels within five years. Why this? Because the western German competitors of the companies privatized by Treuhand didn't want low wage competition on their doorstep. They wanted the Japanese, who were interested in the Treuhand workers, to either stay home or at least pay western German wages if they came. The Japanese chose not to come."[26]

After twenty years of reunification, Dr. Sinn views the situation as a "primacy of politics over the laws of economics," which led to the foreseeable problems in unification policies. A strong "convergence between eastern and western Germany is today only apparent in real incomes; still today the annual net transferred to the new federal states amount to 60 billion Euros."[27]

Measuring affluence by per capita economic output, Germany maintains its coveted position as one of the richest industrial nations; 83 million inhabitants with a per capita GDP of $41,600 in 2012. GDP growth in 2010 reached an impressive 4.2%, in 2001 stood at 3%, but facing the undertow of the global recession and Eurozone crisis since slipped to 0.7% in 2012.[28]

German economic data is still measured in separate statistics for East and West. Transformation of the still-anemic eastern economy has been financed by Germany's state and federal governments.

Specifically Germany's federal budget focused on a huge new package of subsidies extending a Solidarity Pact which began in 1993 and provided the new states 95 billion Euros to 2004. A second Solidarity Pact from 2005 guarantees a further 156 billion Euros up until 2019 for the six eastern states. Programs such as State of the Art Research and Innovation, supporting research in plasma medicine, optical Microsystems, and genetic research are backed by 200 million Euros up until 2014. But despite GDP growth rates of over 10 percent in the early 1990's, growth the Eastern states has slipped behind the West, while the undertow of unemployment in much of the former GDR remains stubbornly .entrenched and nearly double the national average.[29]

Air and water pollution remained a frightful environmental legacy of GDR rule. Major environmental cleanup projects are now aimed at reclaiming polluted mining regions. More than any other region in Europe, Eastern Germany has established itself as a base for renewable energy production and has since become a Green Economy.[30]

German wage levels are the highest in the industrial world. The ratio of direct wages and benefits is almost double the U.S. and British levels. Such costs likewise impinge on long-term competitiveness. Former Chancellor Kohl warned of an economic *malaise* affecting the nation, "Germany's future cannot be secure when our country becomes a collective leisure park."[31]

Critics glibly lament that to bring the five new *laender* into economic parity with the West will take decades. Indeed using an arbitrary formula in which Brandenburg evolves into an economic Bavaria is specious. Even in the FRG the regional characteristics between Hesse and, for example Saarland, are notable. So, too, is the socio/economic differences among departments in France. To assume unification would like a magic wand bring cosmic changes after forty years of GDR misrule is simply *naive*.

Infrastructure renewal has been impressive reflecting quality and vision. Rebuilding and upgrading 2,000 kilometers of *Autobahn* and secondary roads, and modernization of 350 kilometers of railroad have been vital integrating the all-German transportation hub. In road and rail alone, the federal government has allocated DM68 billion for seventeen specifically unification- related projects such as the six-lane *Autobahn* between Kassel in western Germany to Gorlitz on the Polish frontier. Train links between Hanover and Berlin have likewise been greatly improved.

Telecommunications have been modernized and expanded too; *Deutsche Telekom* has invested prodigiously to bring the former GDR's antiquated phone system up to date, and creating an *Infobahn* which has become the most comprehensive cable and fiber optics network in the world.

Germany's economy remains Europe's manufacturing powerhouse with 30 percent of the EU's manufacturing production. As illustrated by the "Industrial Performance Scorecard," Germany along with Sweden and Denmark remain EU's leaders on the Innovation Union Scorecard too in human resource development, intellectual assets, patent applications, and research & development investments. Business satisfaction with the quality of the infrastructure is first in France followed by Germany among the 27 states.[32]

Politically too, unification has caused severe strains both domestically as well as internationally. The underlying problem of the economy has been the rapid pace of convergence of wages between Eastern and Western *laender*.

Disappointment in the lack of an "economic miracle" parallel to that of West Germany in the postwar period, overlooks an important difference. The phase of reconstruction that West Germany experienced after WWII involved personal sacrifice and economic hardship, a phase that has largely been circumvented by East Germany thanks to outpouring of help from the West. The key political oversight of Helmut Kohl's government was its failure to prepare the West Germans for the inevitable sacrifices for their eastern countrymen.

Eastern Germany's economy grew 7 percent in 1993 and 9 percent by 1994. But those days are long past it appears. By the global recession of 2009, GDP fell by 3%. Yet by 2010 the GDP had rebounded to 2% growth only to fall in 2012 to 0.2% growth. In the state of Saxony, 2009 GDP fell by 4% only to see a recovery of 2% in 2010 and nearly zero growth in 2012.[33]

Dr. Klaus von Dohnanyi, former Mayor of Hamburg offers a contrarian critique of unification in a *Die Zeit* essay, "The destruction of what had been such a strong eastern German economy did not take place after the fall of the Wall, but long before 1989. It was not primarily the result of the lost war or of the dismantling and reparations, but of absurd, centrally-planned economic self-sufficiency. Whilst in the rest of the world after 1945, rapid progress was made on overcoming national economic borders, the East of Germany was deliberately excluded from this international learning process of political and economic freedom."

He adds, "It was the democratic system of the West and the social-market economy which ultimately proved hugely superior to the 'socialism' of the GDR. And that is why the gates of this self-imposed prison were opened not from the outside but from the inside. No one came to colonize. But the freedom deprived vacuum of the GDR was immediately filled by the free West."[34]

The 1991 *Bundestag* vote to transfer the capital from Bonn to Berlin triggered a host of *emotional and economic issues*. The Federal Republic had always referred to Bonn, the lovely University town on the Rhine, as a "provisional" capital until unification. The official residence of the President of the Republic, for example, was and remains *Schloss Belvedere* in Berlin the *de jure* capital. Such sentiments were ironically shared by the East Germans who referred to Berlin as the Capital of the GDR/*Hauptstadt der DDR*.

The decision to move to Berlin, beyond the formidable logistics hurdle, rekindled a number of political debates of whether given Berlin's connection as the center of the *Third Reich*, it would pose too negative a symbol. The *Bundestag*, now housed in the historic *Reichstag*, itself one of the first victims of the Hitler regime, equally evokes *a nation reborn in democracy*.

The Federal Government formally moved from sedate Bonn, what the author John Le Caree described as *A Small Town in Germany*, to the revived and grandiose metropolis on the Spree. Significantly, the American Embassy in Berlin was rebuilt on its original site on the historic *Pariser Platz*. The majestic *Hotel Adlon*, a jewel of pre-war Berlin but a ruin on the edge of the city's divide, has been restored to its former glory. The Brandenburg Gate, a poignant symbol of the Cold War division, has now come to symbolize Germany's unity.

Observing Berlin both before and after reunification, one cannot help but be amazed and impressed by the extraordinary transformation. A city that symbolized the Cold War even into the 1980's, has evolved into a vibrant, dynamic, and cosmopolitan place. Beyond the building boom and renovation, the vestiges of the Wall are few. Checkpoint Charlie, a flashpoint of East/West tensions remains as does the *Haus am Checkpoint Charlie* Museum, the testament to the escapes and the fallen. The Wall for the most part has become conveniently forgotten.President Ronald Reagan's historic challenge to the Soviets, "Mr. Gorbachev, tear down this Wall!," echoes almost as distantly as does John F. Kennedy's classic call "Ich bin ein Berliner." History has come full circle.

Transferring the seat of government back to Berlin of course, had been a long stated, if never envisaged, FRG policy prior to 1989. Even after the formal move, Bonn retained seven Ministries including the Ministry of Economic Cooperation. After the collapse of the wall the move was intended as an important psychological boost for the East; in fact multifaceted arguments over the move are reinforcing the division. In Berlin a psychological divide separates East from West.

On the socio/religious side, unification also posed new demographics. Prior to unity, the FRG had a near balance of Catholics and Protestants. Following unity, Germany again emerged as a primarily Protestant (Evangelishe/Lutheran) country since the 51 percent of the GDR population considered itself Protestant and 8 percent Catholic. Subsequently Germany's deep secularism saw a new picture emerge with 26 million Catholics, 25 million Protestants, but 27 million non-denominational and smaller number of other faiths including 3 million Muslims.[35]

In fact, in the agnostic and materialist GDR society, secularism produced a considerable ambivalence towards organized religion despite the significant and noble role played by the Protestant churches in the 1989 peaceful revolution. On the other hand, religious reality had a strong impact historically; Chancellor Adenauer, a devout Catholic had favored staid Rheinish Catholic Bonn over decadent and devastated Berlin as the German capital.

Germany's religious roots were reawakened by the election of Cardinal Josef Ratzinger of Bavaria as Pope Benedict XVI in 2005 brought renewed faith to his native Germany. During the Pontificate of Benedict XVI between 2005-2013, the Pope stressed moral renewal for this otherwise highly secular society. On World Youth Day in 2005, some 400,000 young people flocked to the ancient city of Cologne to hear the new Pontiff.

On the temporal side the 2006 FIFA World Football Cup was hosted by Germany. This extraordinary sporting event saw a surge in nationalism and pride for the soccer matches being held in a reunited Germany.

Psychologically too, reunification raised poignant social issues for the Easterners. The respected Allensbach Institute discovered that 63% of Germans view "reunification as a cause for joy." Some 17% see unity as a "cause for concern" while 20% are undecided. Equally a majority of 64%, believe that east and west are growing together successfully. There's more optimism in the West however. Thomas Petersen of Allensbach opines, "The GDR's propaganda apparatus was excellent; unfortunately. And it's still having an effect today." In an answer to the question "how close are West and East Germans today?," only 25% said they are quite close whereas 37% viewed both as "quite far apart." So the old stereotype of *Ossis* or *Wessis* continues.[36]

Beyond the oft-cited bitterness, "the leap from Marx to markets, from the wasteland of the rigid one-party state to a vigorous federal political system s has now succeeded astoundingly well," relates the *Neue Zuricher Zeitung*. Nothing proves this point better that the innumerable polls that repeatedly come to the same conclusion: indeed majority of East Germans support what has transpired since 1989, especially those who view the changes as an opportunity for commercial and cultural creativity.[37]

Reunification altered the very nature of the Federal Republic. Dr. Anne Marie Le Gloannec opines, united Germany is no longer a system, another form of government on German soil. It is a *nation-state*. Unification is the merging of a community whose sole aim is to become a modern society economically and politically. "The comfortable expectations of yesterday of a West German middle class and of its intellectuals are questioned: unification brings the Federal Republic back to the 1950's and 1960's when it was a less democratic society striving to modernize. To put the matter bluntly, East Germans seem to be the West Germans of yesterday."[38]

The merger of the two German states took place on the basis of the Unification Treaty which envisaged the socio/political integration of the GDR into the FRG. The aftermath of reunification has in fact actually highlighted many of the psycho/socio differences. Approximately a third of all citizens in the now enlarged Germany directly experienced one of the most rigid regimes of the former communist bloc. In fact "the Stasi kept files on an estimated six million people, and built up a network of civilian informants who monitored politically incorrect behavior among other civilians," advise Heineck and Sussmuth. Equally since the fall of the communist dictatorship, former GDR residents have experienced life in a market-based democracy.[39]

The legacy of the Stasi secret police haunts the political atmosphere. In its final days Stasi had 97,000 full time employees and as many as 140,000 collaborators, all this machinery for 17 million Germans while the Gestapo, helped by countless voluntary informers, at the end of the Nazi regime had only 32,000 members for 80 million Germans. The one hundred miles of Stasi files offered poisonous proof of a poisoned society.[40]

Decades after Stasi's demise, the spy agency's files still haunt Berlin's political establishment. Joachim Gauck, the longtime dissident and former commissioner charged with maintaining and evaluating the Stasi archive, estimated to John Koehler that "at least 20,000 West Germans had spied for the Stasi. He based his estimate on reconstruction of the dossiers that had been shredded." Such estimates were said to be "conservative." Kohler added that "even if all the spies were exposed, none could be prosecuted because of the statute of limitations for espionage is five years."[41]

East Germans see themselves as drawing many benefits from becoming citizens of a ready made state. Whereas Heineck and Sussmuth stress that despite twenty years of German reunification, "East Germans show a persistently lower level of social trust...they also continue to believe less that other people are fair or helpful." The authors add, "The GDR system habitually imposed unfair moral choices: for example, denounce your neighbor or colleague, or your child will never go to university. It preached altruism but ingrained selfishness." The maze of moral choices which confronted East Germans, including the elites, was brilliantly chronicled in the film *The Lives of Others.*[42]

Such sentiments often bring forth a combination of political *angst* and misplaced nostalgia often highlighted in Germany's mass circulation periodicals; a *Der Spiegel* cover story, "The Eastern Feeling; Homesick after the old Order," reported on how many easterners feel more comfortable with the iconography of the GDR regime ranging from products to political regalia.[43]

Ostalgia has gone beyond the traditional yearning by a minority for the old regime, to a high tech *virtual GDR* with over fifty websites presenting an odd political blend of the National People's Army, the Stasi, Trabant autos, through scores of *Ostalgia* sites which stress socialism less than the sugarcoated haze of history which most former GDR citizens would rather forget! Ironically, two decades after reunification, the former socialist state on German soil remains on the *virtual reality* of the *Internet*!

Residual respect for the GDR underscores a unique facet of the East German populace. Between 1949-1989 more than four million people left, producing both a brain drain and as importantly, an escape valve for organized resistance. Due to the mass exodus, people who stayed and opposed the Stalinist regime were themselves mostly socialists who wanted to replace totalitarianism with democratic socialism. The exodus severely hampered the development of an indigenous anti-communist and pro-liberal democracy elite. Thus the GDR opposition was much more leftist than Poland's Solidarity or Hungary's Democratic Forum.[44]

The Global Context

Internationally viewed, German unification raised two major questions whether Bonn would continue to provide economic aid to the developing world and would a united Germany remain a loyal member of both the EC and NATO?

Addressing these concerns on the eve of unification, Foreign Minister Hans Dietrich Genscher told the United Nations General Assembly, "The reorganization of industry in the new federal states which are about to become part of our country, and our assistance for the reforms undertaken in Central and Eastern Europe confront us with huge problems. Nonetheless we shall make even greater efforts to meet our responsibility towards the Third World. Our contribution to their development will increase not decrease."

"Solidarity with Central and Eastern Europe does not imply that we are turning away from the Third World," he cautioned. Viewing the political equation, he advised, "Ever since joining the U.N. the Federal Republic of Germany has demanded in this forum the unification of our indivisible nation...through their peaceful revolution, the Germans uniting with us have demonstrated their belief in freedom, unity and in democracy and hence in Europe."

"We do not want a German Europe but a European Germany," Genscher stressed, "We belong to the European Community...we want the European Community to be an economic and monetary union and a political union." He warned, "As the EC identity grows on the way to European union, we do not want the Atlantic to grow wider."[45]

Chancellor Kohl regularly underscored Germany's ties to both Europe and North America and stated, "We Germans, we Europeans, want to further expand trans-Atlantic partnership. Europe still needs America, and America needs

Europe... both are of vital importance, the trans-Atlantic partnership and European Union. It is not a question of choice, we must have both."[46]

Yet the very nature of European power relationships has substantially changed since German reunification and the subsequent fall of the Soviet Union. Viewing the process, Zbigniew Brzezinski opined, "The Soviets had no choice it was an inevitable concession...there would have been a prohibitive cost to rupture East/West détente." Brzezinski felt that after the Two Plus Four Treaty, France and Britain "have been marginalized. The end of the Cold war has produced two winners, the U.S. and Germany, and two losers, the USSR and France."[47]

Britain harbored many fears about German unity. Prime Minister Margaret Thatcher related in her memoirs that in a Moscow meeting with Mikhail Gorbachev in September 1989; two months before the Wall fell, "I explained to him that although NATO had traditionally made statements supporting Germany's aspiration to be re-united, in practice, we were rather apprehensive." She added, "If there was any hope of stopping or slowing down reunification, it would come from an Anglo/French initiative." In early 1990, prior to formalizing of the unification process Prime Minister Margaret Thatcher tried to pressure French President Francois Mitterrand to enter into an Anglo/French alliance to "check the German juggernaut" and to ensure that in each stage of unification "and in future economic and political developments the Germans did not have things all their way." The envisaged London/Paris *entente* failed due to French hesitation.[48]

A more proactive German policy both in Europe and the United Nations has naturally encouraged a reappraisal in the traditional Franco/German relationship. For Paris, according to analyst Anne-Marie Le Gloannec, "Objectively, Germany is perceived as being too strong or too weak. While less dramatic than in the 19th century, or the first half of the 20th century, this dimension is always present." A too-powerful Germany in the center of Europe and at the same time one constrained to overcome real economic and political weakness, offers a classic political dilemma.[49]

Helmut Schmidt opined, "The balance of power in Europe has not only shifted between East and West, but also within the EC. The collapse of the Soviet Union and German unification has, at least in the perception of our neighbors, increased Germany's significance. In terms of its population, its economic rank, and its geographical situation in Europe, Germany has become a power factor, which in the eyes of our partners, requires a counterbalance." The former Chancellor conceded, "Since unification, some of our neighbors have expressed worries which one might have thought were a thing of the past. Although it is often left unsaid, the guarantee of security against Germany is one priority goal of our partners."[50]

Such sentiments often have come to the fore. A seemingly innocuous comment by British Foreign Secretary Douglas Hurd illustrated the point. Interviewed in *Der Spiegel*, Hurd stated that "German foreign policy can comfortably become more assertive, I think that's a good thing." His remarks caused a firestorm in the London tabloids and even a mild rebuke from the otherwise supportive *Daily Telegraph.*[51]

In the grip of recession and confronted by the true cost of unity, the Foreign Minister Klaus Kinkel advised, "Our prime task now is to complete the internal unification of our nation. This task pushes us to the limits of our resources. Nonetheless we have contributed more to the economic recovery of Central and Eastern Europe and the CIS states than all other countries together...We are the biggest attraction in Europe for the massive social migration from East to West and from South to North."

Nonetheless, Third World development assistance was not cut despite the heavy price of unification. The FRG's Official Development Assistance (ODA) in 1981/82 stood at $5.8 billion or 0.47 percent of GNP. By 1991/92 the sum reached $6.8 billion or 0.40 percent of GNP. For example, Germany is one of the larger donors to the U.N. Development Program; the majority of aid is slated for Asia and Africa. The aid ratio declined however to 0.31 percent of GNP in 1995, the amount reaching $7.5 billion. By 1998, ODA fell to $5.6 billion or 0.26 percent of GNP.[52]

A growing consensus in Bonn supports a permanent seat on the U.N. Security Council to coordinate multilateral policies. Nonetheless, former Foreign Minister Kinkel stated, "Germany is prepared to assume responsibility as a permanent member of the Security Council," knew that despite conditional international support for the position, Germany will have to take the politically risky role of troop contribution to U.N. peacekeeping operations as well as pay yet larger budget assessments for a New World Order.[53]

In 1994, the German *Bundestag,* as prescribed by the Constitutional Court, gave parliamentary approval to *Bundeswehr* participation in NATO's naval operation in the Adriatic. The *Bundestag* also lifted the restrictions which had been imposed on the deployment of German units because of the unclear constitutional situation. Foreign Minister Kinkel asserted, "Germany is now fully capable of playing its role in international affairs." The constitutional clarification while giving the green light to the deployment of German forces in U.N. peacekeeping missions, became a cautious first step in a very complicated political process concerning overseas deployment of the military.[54]

By the end of the 1990's it was apparent that Germany had largely come to terms with the external use of its forces, beyond the traditional territorial defense role. Participation in the Kosovo conflict, with German combat units playing a key role in the 1999 NATO operation, illustrated the point. The decision of the Red/Green coalition (SPD/Green) to give the *Bundeswehr* a full combat role was supported by a wide political consensus. Nonetheless according to Dr. Heinrich Winkler, "Unlike in 1995, however, in 1999 the parliamentary left too, was nearly united in accepting the consequences of German sovereignty. Germany acted as one among other Western democracies."[55]

Within the United Nations context, the desire by the former CDU/FDP to gain a permanent seat on the Security Council was unequivocal; "If our country is to pursue a responsible foreign policy in today's new global conditions, it must have a seat on the body making those decisions," opined Kinkel before a Bonn audience, "Not of conceit but of concern for our vital interests. As the third largest contributor, we should have a say in the body where major decisions which involve great expenses are made. The German government is seeking a permanent seat on the Security Council."[56]

The diplomatic focus continued under the new SPD/Green government though with less vigor. In his first address before the General Assembly Foreign Minister Joschka Fischer stated "The Security Council must be adapted to the new realities of the global political situation...Reform must involve enlargement... as you know Germany has for some time now expressed its willingness to assume more and lasting responsibility in this connection, We stand by this unreservedly."[57]

Chancellor Gerhard Schroeder speaking before the U.N.'s Millennium Summit stated "I would like to take this opportunity to reaffirm on behalf of the German government that should the number of permanent members be increased, Germany is prepared to shoulder this responsibility."[58]

Dr. Ludger Vollmer, Minister of State added more specifically, "The discussion about Security Council reform has been going on for years and almost everyone involved shares the view that at least Germany and Japan should have a permanent seat." Vollmer added, "We believe that the Security Council should represent today's reality and not the reality of the postwar era. That would mean that strong countries like, Japan and Germany, but also representatives of the three large southern continents, should have some influence on its decisions."[59]

The postwar Federal Republic was very much an American creation. That phase of history has now come to an end. Reunification means that Germans are becoming more German. Germany will remain a friendly but less pliable ally of the United States. The key to the new German foreign policy, advises Jacob Heilbrunn, is a renewed emphasis on the *nation-state*. Far from subordinating itself to a European super-state, Germany, driven by its domestic needs, is fashioning a new national identity for itself.[60]

British historian Timothy Garton Ash opines that "Germany has over the last thirty years pursued one of the most consistent foreign policies of any Western power. As a result it has a well formed foreign policy tradition, a blend of Adenauerian *Westpolitik* and Brandtian *Ostpolitik*. German diplomacy has excelled in the patient, discreet pursuit of goals through multilateral institutions and negotiations whether in the European Community, NATO or the Helsinki process."[61]

Still discussions on the *classical national interest* are more often than not couched in terms of respect for international law, human rights and protection of the global environment. The clear geopolitical focus which would rapidly come to the fore in France or the United Kingdom is notably absent in Germany. For example, since 2002, Germany has provided the third largest troop contingent in Afghanistan as part of NATO forces. Yet discussions on the topic quietly refrain from any stating the national interest or geopolitical reasons but rather focus on German troops providing humanitarian aid and assistance.

Unification has proven to be a far more fragile political flower than even remotely imagined, the psycho/socio cost of unity being particularly high for east Germans, and the socio/economic bill a particular bane to the westerners. Despite the collective *angst* of unification, Chancellor Kohl's ruling CDU/CSU/FDP coalition was nonetheless able to win an impressive fourth term at the polls in October 1994 elections. One of the many lessons of this electoral victory was at least a grudging realization that Kohl's prescription for unity was the right one. Few serious people, after all, on either side of the former intra German frontier would want to turn the clock back to live in a divided Nation.

Nonetheless, the growing economic undertow of unification's cost, the weariness of the CDU/FDP coalition's sixteen-year rule, public uneasiness over Kohl's near theological commitment to the Euro currency, and the political pendulum swing throughout Western Europe, presaged a return to power by the opposition Social Democrats (SPD) under the charismatic leader Gerhard Schroeder. Thus while the September 1998 election was hardly a rout for the CDU, it signaled a return to power by the SPD.

After piecing together a would become a fractious political coalition with the minority environmentalist and pacifist Greens, Chancellor Schroder's SPD/Green government were beset with tumultuous learning curves with ensuing nervousness in Washington and London.

"Unification had numerous fathers and mothers," Chancellor Schroeder stated in a speech marking the Tenth Anniversary of Unification. "Many who held positions of responsibility at the time, in Germany or among our friends and neighbors abroad, doubtless rendered great services. But the crucial factor for the fall of the Wall was the moral courage of thousands of Germans in the GDR who refused to be intimidated any longer by state and secret service repression and went out on the streets to engage in non-violent protest for their rights, for freedom and democracy."

Schroeder added, "On the tenth anniversary of unification, it deserves to be noted that the Wall was not brought down in Bonn, Washington or Moscow. It was pushed open by the people of eastern Germany."[62]

Still keeping the optimism in the once wayward eastern states has not been easy despite large dollops of *Deutsch Marks* and the largesse of the taxpayers which has failed to discover the magic formula of prosperity.

Dr. Klaus von Dohnanyi, writing in *Die Zeit* opines, "Ten years after the fall of the Wall the landscapes of the former GDR have been transformed. Often mockingly quoted, ex-Chancellor Kohl is proving his critics wrong: the landscapes of eastern Germany are indeed beginning to flourish. The roofs are retiled, the facades are painted in bright colors, important buildings have been lovingly restored, roads and railways have been modernized, people can call anywhere in the world: no one familiar with the once depressing appearance of the old GDR would have believed it possible...but ten years after the Wall came down. Unemployment in the new *laender* stands at over 17 percent."

Von Dohnanyi stresses emphatically, "But let us never forget, the West was not responsible for the pre-1989 social and economic destruction of East Germany which made this radical change inevitable, it was the failed communist system. And so no one can place the main blame for the present situation on the West."[63]

Prior to 1990, there was no need for a grand discussion on national interests because no government in Bonn, or in East Germany, had much room to maneuver on foreign policy. German reunification changed this given virtually overnight. Indeed in the slow but deliberate countdown to the confrontation with Iraq's Saddam Hussein, Germany, under the SPD/Green Coalition actively opposed the United States and Britain's march to war in Iraq. During this critical period leading to the invasion of Iraq in 2003, both Chancellor Schroeder as well as French President Jacques Chirac offered formidable political opposition to the Bush Administration. Importantly this political stance coincided with Germany's two year tenure on the UN Security Council in 2003-2004, and thus offered Berlin a global platform on which to join Paris, and in this case, Moscow as well. Germany's posture caused a serious rift with Washington in the wake of the Iraq war.

Franco/German fence-mending with the USA came in the aftermath of the Iraq war largely through the advent of new governments in Paris and Berlin. In September 2009, Angela Merkel, herself from former eastern Germany, won election and became Chancellor of the Christian Democratic Union (CDU/CSU)and Free Democrat (FDP) coalition. The new Chancellor strove to pursue free market oriented economics on the domestic front while repairing the vital transatlantic relationship with the USA.

Addressing a joint session of the U.S. Congress shortly before the 20th anniversary of the fall of the Berlin Wall, Chancellor Merkel outlined the vital post-war relationship between America and a politically free and now reunited Germany. Citing the positive role played by American Presidents from John F. Kennedy through Ronald Reagan and George H.W. Bush, the Chancellor stressed, "We Germans know how much we owe you, our American friends. We as a Nation, and I personally, will never forget that."

Viewing Transatlantic relations through the wider lens, Merkel conceded that while America and Europe had their share of disagreements, "I am deeply convinced there is no better partner for Europe than America, and no better partner for America than Europe." She stressed, "Germany and Europe will also in the future remain strong and dependable partners for America."[64]

On the diplomatic front, Germany focused on and won another coveted two year term on the UN Security Council for 2011-2012. In its campaign for the post the German government stressed its role as the third largest contributor to the United Nations budget, the world's second largest development aid donor in 2007 and 2008, and the second largest global donor to education. Equally Germany contributes 6,800 soldiers serving in UN peacekeeping missions globally.[65]

Human rights and humanitarian issues form a cornerstone of Germany's international posture too. In an address to the UN General Assembly, Foreign Minister Guido Westerwelle told delegates, "As we Germans have experienced what it is to lack freedom in the course of our own history, we will always stand by those who, wherever they are in the world, call for freedom. For Freedom of opinion and for freedom of religion. For freedom of the press and for artistic freedom." He added, "Freedom therefore does not mean freedom from responsibility. Freedom always means freedom to shoulder responsibility."[66]

Importantly Germany sought and gained a seat on the UN's Geneva-based Human Rights Council for the 2013-2015 term. As Foreign Minister Westerwelle stated, "The German government's strong commitment to human rights is a lesson drawn from the darkest chapter of German history…we regard the Human Rights Council as the leading international institution concerned with human rights protection around the world and the further development of human rights standards."[67]

Clearly both a European home (the EU) and an Atlantic mooring (the U.S) should remain Germany's future diplomatic and defense foundation; this is to say that *close political ties to the European Union as well as unambiguous defense links to NATO* remain of paramount importance. Furthermore Germany's focused friendships with France, the United States, and its emerging partnerships with many states in Eastern Europe, guarantee the prescription for peace and security. Germany's vital commitment to NATO must remain the anchor of its security policy.

Germany remains a central pillar of a stable European order. Moreover the Berlin government continues to play a powerful role in the Atlantic Alliance and European Union. President Joachim Gauck, a respected former human rights campaigner from Eastern Germany, stressed that despite its economic might, Berlin had no aspirations of imposing "a German diktat.." He added "It is my heartfelt conviction that in Germany more Europe does not mean a German Europe. For us, more Europe means a European Germany."[68]

Reflecting Germany's economic prosperity and standing, Chancellor Angela Merkel won a resounding third term in the September 2013 *Bundestag* elections. Known for her pragmatism and prudence, Angela Merkel has emerged as a reassuring figure in Germany and equally one of the world's most powerful women.

Regarding the wider issue of reunification and its continuing challenges, as the German proverb says, "All beginnings are difficult." Unification has proven up to this epic task.

ENDNOTES

1. L.H. Gann and Peter Duignan, *Germany: Key to a Continent*, (Stanford: Hoover Institute, 1992), 7.

2. Thomas Lange and Geoffrey Pugh, *The Economics of German Unification*, (Chelenham, UK: Edward Elgar, 1998), 2, 6.

3. Gann and Duignan, 6.

4. *Foreign Affairs Bulletin*, November 1989, 245.

5. *Author Interview*, Ambassador Vernon Walters, May 1994.

6. Timothy Garton Ash, *In Europe's Name: Germany and the Divided Continent*, (New York, Random House, 1993), 346.

7. *Foreign Affairs Bulletin*, June 1990, 98-99.

8. Philip Zelikow and Condoleezza Rice, *Germany Unified and Europe Transformed: A Study in Statecraft*, (Cambridge: Harvard University Press, 1995), 366.

9. Robert Blackwill, "German Unification and American Diplomacy," *Aussenpolitik* 45, 3/1994, 214-215.

10. Claus Duisberg, "Germany: The Russians Go," *The World Today* 50 October 1994, 191-193.

11. Manfred Worner, "German Unification" *NATO Review* 5, October 1990, 1.

12. Heinz Schulte, "What Happened to the East German Armed Forces?" *Jane's Intelligence Review*, April 1992, 185-186.

13. Ibid, 187.

14. *The Unity of Germany and Peace in Europe*, Treaty of 18 May 1990 between the Federal Republic of Germany and the German Democratic Republic Establishing a Monetary, Economic and Social Union, (Bonn: Press and Information Office/BPA, 1990), 13-14; 67-68.

15. Lange and Pugh, 72.

16. *This Week in Germany* (TWIG), 4 December 1992, 8 January 1993.

17. Lange and Pugh, 76; Eric Owen Smith, *The German Economy*, (London: Routledge, 1994), 481-482.

18. Ibid, 476.

19. *"Schnell Privatisieren, entschlossen sanieren, behutsam stilllegen" Ein Ruckblick auf 13 Jahre Arbeit der Treuhandanstalt und der Bundesanstalt fur vereinigungsbedingte Sonderaufgaben*, Abschlussbericht der Bundesanstalt fur vereinigungsbedingte Sonseraufgaben (BvS) Berlin 2003, 195-197.

20. Lange and Pugh, 40-41.

21. TWIG 12 November 1993, 4; Federal Statistical Office (D STATIS)/Labor Market 2013.

22. Ibid, D-STATIS.

23. Fabien Bornhorst and Ashoka Mody, *Tests of German Resilience*, IMF Working Paper, (Washington, DC: International Monetary Fund, 2012), 9.

24. "Why is East Germany Lagging Behind?" CESifo Group Munich, 30 November 2001, 1.

25. Tests of German Resilience, 10.

26. "Market Order Under Attack: Seizure of Power by Munchhausen," Ifo Viewpoint No. 96, 1 July 2008, 1

27. "Wasted Advantages: A Note on the 20th Anniversary of German Unification," CESifo Group Munich 2010.

28. Ifo Economic Forecast, 13 December 2012.

29. "Developing Eastern Germany," *Magazin Deutschland*, 3/2010, 24-25.

30. "The Green Revolution: How Eastern Germany Became a Green Economy," *Germany Investment Magazine*, Vol. 2, 2010, 15.

31. *Die Welt*, 22 October, 1993.

32. Industrial Performance Scorecard/2012, (Brussels: European Union, 2012).

33. Economic Forecast for Eastern Germany and Saxony 2012/2013, Ifo Economic Forecast, CESifo Munich, 19 December 2012.

34. "Ten Years of German Unity," *Inter Nationes*/Bonn 2000, 2-3.

35. Statistical Yearbook 1991, pp. 108-109; *Magazin Deutschland* 3/2010, 57.

36. Deutschland, 22-23.

37. *Swiss Review of World Affairs*, November 1995, 2.

38. Anne-Marie Le Gloannec, "On German Identidy," *Daedalus*, Vol. 123 Winter 1994, 138-139.

39. Guido Heineck and Bernd Sussmuth, "A Different Look at Lenin's Legacy: Trust, Risk, Fairness and Cooperativeness in the Two Germanies," CESIfo Working Paper No. 3199, September 2010, 4-5.

40. "Freedom and Its Discontents," Fritz Stern, *Foreign Affairs* 72, September-October 1993, 114.

41. *Stasi:The Untold Story of the East German Secret Police*, 150.

42. "A Different Look at Lenin's Legacy," 3, 6.

43. *Der Spiegel* 27/1995, 54-64.

44. "Post-Totalitarianism in Eastern Germany and German Democracy," Burkhard Koch, World Affairs 156 Summer 1993, 26-29.

45. FRG Press/UN 26 September 1990, 6-17.

46. American Newspaper Publishers Association/ UN 5 May 1992, 3.

47. *Le Figaro*, 18 July 1990.

48. Margaret Thatcher, *The Downing Street Years*, New York: Harper Collins, 1993, 792-793.

49. *Le Figaro*, 4 August 1993.

50. Helmut Schmidt, "Deutschlands Rolle im Neuen Europa," *Europa Archiv* 46 November 1991, 613-622.

51. *Der Spiegel* 30/1994, 30-31; *Daily Telegraph* 27 July 1994, 11.

52. UNDP Donor Profiles/1994, pp. 80-86, World Development Indicators 2000.

53. FRG Press/UN, 29 September 1993, 14.

54. Klaus Kinkel, "Peacekeeping Missions: Germany Can Now Play Its Part," *NATO Review* no. 42, October 1994, 3.

55. Heinrich August Winkler, *Germany The Long Road West 1933-1990*, Oxford: Oxford University Press, 2007, 563.

56. FRG Press/UN 3 November 1993, 7.

57. Germany Press/UN 22 September 1999, 4.

58. Germany Press/UN 6 September 2000, 2.

59. Germany Press/UN 6 September 2000.

60. Jacob Heilbrunn, "Tomorrow's Germany" The National Interest no. 36 Summer 1994, 45-47.

61. Timothy Garton Ash, "Germany's Choice," *Foreign Affairs* 73 July/August 1994, 71.

62. Germany-info.org Unification 2000.

63. Ten Years of German Unity, 1-4.

64. Speech by Federal Chancellor Angela Merkel before the United States Congress, 3 November 2009, Berlin: Press and Information Office of the German Federal Government, 11, 15.

65. Germany in the United Nations," Candidate for the United Nations Security Council 2011-2012," Berlin: Federal Foreign Office, 2010, 2-6.

66. Germany Press/UN Speech of Foreign Minister Guido Westerwelle before Annual UN General Assembly September 2012

67. "Candidate for the UN Human Rights Council 2013-2015." Berlin: Federal Foreign Office, 2012.

68. *Deutsche Welle* 2 February 2013, 1-2.

Chapter 4

Republic of Korea/The South

The Division

North/South division of the Korean peninsula resulted directly from military moves by the USSR and the U.S. into the country in the closing days of WWII. Contrary to the occupation of Germany, an enemy state, Korea was newly liberated from Japanese colonial rule, but nonetheless soon became hostage to the vicissitudes of Cold War tensions.

Alas, the fate of Korea had been sealed nearly a half century earlier. "By the end of the 19th century, East Asia had become a stage of imperial competition among the great powers," states Seung-young Kim, adding, "With regard to the Korean peninsula, Japan *Ching* China, and Russia waged a fierce competition to place the weak kingdom under their control....Japan had regarded Korea as a "dagger against the heart of Japan' and constantly tried to strengthen its influence on the peninsula."[1]

Japan's ironfisted rule over Korea between 1910-1945 had nonetheless set the stage for this ancient nation's modern slide into political division. The Korean peninsula had long been under the hegemony or the direct control of China or Japan. In fact Imperial China's assistance had guaranteed Korean Dynastic independence from Japan. Yet with the meteoric rise of Japan as a military power in the *Meiji* period, Tokyo actively meddled in Korean affairs. The Sino/Japanese War and the ensuing Treaty of Shimonoseki in 1895 forced China to relinquish all claims to its old Korean vassal state as well as to Formosa and the Pescadores.[2]

Tokyo's creeping socio/economic hegemony over the Hermit Kingdom became codified after the Russo/Japanese War. The 1905 Treaty of Portsmouth sealed the fate of Russia's Far Eastern influence for forty years. Indeed with the diplomatic blessing of the United States, Japan had checkmated Moscow's influence in Korea thus giving the Empire of the Sun an opportunity for expansion.

"In the era of the Russo-Japanese War, Korea's role as an independent buffer-state could not be sustained because Japan and Russia could not reach any lasting compromise over Korea and Korea itself remained at the mercy of great-power competition," writes Kim. In 1905, Korea became a Japanese protectorate. Tokyo's control of the Chosen Dynasty went so far as to abolish the Korean Kingdom's Foreign Ministry and dissolve its armed forces. In 1910, the Korea Japan Annexation Treaty marked a tragic end to the Chosen Dynasty and opened thirty-five years of colonial status.[3]

Reacting to Korean aspirations for self-determination, a Provisional Government was organized in Shanghai, China, in 1919, and ardent nationalist Syngman Rhee was elected its Prime Minister.

Tokyo's aims in Korea were starkly simple; to integrate Korea into the Japanese empire economically as well as politically. *Chosen* was to be Japan's rice bowl, a springboard for Japanese action in China, and a reservoir of troops for the Imperial Army. Such sentiments were unapologetically described in Tokyo's propaganda of the era; "Outwardly Japan's expansion is a normal phenomenon. But there is idealism behind this expansion and its results are totally different from those achieved by mere aggression or conquest. What burdens Japan has borne through the annexation of *Chosen*! Expansion means to Japan the multiplication of obligations and sacrifice."[4]

The Cairo Conference in November 1943 formed the cornerstone of Allied plans concerning Korea. Kim Koo, of the Provisional government convinced China's Chiang Kai-shek that Korea's status must be specifically enumerated. The *communiqué* later framed by Churchill, Chiang, and Roosevelt, thus stated that the "three great powers, mindful of the enslavement of the Korean people, are determined that in due course Korea shall become free and independent."[5]

Among restless Korean patriots such as Rhee and Koo the phrase "*in due course*" brought a bitter backlash. Franklin D. Roosevelt suggested to Secretary of State Cordell Hull, that "Manchuria and Formosa be returned to China and that Korea might be placed under an international trusteeship with China, the U.S. and one or two other countries participating." Knowing the opposition of Korean nationalists to this formula, Hull consulted against the plan.[6]

Korea was not mentioned in the final *communiqué* of the Yalta Conference in February 1945. Rhee was convinced that his country had been sold out to the Soviets. On 26 July 1945, the Potsdam Declaration defined terms for Japanese surrender and clearly reaffirmed that the Cairo Declaration's terms shall be carried out. The USSR subscribed to the Potsdam Declaration upon entering the war against Japan on 8 August.[7]

The final weeks of the Pacific War brought untold tragedy and confusion to Korea. On 12 August, the Red Army moved into North Korea. On 15 August, VJ Day, General Douglas MacArthur, ordered U.S. forces to accept the capitulation of the Japanese south of the 38th parallel. The U.S. government had decided that Japanese troops north of the 38th parallel should surrender to Soviet units and those south of the line to the Americans.

On 8 September, nearly a month after the first Soviet units entered North Korea, U.S. Army forces of Lt. General John Hodge's 24th Corps landed at Inchon and into the power vacuum in the South. As the surrendering Japanese troops had ceded *de facto* authority to various local political factions, U.S. forces entered a fractious and often hostile political atmosphere.

On 16 October, Syngman Rhee returned to Seoul to a tumultuous reception. Yet, the deed of division had been done. Gregory Henderson a former U.S. Foreign Service officer and Korea scholar opines, "No division of a nation in the present world is as astonishing in its origin as the division of Korea...there is no division for which the U.S. government bears so heavy a share of responsibility as it bears for the division of Korea."[8]

With the peninsula's northern half falling under the Soviets, and the southern half being in the American sphere, the U.S./USSR impasse was complete and division *de facto*. Contrary to Germany's case where an enemy state was defeated in war to be divided among the Four Powers, the map of colonial Korea was likewise divided by foreign hands, nonetheless encouraged by a clear cut civil conflict between communist and nationalist factions.

At the Moscow Summit in December 1945, the U.S., Britain, the Soviet Union, and China agreed to put Korea under trusteeship status for five years. Independence would then follow. Trusteeship was opposed by all parties, particularly the conservatives. When the plan was announced on 28 December, protesters took to the streets. In parallel, the first of fifteen U.S./USSR Joint Conference military meetings was held, part of a strenuous and ill-fated series of negotiations between the U.S. and Moscow on the issue of a Korean trusteeship.

On 17 September 1947, in a momentous step, the United States placed the Korean problem before the United Nations. This initiative before the General Assembly was first in a series of skillful moves in which Washington abdicated sole responsibility for the Korean *imbroglio.*[9]

Secretary of State George Marshall told delegates to the Second General Assembly convened at Flushing Meadows, "The Korean people, not former enemies but a people liberated from Japanese oppression, are still not free. This situation must not be allowed to continue...It is therefore the intention of the U.S. to present the problem of Korean independence to this session of the General Assembly. We do not want the inability of two powers to reach agreement to delay any further the urgent and rightful claims of the Korean people to independence."[10]

American Ambassador Warren Austin and his team then framed the landmark draft resolution "Problem of the Independence of Korea" which called for a U.N. Temporary Commission on Korea to facilitate national elections to convene an Assembly and a National Government. The Occupying powers would withdraw troops from Korea as "early as practicable." The U.N. General Assembly passed the U.S. resolution setting elections for March 1948. The Commission would oversee the voting in each zone.[11]

Significantly, the elections were held in the South in May; the Soviets predictably blocked voting in the North. The Commission later called the vote "a valid expression of the free will of the electorate in those parts of Korea which were accessible to the Commission and in which the inhabitants constituted approximately two thirds of the people in all Korea." Elections provided no clear majority, yet Rhee's National Society won the most seats. Seats proportionate in number to the population, about one third, were left vacant for the later participation of the people of the northern zone. The National Assembly urged the North to hold elections and to join with southern delegates forming an independent government.[12]

According to historian Donald MacDonald, the Americans were anxious to phase out their occupation in order to both re-deploy scarce resources to Europe and avoid the pitfalls of being an occupier. While the occupation between 1945-48, seemed to lack a central philosophy or overall plan, on the whole the display of U.S. goodwill outweighed the mistakes. U.S. forces commenced withdrawals in late 1948 and the Soviets pulled out in December.[13]

Notably, both the State Department and the Pentagon differed in opinion on Korea's importance and of the American ability to keep the south outside the communist orbit. In April 1948, the National Security Council in NSC-8 approved by President Truman, conceded that the U.S. should provide south Korea with at "least the minimum relief and rehabilitation," but only to "forestall economic breakdown." The policy tasked the State Department with forming a government in south Korea "as a means of facilitating the liquidation of the U.S. commitment of men and money."[14]

On 15 August 1948, the third anniversary of VJ Day, the American flag was lowered in front of the capital building in Seoul and the *taeguk* banner of the Republic of Korea (ROK) was raised. The U.S. Military government handed its administrative authority over to the ROK. General Douglas MacArthur and Syngman Rhee sat side by side during the ceremony proclaiming Asia's newest republic. In September, the Democratic People's Republic of Korea (DPRK) was founded under Kim Il-sung's leadership.

The U.N. General Assembly adopted a landmark resolution declaring "there has been established a lawful government (the Government of the ROK) having effective control and jurisdiction over that part of Korea where the Temporary Commission was able to observe...and this is the only such Government in Korea."[15]

Washington soon extended *de jure* recognition to the ROK on 1 January 1949. Similar action was subsequently taken by 37 countries.[16] A major diplomatic and legal hurdle having been surmounted by the South, the ROK's most trying days loomed on the horizon.

Thunder Clouds and War

The first uneasy year of South Korean independence was notable for its economic shortcomings. While most of Korea's industry was located in the North, the South contained a larger proportion of arable land and was historically the nation's rice bowl. Still even agriculture was strained with the influx of over a million refugees from the North. The gap could not be closed even with American aid, $6 million in 1945-1946, $93 million in 1946-1947, and $113 million in 1947-1948[17] (Allen 1960,104).

The continuing military buildup of the Democratic People's Republic, a sealing off of North Korea to the U.N. Commission, and the communist takeover of the Chinese Mainland, created a spiral of events which clearly threatened the territorial integrity of the embryonic Republic. Just days after the establishment of the People's Republic in neighboring China, a resolution before the U.N. *ad hoc* political committee expressed concerns over the situation which "menaces the safety and well being of the Republic."

It defined the Commission's duties as "to observe and report on developments which might lead to involve military conflict in Korea," and to seek the removal of barriers to social and economic contacts caused by the division. Yet, the Commission conceded, "The problem of Korea's unification was further from being solved that it was a year ago and, unfortunately, the spirit of compromise did not seem to exist in Korea."[18]

The predawn attack on South Korea by communist forces on 25 June 1950, was a clearly calculated aggression by the People's Republic to unite the peninsula by force. In fact, the invasion was first of only two instances when one part of a divided nation militarily attacked the other side—the other cases being the Chinese communist attacks on Quemoy and North Vietnam's forcible reunification with South Vietnam in 1975.

While militarily caught off balance, the U.S. was diplomatically surefooted. At 3 AM Sunday morning 25 June, the U.S. requested a meeting of the Security Council. Later that day stunned and anxious delegates convened at Lake Success to adopt a resolution declaring a breach of the peace and calling for a cessation of hostilities and a withdrawal of North Korean forces to the 38th parallel. The resolution propitiously passed given that the Soviets were boycotting the meetings in deference to their Chinese communist allies not having membership in the Security Council. Nationalist China still held the seat.

The U.N. Commission later reported that all evidence pointed to the invasion being "a calculated, coordinated attack prepared and launched with secrecy." CIA estimates just days before the attack, had totally miscalculated North Korean plans.[19]

The Security Council responded boldly, passing a landmark enforcement resolution #83 (1950) of 27 June which recommended "members of the United Nations furnish such assistance to the Republic of Korea as may be necessary to repel the armed attack and to restore international peace and security in the area." Despite the ROK not being a U.N. member state, the resolution referred to the "armed attack on the Republic of Korea by forces from North Korea."[20]

President Harry Truman, speaking after the U.N. vote, forcefully outlined U.S. military support for South Korea. He stressed, "The attack on Korea makes it plain beyond all doubt that communism has passed beyond the use of subversion to conquer independent nations and will now use armed invasion and war. In these circumstances, the occupation of Formosa by communist forces would be a direct threat to the security of the Pacific area...accordingly, I have ordered the Seventh Fleet to prevent any attack on Formosa."[21]

The Council called for the establishment of a unified military command, authorized the U.N. flag to be used concurrently with the flags of participating military units, and requested that the U.S. designate a force commander.[22]

Truman's mention of Formosa was directly related to a foreign policy *faux pas* earlier in the year when Secretary of State Dean Acheson, addressing the National Press Club, outlined America's "defense perimeter" in Asia as Japan, Okinawa, and the Philippines. Referring to other areas in the Pacific, he said in case of attack initial reliance "must be on the people attacked." Significantly, the response *excluded mention* of Korea or Formosa leading many observers to opine that Acheson's oversight provided North Korea and China with a dangerous misperception as to American interests in East Asia.

Yet, ironically, it was Dean Acheson as both Under Secretary and Secretary of State, who had proven himself as a firm proponent of massive Korean economic aid and a growing security commitment as emphasized in a revised NSC 8-2. "Although Acheson at once accorded Korea a much higher priority, the Defense Department did not."[23]

The Korean war enforcement operation between 1950-1953 saw the participation of units from sixteen countries among them Australia, Belgium, Britain, Canada, Ethiopia, France, Greece, the Philippines, South Africa, Turkey, and the United States. A sanguinary seesaw struggle of epic proportions engulfed the Korean peninsula. America came face to face both with North Korean aggression and Chinese communist "volunteers." Losses were staggering; 3 million Koreans, 900,000 Chinese killed or wounded, 33,000 Americans, 1, 000 British and 4,000 other allied forces.[24]

Nearly a year to the day after the attack, Moscow's U.N. Delegate proposed a truce. Talks commenced at Kaesong which eventually, and after further fighting, led to the Armistice of 27 July 1953.

The Phoenix Rebuilds Economic Development 1953-1999

The devastation upon the Korean peninsula after three years of war appeared near apocalyptic. South Korea was shattered and stunned. A resource weak and industry-starved economy was further hampered by a lack of functioning infrastructure and an unstable political situation. Noted economist Il Sakong recounts, early efforts to revive the South Korean economy rested with the United States. In the 1950's massive aid transfers and public works programs were the order of the day. The South Korean economy began a solid recovery after the war. From 1953-57, GNP in real terms grew about 5 percent a year.

During this period foreign aid was an important factor in the nation's growth. "From the nation's liberation in 1945 to the late 1950's, foreign aid was virtually the sole source of foreign capital. More than 70 percent of imports were financed by foreign aid during the reconstruction period of 1953-60, the U.S. being the major source of this aid."[25]

The May 1961 military coup ushering Gen. Park Chung-hee into power, remains a seminal turning point. Historian Frank Gibney writes, "Park ran his economy like a military operation. If the Japanese high growth era was primarily the work of bureaucrats, South Korea's was that of the military. At the onset ex-officers made up seventy percent of South Korea's bureaucracy. In turning from military to economic pursuits, they evoked comparisons not so much with modern Japanese bureaucrats, but with the *samurai* bureaucrats who had executed Japan's *Meiji* Restoration a century before...Park assembled a group of technocrats and economists to act as a kind of general staff for national mobilization."[26]

Park's assumption of power coincided with the arrival of a new USAID mission director mission in Seoul who proposed Park shift focus from producing agricultural too industrial products for export. According to historian Andrew Natsios, "This appealed to Park who adopted the strategy and approached the effort as a military commander." The strategy was part Korean and part American but had its origins in a book, *Stages of Economic Growth* by Walter Rostow which focused on development economics. Indeed the formula worked; between 1961 and 1979 per capita income rose eight fold and the economic growth rate exceeded 1400 percent.[27]

Since South Korea launched its first five-year development plan in 1962, real GNP has expanded by an average of 8 percent a year. As a result, GNP rose from $2.3 billion in 1962 to $170 billion in 1988. An aggressive export strategy maximized growth.[28]

In 1966 South Korea total trade was $1 billion; within half a century it topped $1 trillion. Total trade increased from $477 million in 1962 to $153 billion in 1991. Per capita income in 1990 surpassed the $5,000 mark, a big leap from the meager $87 recorded in 1962, related economist Il Sakong.

By the 1970's export success rested more with heavy industry and the *Chaebol*, the family owned mega companies such as Hyundai, Samsung and Lucky Goldstar. The rise of the *chaebol* was an inevitable byproduct of Park's economy in armor. Park did not make the mistake of other third world authoritarian governments by nationalizing the country's industry—he needed the skills of the entrepreneur. He had studied the postwar "economic miracles" of Germany and Japan and had seen that the government had helped the private sector but did not invade it. The same was true of the *Mieji* reformers in Japan a century before; they had moved quickly to privatize industry.[29]

Between 2003 to 2007, exports increased by 17.7% each year and amounted to $371 billion. During the same period imports increased by nearly 19%

annually to $357 billion. Interestingly China has become the ROK's largest trading partner placing the USA in second place.[30]

The ROK is now the tenth largest trading economy in the world. Yet the trading patterns and partners have changed dramatically. In 1986 the U.S. took the largest share of South Korea's trade with 31% followed by Japan. Trade with China stood at 1%.

By 2011, Korea's trade with China was 20 %, followed by ASEAN 11.6%, by Japan 10%, the European Union 9.6%, and the USA 9.3%. Indeed compared to trade structure in 1971, by 2011 Korea traded much less with advanced countries, and more with emerging and developing economies. According to economist Lee Junkyu, in 2011 Korea achieved one trillion dollars in international trade amidst the global crisis...only eight countries are ahead of Korea in terms of achieving one trillion dollars in trade.[31]

On the individual scale the economic fruits have been truly impressive. By the 1990's South Korea had "*made it.*" In 1945 automobile ownership was negligible; today car ownership is ubiquitous and Korea remains a car producer of global standing. In 1959, there were only 25,000 telephones; today South Korea is a world leader in Samsung cell phone/Smart phone ownership, innovation and production. Equally firms like Samsung and LG are global market players in widescreen TV's.

Despite material success, the Seoul government has expanded its Overseas Development Assistance (ODA). Starting modestly in 1987,the system has been organized into the Korean International Cooperation Agency. In 1999, Korea provided $318 million, equivalent to 0.079% of GNP. This was nonetheless far below the average rate of 0.24% of OECD member states and equally noticeable given South Korea's stellar global standing. Since 2008, ODA allocations have jumped dramatically. By 2010 ODA stood at $1.17 billion the equivalent of 0.12 percent of GNI. The majority of aid is focused on Asia and Africa. As President Lee Myung-bak told the UN, "The Republic of Korea will be an active participant in the international development cooperation as pursued by the MDG's (Millennium Development Goals) We will faithfully implement our plan to double our current level of ODA by 2015."[32]

The Korea-U.S. Free Trade Agreement (KORUS) came into effect in March 2012. U.S./ROK commercial relationship saw two-way trade reach $101 billion in 2012. The volume of bilateral trade between the U.S. and South Korea made Korea 7th largest trading partner. The USA has slipped to number five among South Korea's trade partners. This still remains remarkable given that U.S./Korean trade amounted to several hundred million dollars in the early 1960's.[33]

"In 2003, China became South Korea's largest trading partner, surpassing the United States in a position held by Washington since the 1960's,"advises Heo and Roehrig. Trade jumped from $5 billion in 1991, just before the establishment of formal diplomatic relations, to $20 billion in 1996, exceeded $31 billion in 2000, and reached $168 billion in 2008.[34]

"Korea's economic reliance on China has sharply increased since the global financial crisis erupted, the nation's post-crisis export growth rate to China and its dependence on trade with China to fuel economic recovery are the highest among major economies," write Kang and Lee. The export boom to China has expanded since 2008 and comprises over 30 percent of all Korean exports. China is also the largest destination for Korea's foreign investment.[35]

Unlike other former Asian tiger economies, Korea shunned foreign investment during its thirty years dash from one of the world's poorest nations to one of its richest. Closed markets and heavy regulation kept foreign investment to a trickle. Investment increased rapidly in 1999, setting an all time record of $15 billion. Korea attracted $9 billion in FDI in 2004 but then saw a steady decrease to $2.6 billion by 2007 during the business-hostile Roh Moo-hyun administration. Conversely, China is the number one destination for Korean investment reaching $6.5 billion in 2007 and forming what observers see as over $100 billion in South Korean investment on the Mainland.[36]

The most important task remains globalization of the Korean economy. At the same time, emerging links with North Korea will evolve, proceeding from the view of market proximity/low labor costs. In the aftermath of German unity, the World Bank opined that the main uncertainty in the medium term outlook for the Korean economy arises from the prospects for unification. Irrespective of its timing, reunification would impose high economic and social costs in the short and medium terms as illustrated by the German experience.[37]

Thus unification beyond its political component likewise offers the undeniable lure to South Korean *chaebol* of turning a united Korea into a serious economic competitor to Japan.

Korea Welcomes the World — The 1988 Seoul Olympics

The 1988 Seoul Olympiad represented an extravagant "coming out" party for Korea, the former Hermit Kingdom. As in the case of the 1964 Tokyo Olympiad, the Summer Games were as much a sporting event as a proud sociopolitical statement of South Korea having arrived on the world stage.

Needless to say given the tense military standoff only an hour's drive north of the sporting stadiums, the Seoul Olympics had a security and defense dimension. The ROK was understandably intent on making the Games an overwhelming success—in direct juxtaposition to the severe loss of face for Kim Il-sung's bellicose regime in the North.

The quest for security in the pre-Olympic period was thus paramount and clearly enunciated by the U.S. and Japan. The Declaration of the 1986 G7 Tokyo Summit pledged support for the Seoul Olympics proceeding peacefully. In a well-calibrated bid to stave off the very real possibility of state-sponsored terrorism or overt military aggression from North Korea, both the Chun Doo-hwan and Roh Tae-woo governments laid a careful groundwork of overlapping diplomatic interests, promises of trade, and even an olive branch to the recalcitrant North.

Importantly what evolved as Seoul's *Nordpolitik* focused on the USSR and China, variously patrons of North Korea's mercurial Marxist monarch Kim. Seoul planned to isolate Pyongyang via discreet diplomatic initiatives towards both Moscow and Beijing. Similarly, Seoul opened contacts with East Bloc regimes, especially Hungary, in a bid to widen participation in the Olympics.

The ROK's U.N. Observer Mission pursued political contacts with the organization's multifaceted membership in a bid to cultivate political sympathy, diplomatic recognition, and wider participation in the Olympiad. In a sense, the Observer Mission played political adjunct to the Olympic Committee.

On the domestic front, Chun Doo-hwan's authoritarian rule, buffeted by raucous student demonstrations and increasingly bitter rioting, chose the path of political decompression. The *demarche* was due in large part to the Reagan Administration's pressures put on the Blue House. In his concession of June 1987, Chun announced that there would be direct Presidential elections and other reforms, thus defusing a volatile domestic situation on the eve of the Games. Roh Tae-woo was elected President in December.

In the nervous countdown to the 24th Olympiad, Roh originally coordinator of the Seoul Olympic Organizing Committee, aimed at attracting maximum participation in the Games, thus indirectly guaranteeing that through political universality, the games were "insured" against North Korean terrorism. Efforts to share some Olympic events fell on fallow ground. Nonetheless Pyongyang's boycott of the games was a dismal failure, eliciting support from a handful of countries including Cuba and Nicaragua.[38]

"We want the 24th Olympiad to be an Olympics which creates unity between East and West," became the Committee's mantra. The gala events of September/October 1988 opened amazing new political vistas for the ROK.

Soviet participation in the Games opened a new phase in relations with the communist world; the USSR team was feted and Soviet cultural events were given accolades by the local media. China, a country not having relations with Seoul, and closely tied to Pyongyang ideologically, also participated. Developing commercial ties between South Korea and the socialist states began to be *openly* acknowledged.

Thus, through the Olympics, the USSR and its allies had pried open a political door to Korea which would have been unimaginable following the 1983 Soviet shoot-down of Korean Airlines flight 007. The Games likewise illuminated the cross-ideological and commercial interests both Moscow and Peking shared with Seoul, despite the communist powers offering perfunctory ideological solidarity with Pyongyang.

Nordpolitik/Northern Diplomacy

The roots of the ROK's *Nordpolitik* or Northern Diplomacy rested with President Park Chung-hee and the June 1973 Declaration outlining the *Yushin* regime's foreign policy guidelines. The declaration put forward a policy of peaceful coexistence between the Korean states and disclosed that Seoul would not object to the simultaneous entry of both *de facto* Korean states into the United Nations. Seoul likewise established willingness to open diplomatic ties with all countries irrespective of ideology.

Significantly, *Nordpolitik* emerged as a diplomatic move on par with the Brandt government's *Ostpolitik* policies of the day. In December 1972, both the FRG and GDR had recognized each other's *de facto* status through the Basic Treaty. The ROK's flexibility towards dual U.N. membership was very likely inspired by the Security Council's move to accept the dual German membership.

The June 1973 Declaration provided the momentum for Seoul to break out of its "Hallstein Doctrine," and as a result South Korea entered full diplomatic relations with Finland and Indonesia. Seoul later proposed an "Inter-Korean Agreement on Non-aggression" (1974) and the "Three Principles of Peaceful Unification."[39]

Seoul's abandonment of the Hallstein-type model allowed the ROK to establish diplomatic ties with communist countries in theory and on a more practical side, take advantage of "dual recognition" among the myriad of the U.N. member states with no direct ideological or economic interest in the Korean imbroglio. Following vigorous North Korean diplomacy, and especially after the admission of the People's Republic of China into the U.N., Seoul perceived that the diplomatic fulcrum favored Pyongyang, Beijing's close ideological ally.

Seoul's *Nordpolitik* goals were based on a policy premise of isolating North Korea by cultivating commercial and consular ties with its friends, carrying out a security policy to neutralize the DPRK's major arms suppliers and ideological supporters, and insuring a safe and well-attended Summer Olympiad. The changes were induced largely by the emergence of the ROK as a major economic force and the benefits accrued by trading with it.

The latter half of 1988 proved a political watershed. The July Declaration outlining Unification Policy, the September Olympics, and the October U.N. foreign policy address, made the ROK an active player on the world stage.

The July 1988 Declaration by President Roh Tae-woo represented a landmark effort to promote national unity, defuse intra-Korean tensions, and open trade and diplomatic ties with North Korea's traditional allies. Significantly, the Declaration for "National Self Esteem, Unification and Prosperity," came on the eve of the sporting extravaganza of the Seoul Summer Olympiad. The Declaration emerged as a recalibration of the ROK's political policies and emerged as the seminal statement on the foreign policies of the Sixth Republic.

Roh's speech, to "My 60 million compatriots," translated into a poignant political appeal to the both halves of the divided nation to set their sights on peaceful unification. Importantly the Declaration defined the DPRK not as an adversary but as part of the *same ethnic family* to be embraced. Of the six measures proposed by Roh, three dealt with intra-Korean relations, exchange of visits, humanitarian measures, and internal trade. Three other steps concerned the international aspects of the problem; trade between Pyongyang and Seoul's allies, an end to diplomatic confrontation and competition, and an improvement in relations with China and the Soviet bloc.[40]

During his address before the U.N. General Assembly months later, Roh spoke of pursuing "a relationship of partnership with North Korea." He added, "it is our wish that our allies and friends will contribute to the progress and opening of North Korea...it is also our position that those socialist countries with close ties to North Korea will continue to maintain positive relations and cooperate with North Korea even as they improve relations with us." He outlined his government's efforts to "improve relations with countries such as the PRC, the USSR and many East European nations with which we have had only remote relationships due to ideological differences."

Roh also called for a "city of peace in the DMZ," a Summit with Kim Il-sung to conclude a non-aggression pact, and an end to the military confrontation to "transform the Armistice Agreement into a permanent peace."[41]

Seoul's ties with socialist states, spurred on by the approaching Olympiad, first came to fruition in Hungary. The establishment of relations between Seoul and Budapest belied the fact of two years intense behind-the-scenes contacts, primarily commercial but likewise secret political discussions between the ROK and Socialist Hungary. A trade office opened in September 1988 was followed by full diplomatic relations the following February. ROK/Hungarian detente sparked a negative response from Pyongyang whose shrill communist party paper *Rodong Shimum* declared "Seoul's *nordpolitik* has been instigated by the U. S. through a cross-recognition policy to perpetuate division and alienate the socialist camp."

Nordpolitik resulted in pushing Pyongyang farther into isolation. Contrary to Germany's *Ostpolitik* which to a degree isolated East Germany from its political comrades, the key difference remained that the GDR was a far more established international player than was the DPRK. While North Korea was essentially outmaneuvered by the South, East Germany kept its identity in parallel to the West and often with Bonn's active subsidy.

By the end of 1990, Seoul had opened full diplomatic relations with most of Eastern Europe, a region itself embroiled in a dramatic sea change of political regimes, and established full diplomatic ties with the Soviet Union. "Our major objective in Northern Diplomacy is a reduction of tensions on the Korean peninsula where 1.5 million troops face off over the DMZ and unification of our divided country," stated ROK Foreign Minister Choi Ho-joon. "The major part of our Northern Diplomacy is directed to China and the Soviet Union," he continued, "appealing to North Korea's friends serves to influence North Korea to change."[42]

The policy parameters of Seoul's Northern Diplomacy rested on a tripartite premise; develop economic links with the socialist states, open diplomatic relations, defuse DPRK military political potential through economic/political entente with East Bloc/China.

In direct proportion to evolving economic/political ties between Seoul and the socialist states, North Korea was increasingly facing diplomatic checkmate. The opening of ROK/USSR relations in September 1990 and the ROK/PRC ties in August 1992, served as ideological body blows to the DPRK regime. Pyongyang's two ideological and military pillars, Moscow and Beijing, were teetering.

Yet, the changes were primarily due to the overall thaw in the East/West relationship and the ensuing seismic changes in the East bloc and USSR. Had the world situation not been undergoing a profound realignment of power structures, Roh's policies might have fallen on fallow ground and certainly would have produced anxiety and concern in Washington.

Northern Diplomacy as a theory worked splendidly, *precisely because* of a thaw in East/West tensions and the corresponding downshift in traditional East Bloc hostility to the ROK. *Nordpolitik*, through unabashedly using a wedge of business incentives to the bankrupt socialist states, adroitly isolated North Korea from her traditional comrades. But success of this policy likewise raised the ante for North Korea, isolated save for a few friends such as Cuba and Burma, to contemplate a desperate gamble.

Quest for a U.N. Seat; North/South Confrontation

It remains richly ironic that South Korea, a country whose sovereignty was preserved by multinational U.N. forces in the early 1950's, and whose socioeconomic progress is admired worldwide, was only admitted to the United Nations in September 1991. Not surprisingly, the complicated case of Korean U.N. membership was mired in a longstanding political imbroglio; namely, would the ROK the DPRK or both be allowed to join the world body?

For a country to gain U.N. admission, the prospective member must pass the Security Council without the veto of the any one of the Permanent five members (China, France, U.S. USSR, U.K.). Thus owing to the political alignment of the two Koreas and the DPRK's opposition to separately joining the U.N., it remained highly improbable that either Korean state could pass the Council. A long litany of membership vetos had hung over Korean admission like a diplomatic Damoclean sword. The newly-born Republic of Korea first applied for U.N. membership on 19 January 1949. In the period between 1949 and 1955, the ROK applied for U.N. admission eight times, five applications being made by Seoul itself and the remainder through friendly governments. Four applications were vetoed by the Soviets while no action was taken on the other four.[43]

The DPRK first applied for U.N. membership on 9 February 1949; between 1949 and 1957, two applications were made by Pyongyang and two others by Moscow. Two applications were vetoed by the U.S. and no action was taken on the others.[44]

Interestingly in January 1957, the Soviets proposed that both North Korea and North Vietnam be admitted as a "package deal" concurrently with South Korea and South Vietnam. The concept was viewed by the West as a maneuver by Moscow to gain new allies in the world body as much as to deflect attention from the ongoing communist crackdown in Hungary.[45]

In May 1961, expecting that ROK membership could be achieved through the wave of new admissions in the wake of de-colonization, the ROK Foreign Minister made another application; ironically the document was presented days after Park Chung-hee's military coup.[46]

Again in 1975, shortly after the fall of Indochina to communist forces, the ROK Foreign Minister submitted a telegram to U.N. Secretary General Kurt Waldheim, concerning the ROK's admission to the U.N. The mood was anxious and now the U.S. was confronted with membership applications of two Vietnamese *de facto* entities, the Democratic Republic of Vietnam (DRV) and the Republic of South Vietnam (a provisional Vietcong regime). U.S. Ambassador Daniel Patrick Moynihan recounts that "we would vote to admit both North and South Vietnam, and also North Korea, but that our condition was that South Korea come in too. But the balance of force was now with the Soviets and they would give nothing."[47]

Later on 30 September the U.S. vetoed the two Vietnamese applications. Moynihan retorted, "The Security Council has again declined to consider the application of the Republic of Korea, a state fully qualified for membership."[48]

The U.S. Ambassador had proposed linkage of ROK admission. Washington thus was conceding to membership of three Soviet client states in exchange for ROK admission, but Moscow would not relent. Thus in classic cold war political patterns, Seoul stood with the support of three Security Council members (France/ U.S./ U.K.) and Pyongyang with two (China/USSR).

While both the ROK and DPRK maintained U.N. Observer Missions in New York and Geneva, it was not until 1989, while still basking in the Olympian limelight and benefiting from a meltdown in the cold war, did Seoul actively invigorate its quest for the U.N. seat, despite the looming veto roadblocks from both Moscow and Peking. Looking to the example of dual German admission in 1973, Seoul stressed that concurrent admission of the ROK and DPRK as a *modus vivendi* pending unification would help increase the opportunities for peaceful cooperation.[49]

Pyongyang's position reflected an opposite approach, "The fair way for Korea to gain admission to the UN is to enter that organization with a single state name and one seat after the reunification of the country through a confederation."[50]

Despite having Observer status, the ROK held membership in fifteen specialized U.N. agencies; the DPRK had membership in eleven. At the same time the ROK's financial assessment for the regular budget in 1990, the last full year of Observer status, came to $4.97 million. The DPRK's dues amounted to $440,000.[51]

A decade into UN membership the ROK was assessed at 1.72 percent or $17.8 million; the DPRK's dues stood at 0.009 percent or $93,085. By 2013, the ROK was assessed at 1.99 percent or $56 million. DPRK assessment in the same period dipped to 0.006 percent or $168,000. Budget assessments are compiled by a complex formula of GNP, commercial accounts, and national reserves.[52]

Yet, the possibility of a Soviet or Chinese veto of Seoul's application had diminished greatly in direct proportion to the burgeoning business ties between South Korea and the Soviet Union and the PRC. The Gorbachev era opened new vistas for the once frozen relations between Moscow and Seoul. As crucial, Soviet *entente* with Seoul leading to full diplomatic relations in September 1990, removed the prospect of the Kremlin's veto.

Seoul stressed its qualifications for U.N. membership while at the same time opening the door to Pyongyang's concurrent admission. "If North Korea wants to become a member we welcome that," stated Foreign Minister Choi. The Minister added, "Germany and Yemen had separate seats for separate governments. They are now both one. This did not hinder unification. North Korea says if we join before unification, it must be a single seat, this is impossible," he advised.[53]

In February 1991 the pace quickened with the ROK Foreign Ministry statement of intent to join the U.N. under an option of either dual membership or unilaterally if "in the case that North Korea is unwilling to or not ready to join the United Nations, the ROK intends to seek U.N. membership during this year."[54]

Pyongyang while still holding to a single seat formula was soon bypassed by events; the die had been cast. The April Summit between ROK President Roh Tae-woo and Soviet President Mikhail Gorbachev solidified Soviet support for Seoul's entry into the U.N. A $3 billion loan from the ROK to the cash-strapped Soviet Union gave the final diplomatic green light to Seoul's entry. ROK/USSR trade during this period had jumped from $600 million in 1989 to $1.5 billion in 1991.[55]

The prospect of Beijing's veto still haunted Seoul on the final approach to membership. After all PRC did not have diplomatic ties with the ROK and the Chinese communists were close ideologically with Pyongyang. Here, too, the logjam eased; lucrative commercial ties rationalized the political juxtaposition. ROK/PRC two-way trade stood at $1.1 billion in 1987, $2.9 billion in 1990, and $16.5 billion in 1995. Seoul and Beijing's political relations improved greatly in this period despite still close PRC ties to the DPRK.[56]

During a visit to Pyongyang in early May, PRC Premier Li Peng signaled his government's intent not to block South Korea's U.N. membership. Li warned his intransigent North Korean allies that a "one people, one nation, two governments, two systems" formula should be applied to Korea. Despite this policy, Kim Jong-il made a secret trip to Peking in a last ditch but vainglorious attempt to convince the Chinese to use their Security Council veto.

Now uncertain of China's diplomatic support, North Korea in a major diplomatic *demarche* announced on 28 May that had "decided reluctantly" to join the United Nations. Thus, the way was cleared for the two Koreas to join the world body. The Security Council recommended, and the General Assembly approved the membership applications of the ROK and DPRK concurrently. On 17 September 1991, the flags of both Korean states were raised at U.N. headquarters in New York. At the time of its U.N. admission Seoul was recognized by 151 countries and Pyongyang by 114.

Addressing the 46th session of the U.N. General Assembly ROK President Roh stated, "Imperfect as it may be, the separate membership of the two Koreas in the U.N. is an important interim step of the road to national unification. It has taken more than forty-five years to move the short distance from the Observer's to the member's seat. It took the Germanies seventeen years to combine their U.N. seats. I sincerely hope it will not take as long for the two Korean seats to become one."[57]

United Nations membership for the Koreas proved fruitful for Seoul but achieved little more than marking time for Pyongyang. The ROK has played an active role in the U.N. and has furthermore acted as a model global citizen. A South Korean Ban Ki-moon was elected as UN Secretary General in 2006 and later gained a second term. The DPRK has been less than adroit in using its U.N. political pulpit. Interestingly cooperation between the two delegations and joint initiatives, have been few and far between.

Unification: Seoul's View

In his landmark July Declaration, Roh Tae-woo made a nationwide appeal to the sixty million Koreans, "I am confident that we will accomplish the great task of unifying into a single social, cultural and economic community before this century is out." He likewise spoke of "unifying into a single national entity in the not so very distant future." Curiously Roh did not outline *any specific political system* as a reference point for the future Korean nation-state.[58]

Unification policies for Syngman Rhee's First Republic were formed through the crucible of the independence struggle against Japan and the natural aspiration for a unified Korea. Given that North Korea had tried to forcibly unify the peninsula, he felt that the struggle against the Pyongyang communists must be carried out until final victory, that of a unified free Korean nation. Although Rhee feared that the 1953 armistice agreement reestablishing the 38th parallel was a serious setback to unification efforts, the ROK government gained a Mutual Defense Treaty with the U.S. as well as vital economic assistance.

Interestingly in the ROK's 1948 Constitution, unification is cited only in the Preamble, "To consolidate national unity by Justice, Harmony, and Fraternity."[59]

It was Park Chung-hee who discarded the idea of employing force to reunify Korea, emphasizing the importance of building up national strength under the slogan "construction first, unification later." In 1970, Park embraced the concept of "peaceful unification" while demanding the North abandon attempts to communize the South.[60]

Indeed since the early 1970's the ROK unification policies have presented seemingly generous and bold proposals for non-aggression pacts, economic cooperation and a myriad of humanitarian and sporting dialogues, all of which have to various degrees fallen on fallow ground. Park Chung-hee's "Three Principles of Peaceful Unification." called for a non-aggression pact, progress in North/South dialogue to recover mutual trust and exchange between the two societies, and free nationwide elections to "set up a unified government." Park seemingly confident of the vote implored, "once Korea is reunified under our leadership, the wounds of division should be healed through collective efforts."[61]

In 1982, Chun Doo-hwan in his "Formula for National Reconciliation and Democratic Unification" proposed the formation of a Korean Unification Council with members from both sides to be tasked with writing a constitution for a unified democratic republic.

Realistically the reunification efforts of the *Yushin* regime and Chun Doo-hwan's Fifth Republic were moribund despite a myriad of gestures, proposals, and olive branches. This was partly due to Pyongyang's close ideological/political relationship with Beijing and Moscow as well as the rigid bipolar nature of the division. Roh Tae-woo would make a political chess-move.

Roh's July 1988 Declaration, the blueprint for *Nordpolitik*, was set in an historical period in which the static political confines of the Korean alliance systems were exhibiting flexibility, due to geopolitical and economic factors, thus offered an opportunity for success. While meaningful *entente* between Seoul and Pyongyang was lacking, it could be induced by focused diplomacy.

Roh called for a Korean Commonwealth in which both states would merge socio/political functions in a step by step plan leading to unification. He stated, "The Korean people are one, a unified Korea must be a single nation. No system for bringing the two parts of Korea together will accomplish genuine unification so long as it aims at perpetuating two states with differing ideologies."[62]

Constitutionally, the ROK maintained a legal mandate for unification. In the revised 1987 version, the Preamble exhorted majestically, "We the people of Korea, proud of a resplendent history and national traditions, having assumed the mission of democratic reform and reunification of our homeland, and having determined to consolidate national unity," which would be carried out with justice and brotherly love.

Article 3 states, "The territory of the Republic of Korea shall consist of the Korean peninsula and its adjacent islands." Clearly the constitution views the geographical entity of the historic nation as comprising the ROK state. Article 4, exhorts the ROK to "seek unification and formulate and carry out a policy of peaceful unification based on the principle of freedom and democracy."

Curiously, this became the first *de jure* call for national unification in ROK constitutional history.[63]

Importantly the first step in the proposed North/South dialogue occurred in September 1990, when the two countries' Prime Ministers met for the first time since the division. Follow-up rounds of talks held alternatively in Seoul and Pyongyang stressed confidence building measures. By the fifth meeting in December 1991, the Premiers signed an Agreement on Reconciliation, Non-aggression, Exchanges and Cooperation Between North and South. The so-called "Basic Agreement," hailed as an epic event in both Seoul and Pyongyang was the first document signed by both Koreas since 1948. The Meetings also held to the 31 December Declaration in which both the ROK and DPRK stipulated that both sides were prohibited from possessing or developing atomic weapons, or nuclear fuel reprocessing and uranium enrichment facilities.[64]

Neither Agreement has been implemented. Pyongyang's nuclear proliferation subsequently caused continuing regional security concerns in the wake of North Korea's continuing nuclear and missile tests. Yet, the remarkable proposals towards reunification put forward during Roh's tenure in the Blue House, placed the once seemingly moribund issue into the limelight of national aspirations. Unification fever following Germany's dramatic reunification in October 1990, furthermore, made Koreans keenly aware of the political hurdles and the economic price of such a move.

When Kim Young Sam assumed office at the Blue House, most of the external impediments to Korean unification had been removed; relations were good and business was thriving with the Russian Republic and People's China. Ties were close with Washington and Tokyo. The Soviet Union had disappeared as a geopolitical patron of Pyongyang; Beijing, engaged in massive trade with Seoul, did not support its DPRK comrades' political/military adventurism.

Kim Young Sam, the ROK's first freely elected civilian President in a generation took the Oath of Office; "I do solemnly swear before the people, that I shall execute the duties of the President by observing the Constitution, defending the State, *pursuing peaceful unification of the homeland,* promoting the freedom and welfare of the people and endeavoring *to* develop national culture." This oath exhorting unity, which first appeared in Article 69, was unique in Korean constitutional history.

Kim later told a hopeful audience that he would fulfill the mandate for national reconciliation and unification but that "what is needed now is not emotionalism but reasoned national consensus...South and North Korea must be genuinely willing to cooperate with each other." He implored, "My 70 million fellow Koreans, I say the motherland will be unified before the present century is over and will eventually become a land of freedom and peace."[65]

President Kim's unification policy goals reflected initial optimism followed by near neglect. As if to ensure optimism, Kim's inauguration stamp, featured a portrait of the 14th President of the Republic aside the ROK flag, its *taeguk* symbol hovering over the legendary Mt. Paektu in North Korea.

President Kim, speaking on the 50th Anniversary of the liberation from Japan outlined key policies; 1) the establishment of a peace regime on the Korean peninsula must be reached through direct consultations between the South and North;

2) the development of a permanent peace structure on the peninsula will require the cooperation and support of all the countries, but especially the major powers with interests in Korea;

3) a lasting peace will require the implementation of the previously concluded inter-Korean agreements, including the South-North Basic Agreement and the Joint Declaration on the De-nuclearization of the Korean peninsula.[66]

Securing stability on the peninsula remains as much a function of the ROK/U.S. defense treaty as the 1953 Military Armistice Agreement. The DPRK has consistently striven to nullify the 1953 Military Armistice and to sign a formal peace treaty directly with the United States thus shutting out South Korea. Pyongyang has pressed for a new peace mechanism which would essentially be a bilateral pact between the DPRK and U.S. Until that time, the 1953 ceasefire remains the operative agreement.

The landmark election of Kim Dae-jung, a former dissident and longtime labor leader, as ROK President changed the style and substance of Seoul's Northern policies. The new "Guidelines for North Korea Policy," were outlined at the onset of Kim's Administration in 1998; South Korea will never tolerate any armed provocation which destroys the peace; South Korea does not have any intention of pursuing unification by absorption of the North; and South Korea will expand reconciliation and cooperation with North Korea.[67]

President Kim's early days were burdened by the bad fortune of the East Asian economic collapse which faced the millstone of domestic business over regulation and governmental meddling in the economy. Equally the fast eroding economic situation in North Korea would preoccupy Kim's early tenure.

The Kim government adopted a "Sunshine Policy" of engagement towards the North. The policy treats political relations separately from economic exchanges, encourages greater private sector contacts with the North, and gives a green light to South Korea allies, the U.S. and Japan, to proceed with improving relations with North Korea.

According to Han Sung-joo, a former Foreign Minister, "initially the Sunshine policy received little resistance from the generally conservative South Korea public, most likely because the public felt that the dire situation in the North made it less of a threat." Han added that constituencies for inter-Korea exchanges, businessmen, nationalists and refugees from the North who wanted to have the opportunity to visit their home, supported the policy.[68]

The significant if highly scripted journey by South Korean President Kim Dae-Jung to Pyongyang was indeed extraordinary. Beyond heralding the highest level contacts between the estranged Korean governments in a half century, the State visit produced a kind of political euphoria or *Kimraderie* as the *Economist* dubbed it.

Though the two Kim's signed a wide-ranging communiqué during the three day visit, there remains a long way to go. They agreed in principle in ways to promote economic integration, achieve reconciliation, and eventually reunify their two countries.[69]

The subsequent enthusiasm sweeping Seoul saw North Korea's once vilified Marxist despot being politically *morphed* into a jocular if quirky politician. South Korea had allowed an almost giddy enthusiasm to overdrive its once cautious and calibrated relations with its northern cousins.

In the meantime Kim Dae-jung, the dissident turned statesman, was awarded the 2000 Nobel Peace Prize for his extraordinary political efforts to bring accord to the divided peninsula. Upon accepting the Peace Prize in Oslo, President Kim advised, "Unification, I believe, can wait until such a time when both sides feel comfortable enough in becoming one again, no matter how long it takes."

Donald Gregg, former American Ambassador to the ROK opined, "Of the nations in Northeast Asia, only South Korea has positive relations with all of its neighbors. It is clearly becoming the hub of the region, to thanks to President Kim's proactive diplomacy with Tokyo, Beijing, Moscow and Pyongyang."

Despite his landmark opening to the DPRK, follow-up relations with Pyongyang proved difficult and caused a subsequent reappraisal of Sunshine Policy. Moreover balancing the unique intra-Korean dialogue with very genuine security concerns from Seoul's major military and political ally, the USA, put Kim Dae-Jung on a political tightrope.

In the last year of the Clinton Administration there was genuine political momentum seeking rapprochement with communist North Korea in exchange for Pyongyang's purported pledges on missile non-proliferation. The moves which led to the visit of Secretary of State Madeleine Albright to Pyongyang, only to be feted at a classic DPRK propaganda spectacle with Kim Jong-il, were ultimately aimed at a political opening with North Korea.

The dialogue was based on the assumption that the DPRK, in dire economic straits, was apparently ready to agree to American demands.

The transition to the Bush Administration saw more focused and realistic view of both North Korea's missile capabilities, and as importantly the genuine willingness to pursue a verifiable non-proliferation regime. Nonetheless the Administration was in no hurry to sign an agreement with Pyongyang unless there could be genuine verification.

Transparency into the reaches of reclusive North Korea remains an imperfect science and thus the U.S. is correct to tilt to the side of caution more than to allow exuberant optimism to blur the politico/security agenda. The Bush logic was *not tainted by illusion* nor prompted by the need for a quick political fix; Pyongyang remains a major producer and exporter of missile technology to many Mid-Eastern states. The missiles moreover pose a direct and unambiguous regional threat not only to South Korea, but to Japan as well.

The evolution of North Korea's missile capability has prompted Japan to consider closer cooperation with the U.S. on theatre missile defense options.

Few Japanese don't recall the psychological trauma caused by Pyongyang's reckless missile test over the Japanese islands in 1998 or in subsequent tests.

Kim Dae-jung strove to ease strains with Washington and equally to continue a dialogue with Pyongyang. Such sentiments are not contradictory. While the ROK/U.S. Defense Treaty remains the lynchpin of Seoul's security, ongoing *Sunshine Policy* strove to find a political formula to lessen the mistrust, bridge the economic chasm, and defuse the massive intra-Korean military standoff, one of the remaining legacies of the Cold War.

The record was decidedly mixed. Indeed the left-leaning of Roh Moo-hyun would not only see rocky relations with Washington but as importantly, misjudge many of the signals from Pyongyang. "Kim Dae-jung and Roh Moo-hyun sought to transform Korean national identity. The Sunshine policy was presented as consistent with alliance, relations, international responsibilities and improved ties to each of Seoul's neighbors," writes Dr. Gilbert Rozman. "Offering bribes to Pyongyang with the expectation that they would be forthcoming at each stage of improved relations even if reciprocity was meager while empowering nongovernmental organizations with an idealistic worldview meant a distorted kind of *Koreanization.* Pyongyang could set the terms of the relationship," Rozman argued.[70]

While Kim Dae-jung "concentrated on the Sunshine Policy, thus transforming the image of North Korea into one of a partner able to embrace reunification, even when its domestic policies, development of weapons of mass destruction and belligerent rhetoric cast doubt on this decision," stated Rozman, adding, viewing Roh Moo-huyn's tenure between 2003 and 2008 saw the president cater to anti-Americanism and moreover "manipulating views on North Korea for domestic and international objectives with insufficient regard for national security."[71]

During Lee Myung-bak's presidency, ROK relations with the DPRK deteriorated. Under Lee Seoul had pursued a policy of "conditional engagement" as opposed to what Lee's conservatives considered the previous two administrations' "naive and dangerous unconditionally." After assuming office, Lee restated his policy as a 'grand bargain' in which Seoul would offer North Korea economic assistance and security guarantees in exchange for the DPRK's denuclearization.. North Korea's sinking of the South Korean Navy vessel *Cheonan* in March 2010 and the subsequent shelling of Yeonpyeong island changed the tone. Prof. Charles Armstrong asserts, "More than any previous South Korean Administration, the Lee Myung-bak administration has aligned itself fully with the U.S. priority on the threat of North Korea's nuclear program. South Korea has called repeatedly for North Korea's denuclearization as a prerequisite for diplomatic engagement and economic cooperation."[72]

The advent of Park Gwen-hye's administration in 2013, to the drumbeat of escalating North Korean rhetorical bombast and nuclear threats, edged the divided peninsula back from the brink. President Park, the daughter of the late leader Park Chung-hee, brought a steely resolve back to the *Blue House.*

In a diplomatic move to defuse tensions, Seoul's policy towards Pyongyang was recalibrated. Foreign Minister Yun Byong-se told the UN General Assembly, "The Repbulic of Korea is pursuing a policy called *Trustpolitik* to establish a regional order of reconciliation and cooperation in the Korean Peninsula as well as in Northeast Asia. *Trustpolitik*, in turn, is implemented through the Korean peninsula Trust Building Process."[73]

Containing any crisis and managing tensions with the unpredictable DPRK rulers remains a paramount focus for the Republic of Korea.

ENDNOTES

1. Seung-young Kim, "Russo-Japanese Rivalry over Korean Buffer at the Beginning of the 20th Century and its Implications," *Diplomacy & Statecraft* Vol. 16 December 2005, 620.

2. *Treaties Between China and Foreign States*, 1917, 590-591.

3. Kim, 639.

4. Tatsuo Kawai, *The Goal of Japanese Expansion*, (Tokyo: Hokuseido Press, 1938), 16.

5. U.S. Department of State (USDS), Korea's Independence, (Washington DC: Far East Series, 1947), 16.

6. Cordell Hull, *Memoirs of Cordell Hull*, (New York: Macmillian, 1948), 1584-1596.

7. USDS, Korea's Independence, 17.

8. Don Oberdorfer, *The Two Koreas; A Contemporary History*, (New York: Basic Books, 2001), 7.

9. Rosalyn Higgins, *United Nations Peacekeeping 1946-1967/Vol. 2 Asia*, (Oxford: Oxford University Press, 1970), 155.

10. United Nations General Assembly (UNGA) Verbatim September 1947, 22.

11. United Nations General Assembly (UNGA) Resolutions, 1947, 16-17.

12. USDS, The Record on Korean Unification 1943-60, (Washington DC: Far East Series, 1960), 10.

13. Donald MacDonald, *The Koreans: Contemporary Politics and Society*, (Boulder, CO: Westview, 1990), 48-49.

14. Ronald McGlothlen, *Controlling the Waves: Dean Acheson and U.S. Foreign Policy in Asia*, (New York: Norton, 1993), 60-63.

15. UNGA Resolutions 1948, 25-27.

16. Record on Korean Unification, 11.

17. Richard C. Allen, *Korea's Syngman Rhee: An Unauthorized Portrait*, (Rutland, VT: Tuttle, 1960). 104.

18. UN/Bulletin October 1949, 450.

19. *New York Times*, 1 October 1993.

20. UNSC, Resolutions, 1950, 4-5.

21. Record on Korean Unification, 99.

22. UNSC, Resolutions, 1950, 5.

23. McGlothlen, 67-74.

24. Michael Breen *The Koreans*, (New York: St. Martin's Griffin, 2004), 124.

25. Sakong II, *Korea in the World Economy*, (Washington DC: Institute for International Economics, 1993), 2, 96.

26. Frank Gibney, *Korea's Quiet Revolution; From Garrison State to Democracy*, (New York: Walker and Company, 1992), 54-55.

27. Andrew Natsios, "The Secret Success of U.S. Aid to South Korea," Korea's Economy 2012, (Washington DC: Korean Economic Institute of America, 2012), 43-44.

28. *Handbook of Korea*: 1990, (Seoul: Korea Overseas Information Service, 1990), 363-364.

29. Gibney, 56.

30. *International Trade Statistics Yearbook; 2008*, (New York: United Nations, 2009), 222-223.

31. Junkyu Lee, "Korea's Trade Structure and Its Policy Challenges," Korea's Economy 2012, 21-22.

32. Kye Woo Lee, "Aid by Korea: Progress and Challenges," Korea's Economy 2012, pp. 46-47, ROK Press/UN, Address by Lee Myung-bak to the 66th Session of the General Assembly of the United Nations, 21 September 2011.

33. Referenced: census trade/statistics/highlights/2012.

34. Uk Heo and Terence Roehrig, South Korea Since 1980, (Cambridge: Cambridge University Press, 2010), 187-188.

35. Du-yong Kang, Lee Sang-ho and Hwang Sun-oong, "Korea's Post-Crisis Economic Reliance on China and Policy Suggestions," *Korea Focus*, 19 (Spring 2011), 106-110.

36. South Korea Since 1980, 119 and 188.

37. World Bank/*Trends in Developing Economies*, 1993, 266.

38. John J. Metzler, *Korean Diplomacy*, Global Affairs (Winter 1990), 130-131.

39. Geydong Kim, "South Korea's *Nordpolitik* and Its Impact on Inter-Korean Relations," East Asian Review 4 (Spring 1992), 47.

40. July Declaration, 1988, 3-8.

41. ROK Press/UN October 1988, 7-12.

42. Author Interview/Foreign Minister Choi, October 1990.

43. UN/ Secretariat 238 1990, 1.

44. UN/Secretariat 1247, 1990, 1.

45. "Korean Diplomacy, " 137.

46. UN General Assembly (UNGA)/4769 1961, 1-2.

47. Daniel P. Moynihan, *A Dangerous Place* (Boston: Little, Brown and Company, 1978), 143-144.

48. UN Security Council (UNSC) PV 30 September 1975, 23-25.

49. UNSC 20830, 5 September 1989, 3.

50. UNSC 20858, 21 September 1989, 6.

51. UNGA Committee on Contributions 1991, 18-19.

52. UN Secretariat 28 February 2001, 7-9, and UN Secretariat ST/ADM/ser.b/966, 24 December 2012, 3-5.

53. Author Interview/Foreign Minister Choi, October 1990.

54. ROK Press/UN June 1991.

55. *Far Eastern Economic Review*, 11 June 1992, 8.

56. South Korea Since 1980, 188.

57. "Towards a Peaceful World," 1991, 13-15.

58. July Declaration 1988, 7.

59. ROK Constitution 1955, 1-3.

60. Kim Hong Nack, "The Koreas in Search of Reunification," 430.

61. Chung-hee Park, Korea Reborn: A Model for Development, (Englewood Cliffs, NJ: Prentice Hall, 1979), 120-122.

62. *Korea: A Nation Transformed; Selected Speeches of President Roh Tae-woo*, (Seoul: The Presidential Secretariat, 1990), 90-92.

63. ROK Constitution 1987, 5-6.

64. "The Koreas in Search of Reunification," 430-432.

65. ROK Constitution 1987, 24 and ROK Press/UN 25 February 1993.

66. *Korea Update* 1996, 1.

67. *Korea Update* 1998.

68. Zoellick, Robert and Philip Zelikow/Editors, *America and the East Asian Crisis; Memo to a President*, (New York: Norton, 2000), 94-95.

69. Myers, B, The Cleanest Race; How North Koreans See Themselves and Why it Matters, (Brooklyn, New York: Melville House, 2010), 55.

70. Gilbert Rozman, "South Korea's National Identity Sensitivity: Evolution, Manifestation, Prospects," Academic Paper Series on Korea Vol. 3 Korea Economic Institute, 2010, 71.

71. Ibid, 73.

72. Charles Armstrong, "South Korea and the Six Party Talks: The Least Bad Option?" Joint U.S.- Korea Academic Studies, Vol. 21, 2011, (Washington DC: Korea Economic Institute, 2011), 172-175.

73. ROK Press/UN 27 September 2013, 2.

Chapter 5

Democratic People's Republic of Korea/ The North

Kim/Stalin/Mao and the War

The roots of the Korean War rest in the still controversial events resulting from the peninsula's division in 1945. The collapse of Imperial Japan and the rapid occupation of north Korea by Red Army units and south Korea by American forces, presented Koreans with a *de facto* situation. The 38th parallel has since divided the peninsula into a North/South political configuration, an enduring legacy of WWII. The line was intended as a temporary demarcation.

When the Soviet XXV Army moved into Pyongyang on 24 August 1945, they found the "Committee for the Preparation of Korean Independence" was already in existence. Led by the Christian nationalist Cho Man-sik, it had received a direct transfer of power from the Japanese provincial Governor. It consisted of eighteen rightwing nationalists and two communists.

The first actions of the Occupation forces were to undermine Cho's leadership. On 26 August a Committee was established with Cho as Chairman but with members equally divided between communists and nationalists. On 14 September, the Soviets outlined their policy guidelines; the establishment of a government representing the workers and peasants, land redistribution, confiscation of Japanese-owned industry; and a purge of pro-Japanese Koreans.[1]

North Korea's complicated communist political hagiography dates to the anxious days when four rival factions vied for power under the mantle of Soviet Occupation—the Yenan Faction, the Soviet Faction, the Partisan Faction, and the South Korean Worker's Party/Nampo Faction.

On special instructions from the Soviet and Chinese Communist Party, cadres from the Soviet Union and Yenan were to remain north of the 38th parallel, gathered in the small capital of Pyongyang. In terms of training, personalities and exploits, the Yenan and the Soviet factions were most formidable, according to Lim Un. The Yenan members were Chinese Communist Party cadres with military and ideological experience. The Soviet cadres were specialists with administrative ability; most were members of the Soviet Communist Party. The Partisan Faction, of which Kim Il-sung, a Red Army Captain was a member, was comprised of Koreans who had fled to the Soviet Union in the early 1940's and who had later served in the Red Army.[2]

Moscow trained about 300 cadres from each group to assume administrative duties following the Japanese capitulation. Many held USSR citizenship and Soviet Communist Party membership. Following the Leninist policy of party supremacy over administrative structures, and intended to weaken the indigenous political forces, the Soviets set about political control of North Korea.[3]

On 14 October, amid great fanfare to welcome the Red Army, Pyongyang citizens were surprisingly introduced to their "liberator" General Kim Il-sung. Curiously, the 33-year old partisan had faced clear competition from both the respected nationalist Cho Man-sik and other communists. Kim the son of a Presbyterian elder, was actually educated in Chinese and over the next twenty years saw his loyalty swing between the Chinese and Soviet Communist Party. Indeed many ethnic Koreas fought in Mao's armies in China while others served the Soviets. Kim was selected from several candidates presented to NKVD Chief Beria, who met him several times before Stalin gave the final blessing. Stalin selected Kim being convinced that General Kim would obey Soviet orders, and because according to Becker, "they could rely on him to show total obedience."[4]

Significantly, Kim Il-sung was favored by Stalin over the stalking horses of the fractious factions. Here one finds the roots of two major trends in the iconography of Kim's rule; his selection by Marshall Stalin and his playing off the domestic Yenan, Soviet, and Nampo Factions. Kim's later political gyrations between Beijing and Moscow, and his indigenous *Juche* ideology, were part of his political iconoclasm.

The Moscow agreement in December 1945 sought to implement the Four Power Trusteeship Status (U.K. U.S., USSR and Nationalist China) which would continue for five years. The clumsy move sparked a wave of peninsula-wide resentment by Koreans who saw it as a tactic to delay long awaited self-determination. Cho Man-sik called the accord a "sellout of Korea to the Soviet Union." Kim accepted the Soviet trusteeship but rejected the UN decision to hold elections that he knew he would not win. "By 1949, his DPRK was a fully-fledged Stalinist dictatorship with labor camps, purges, arbitrary arrests, public executions, and a personality cult. Kim erected a statue to himself before he was even 40 and began calling himself 'The Great Leader' or *Suryong*.[5]

Kim Il-sung and Syngman Rhee were the dominant political figures in the two zones. As Bruce Cummings writes, "Rhee was a septuagenarian who had lived in the U.S. for nearly four decades, had a Ph.d from Princeton, and had taken an Austrian wife; a patriot well known for devoting his life to Korean independence, he was also a willful man of legendary obstinacy and strong anti-communist beliefs. Kim Il-sung as had begun armed resistance in the Sino-Korean border region shortly after the Japanese established the puppet state of Manchukuo in 1932, and was fortunate enough to survive a rugged guerilla war that had killed most of his comrades by 1945. Although both leaders had the support of the respective superpower, neither was an easily malleable person, let alone a puppet."[6]

The U.N. mandated elections in South Korea in May 1948 and the subsequent establishment of the Republic on 15 August under President Syngman Rhee, presented the Pyongyang communists with a *fait accompli* and a *de facto* foe in the newly-born Republic of Korea. Although the North boycotted the U.N. sponsored vote, the communists supported "elections" to the Supreme People's Assembly throughout North and "secretly" in South Korea on 25 August 1948. The Supreme People's Assembly proclaimed the Democratic People's Republic of Korea (DPRK) on 9 September; predictably Kim Il-sung was appointed as its first leader. Korea's division thus became formalized with the *de facto* establishment of the ROK and the DPRK.

Meantime in the South, in 1948 local communists were carrying out a low level insurgency against the ROK; a Democratic Front for Unification of the Fatherland was founded in Pyongyang. The group's goals included support for the DPRK, a pullout of U.S. forces and the U.N. Commission, and a call for national elections in 1949. The plan seen as a classic Trojan Horse, was combined with Pyongyang's spurious claim that Supreme People's Assembly elections had been "secretly" carried out in South Korea, thus setting the pretext for unification. Political rumblings in the South combined with Pyongyang's covert military plans for an invasion proceeded accordingly.

On New Year's Day 1950, Kim Il-sung addressed Koreans, "In 1949 our mission of unifying the fatherland was not accomplished. The circumstances made us build a strong base in the northern half to lay the groundwork for unification. The People's Army should be combat-ready to eliminate the enemy anytime...1950 is hoped to be a year of national reunification, bringing hope and honor to the whole Korean people marching forward towards victory."[7]

In May 1950, Kim opined on unity in classic communist lexicon, "The Worker's Party, the Democratic Front for The Reunification of the Fatherland led by the Party, the government of the DPRK, and all the Korean people who are rallied around it, will advance vigorously for the complete independence and reunification of their country and for peace and democracy. They will certainly win the final victory."[8]

Traditionalist historians hold that the Korean War was hatched and directed by Moscow, Beijing or both. Such viewpoints attach too much importance to the role of big powers. Yet, it was hardly likely that North Korea acted on its own without the knowledge of the Soviets, their main source of aid and guidance. *Glasnost* in Gorbachev's USSR shed new light into the war's murky origins. A Radio Moscow interview with historian Mikhail Sminorov stressed; North Korea had been building its military since 1945 for an invasion of the South, in early 1950 Kim Il-sung made a secret trip to Moscow to meet with Stalin to discuss the invasion, the war was clearly begun as a surprise attack by North Korea on the South.[9]

While seemingly rhetorical, Moscow's admissions broke with the official Soviet line that the U.S. had attacked North Korea. While Kim had met with Stalin in 1949, only recently did the 1950 trip became known. "The birth of the two Koreas has the same origin as the two Germanies," according to the Moscow magazine *New Times*, "Josef Stalin quickly established socialist style states in East Germany and North Korea under the control of Soviet occupation forces." *New Times* added, "With the full approval from Stalin and Mao, Kim Il-sung launched the Korean war which cost four million lives. Stalin helped Kim not only by supplying weapons but also by dispatching air force pilots and military advisors."[10]

Viewed in the context of the times, 1950 seemed to favor the DPRK's revolutionary momentum. A year earlier the Soviets acquired the A-Bomb and Mao conquered Mainland China, two extraordinary geopolitical events *tilting* East Asia's balance of power.

The decision to dispatch Chinese "volunteers" to Korea was made arbitrarily by Mao Tse-tung. On 2 October 1950, a year and a day after the founding of the People's Republic of China, Mao made the decision to send "volunteers" to Korea. "If we allow the United States to occupy all of Korea, Korean revolutionary power will suffer a fundamental defea...and have negative effects on the entire Far East," Mao cabled Stalin on 2 October. Mao's telegram recognized the very real possibility of a major war with Washington; the document implied that Peking acted out of fear that a U.S. victory in Korea could reverse the communist revolution on the Chinese Mainland itself.

While Stalin had offered air cover for the Chinese "volunteers," the Soviet leader soon reneged on the promise, sowing the seeds of the Sino/Soviet rivalry. Premier Zhou Enlai made a secret visit to Moscow to persuade Stalin to support the Chinese initiative but to no avail. The PRC Politburo decided to go ahead with the operation anyway; it commenced on 19 October.

Approximately 20,000 Soviet military personnel were estimated to have taken part in the Korean war, although never on the front lines. "Stalin sent Soviet Mig-15's with Chinese markings and Soviet pilots, mostly WWII veterans dressed in Chinese uniforms," writes Becker. In November the PRC dispatched 300,000 "volunteers," who soon overwhelmed the UN forces.[11]

Building Socialism/The Early Victory

Economically speaking, northern Korea was the nation's industrial heartland; heavy industry, factories, and port facilities were part of the infrastructure Kim Il-sung's communists inherited from the Japanese. Thus, on one level, North Korea had a firm socio/economic footing on which to expand.

Immediately after the Korean War in 1953, Pyongyang launched an industrialization drive stressing iron and steel, machine tools, shipbuilding, mining, electric power. In 1956, the three-year plan (soon to follow the Soviet-style five year plan) was declared over-fulfilled. Heavy industry had received 80 percent of the funds; by 1959 agricultural collectivization was complete. While adopting the Soviet command economy, output in the early years reached dizzying growth rates, 42 percent during 1954-56 and 37 percent annually during the 1957-61 Five Year Plan.[12]

The Flying Horse Campaign, *Chollima,* begun in 1958, coincided with China's equally vainglorious Great Leap Forward. *Chollima* stressed socialist competition, worker exhortation, with a corresponding statistical exaggeration in a bid to keep pace with *Stakanivite* goals. A major factor contributing to high growth rates in the 1950's was the injection of substantial foreign aid from the

Communist countries. This aid dwindled during the 1960's. Yet the high growth rates reflected the reality that rebuilding the war-ravaged country would spur initial growth. They slowed later when the inherent inefficiencies of the Soviet model began to take hold.[13]

According to Seoul's Research Institute for National Unification, a study of the DPRK and ROK economic aggregates from 1953 to 1990 illustrate that while ROK per capita income was higher in 1953 ($76 versus $58) in 1960 the numbers soon narrowed;

1960	ROK	$94	DPRK	$137
1962	ROK	$87	DPRK	$168
1970	ROK	$248	DPRK	$286
1975	ROK	$591	DPRK	$579

But by the 1980's South Korean growth surged—

1980	ROK	$1,589	DPRK	$758
1985	ROK	$2,047	DPRK	$765
1990	ROK	$5,569	DPRK	$1,064

While South Korea was nearly completely devastated by the 1950-53 War, rebuilding was not initially so dynamic largely due to Seoul's over-dependence on U.S. foreign aid. Economic reliance on official aid rather than on productive capacity, posed a serious structural obstacle overcome by Park Chung-hee.[14]

North Korea experienced uncommonly rapid growth up to the early 1960's. Once a certain stage of economic development and complexity was reached, however, the Stalinist model exhibited systematic limitations.

Yet, the estimates for DPRK growth averages are:

9.8%	Between	1961-65
5.5%	Between	1966-70
10.4%	Between	1971-75
4.1%	Between	1976-80

1.7%	Between	1981-84
2.4%	Between	1985-86
-1.3%	Between	1987-92
-2.2%	Between	1993-99

Prior to 1960, ROK growth rates were anemic as compared with the DPRK's average of 20 percent.[15]

Unlike China and most communist states of Eastern Europe, North Korea adhered to rigid authoritarianism and Stalinist state planning more closely than the Soviet Union itself. Yet, North Korea made modifications. Desiring an independent national personality and reacting to foreign aid reductions from the Soviet Union and China, Kim created the *Juche* or self-reliance doctrine. By 1975 a falling North Korean growth rate coincided with an expanding South Korean rate.[16]

In 1984, in a bid to encourage needed foreign investment, Pyongyang promoted its only flexible economic policy in a generation, the Joint Venture Law. The plan intended to open the closed economy to the outside world. Focused on the pro-DPRK General Association of Korean residents *Chongnyon* in Japan, the scheme had limited results in revitalizing the moribund economy. The plan was rooted in a bid to copy China's economic opening and to use economic revitalization to revive the moribund socialist political system. Pyongyang later promulgated three foreign investment laws in 1992; Law on Foreign Investment, Law on Joint Ventures, Law on Foreign Enterprises. This action signaled a cautious open door policy.

Chongnyon business activities in Japan, particularly in Osaka's game parlors, have been a major conduit for cash to the DPRK, an estimated $600 million annually going to the Hermit Kingdom to among, other things, fund the Yongbyon nuclear complex. Such money laundering, according to the police, comes from among the Koreans in Japan loyal to Kim. Trade with Tokyo remained the major non-communist commercial conduit for the North Koreans.

Prior to the political collapse of the East Bloc/USSR, economic ties between the DPRK and the socialist states were already in flux, due to the ROK's remarkable commercial inroads into the communist world, as well as a clear inability to offset "solidarity trade," namely, barter for petroleum. Although Kim Il-sung had trumpeted his doctrine of *Juche*, in reality North Korea's economy was being propped up by large dollops of aid from the Soviet Union and China. Even before the USSR collapsed, North Korea was beginning to learn what real self-reliance meant.

A deterioration in DPRK commercial relations with the communist states is best exemplified by the Soviet demand in 1991 that Pyongyang must pay for crude oil in convertible currency. This reality triggered a precipitous drop in DPRK petroleum imports from the former Soviet Union but likewise opened a new political/economic relationship with the Islamic Republic of Iran. Since 1993, PRC/DPRK trade has been conducted through a cash not barter basis. The PRC was North Korea's main trading partner with $624 million in 1994 falling from $900 million in 1993. DPRK trade with the ex-USSR in the same period sank from $1.1 billion in 1990 to $365 million in 1991 and $140 million in 1994. China, South Korea, and Russia remain the DPRK's major trade partners.[17]

Pyongyang's global trade volume has exhibited a dangerous decline in recent years ranging from $800 million in 1970, $2.1 billion in 1975, $4.8 billion in 1988 and $4.7 billion in 1990, and $2.6 billion in 1993 according to the Korean Trade Promotion Corporation in Seoul. Although the regime has not placed the same emphasis on exports as the ROK, the volume has been in clear decline. By 2010, two-way trade had reached only $4 billion.[18]

The DRPK trade numbers have since soured. Though North Korea does not publish trade statistics, the Korean Trade-Investment Promotion Agency (KOTRA) in Seoul has tabulated estimates. In 2009 North Korea only exported $2 billion of which $793 million went to China, $934 million to South Korea and a piddling $21 million to Russia.

Most of the South Korean "imports" were finished goods which originated in the Kaesong Industrial zone. North Korea imported $3 billion in the same year with $1.8 billion most crude oil from the PRC, $745 million from South Korea and $41 million from Russia. Notably absent was trade with Japan or the USA. The $1 billion trade deficit is mostly funded by the ethnic Korean *Chongnyon* organization.[19]

North Korean economic growth rates equally exhibit near free-fall in recent years:

Seoul's Bank of Korea lists North Korean growth rates:

DPRK		ROK	
2.7%	vs	7.0%	in 1985
3.3%	vs	12.8%	in 1987
-3.7%	vs	9.0%	in 1990
-5.2%	vs	8.4%	in 1991
-4.2%	vs	5.5%	in 1993
-4.1%	vs	8.9%	in 1995
-6.3%	vs	5.0%	in 1997
-1.1%-	vs	-6.7%	in 1998
6.2%	vs	10.9%	in 1999
1.3%	vs	8.8%	in 2000
3.7%	vs	3.0%	in 2001
2.1%	vs	4.6%	in 2004
3.8%	vs	4.0%	in 2005
-1.0%	vs	5.2%	in 2006
3.1%	vs	2.3%	in 2008

(Bank of Korea, Seoul, November 2011)

DPRK   **ROK**

-0.9%	vs	0.3%	in 2009
-0.5%	vs	6.2%	in 2010
0.8%	vs	3.7%	in 2011

(Bank of Korea, Seoul, 2012)

In 1990, the DPRK's population was estimated at 22 million; the ROK's at 43 million. The National Unification Board in Seoul estimates that North Korea's 1990 GNP $23 billion (ROK $238 billion) and DPRK per capita income at $1,064 (ROK $5,569). Thus North Korea's GNP and per capita income stood at ten percent and twenty percent of South Korea's respectively.[20]

By 2010, the chasm grew with North Korean GNI at 2.6 percent the size of the South Korean economy and its per capita GNI at only 5.3 percent of the South.[21]

Viewed over the period 1990 to 1999, the DPRK economy faced the stark *triple witching* of socialist stagnation, natural disasters, and the East Asian economic crisis. The population remained static at 23 million.

The North Korean economy shrank in 2010. Indeed the per capita income stands at 25 percent below the 1990 peak. "Today's North Korean economy is characterized by macroeconomic instability, an uneven track record on policy change, and growing inequality and corruption," writes Marcus Noland. Based on Transparency International analysis of corruption, the DPRK holds the dubious distinction of being the world's most corrupt state.[22]

Economic deterioration is the order of the day in the DPRK. Statistical abstracts which invariably must make a synthesis of varied and disparate sources, conclude that the widening GDP gap between the North and South, poses a serious socio/economic roadblock to national reunification.

Kim Il-sung and Kim Jong-il/ god the Father and the Son

It is perhaps an understatement to say that the Great Leader Kim Il-sung, *Suryong*, Sun of the Ages, and Supreme and Beloved Leader of Korea cannot be described. For in the *bizarre political iconography* of North Korea, a land founded by Stalin, "Sun of Mankind," one should perhaps expect no less a vainglorious tradition.

Nowhere in the Communist world excepting the personality cult of Stalin and Mao Tse-tung, did the leader of an East Asian state bathe himself in the epic saga that has become the *Cult* of Kim Il-sung. In the modern political hagiography of socialist states, nowhere but in Nicolae Ceausescu's Romania did the Cult of Leadership reach the dizzying heights and absurdity grandly exhibited in the DPRK. North Korea exalts a bizarre political tradition of leader worship, political exhortation through *Juche*, and a dynastic succession unknown anywhere. To concede that North Korea is a classic totalitarian regime presents an understatement; the Democratic People's Republic of Korea is *ruled by a unique form of Marxist monarch, the Kim Dynasty.*

Setting aside the customary usage of miscellaneous modifiers such as the "Sun of the Nation," and "The Great Chieftain," which are put before and after his name to glorify him since the 1970's, the Cult of Kim, according to defector Lim Un, has become "a world of fantasy based on leaps of lies."[23]

Kim was born 15 April 1912, and played a modest resistance role, later inflated by the Soviets to make him the leader of the anti-Japanese movement. Today 50,000 Kim statues, many of marble and granite, grace the countryside. The Museum of the Revolution in Pyongyang has 95 halls with three miles of exhibits glorifying the Great Leader. In 1992, his 80th birthday celebration extravaganza cost $1 billion. In 2012, the Centennial of his birth was feted in the impoverished DPRK.

Pyongyang, the capital of the Red Dynasty, has grown into a shining symbol to the *Kim Cult*. An Arch of Triumph twice the size of the Paris monument, wide boulevards which resound to the martial music of the Kim Il-sung Song and goose-stepping troops and cadres, and the Golden Kim Statue all evoke *an Oz-like charm*.

Yet, in a calculated move to preserve the dynastic rule, from the early 1970's the personality cult which deified Kim Il-sung, began to focus adulation on his first son Jong-il, born 16 February 1942. "When Kim Jong-il became the apparent heir in 1974, there was a two-tier structure or a sort of co-kingship; with the father leading," advises Becker.[24]

Jong-il became known as *Dear Leader*. North Korean literary lexicon imbibes deification based on historical connections with the legendary Mt. Paekdu as in this *Ode to the Leader*:

> On the top of Mt. Paekdu Three Great Stars Rose;
> the Great General Star (Kim Il-sung)
> the Mother Star (Kim Jong-suk/his first wife) the
> the Lodestar of Mr. Paekdu (Kim Jong-il)

Although born near Khabarovsk in Soviet Siberia, Korea's sacred Mt. Paekdu has emerged as Kim Jong-il's "birthplace." Appropriately, as reported by the Korean Central Broadcasting Station in Pyongyang, "During the February Festival celebrating Jong-Il's birthday, very clear and beautiful *double rainbows* had mystically appeared in the skies over the sacred site of Milyong and Jong-il Peak, a pinnacle of Mt. Paekdu renamed for *Dear Leader*." Another account adds, "When he was born at the foot of Mount Paektu on February 16, 1942, a double rainbow appeared and a comet traversed the sky."[25]

Jong-il was officially anointed his father's successor in 1980, by 1982 joined the Supreme People's Assembly and assumed the title of *Dear Leader*. He became the object of his own personality cult, relates Myers, and "much has been made of his birth on scared Mount Paektu (though he had actually been born in the USSR).[26]

World Leaders and common-folk alike pay homage to the Kims. The Museum on Mount Mohyang has a six story building in appropriate socialist realism with tribute treasures from around the world; gifts of a crocodile leather attaché case from Castro, a bearskin from Ceaucescu, a plush railway car sent by Stalin, and a smaller railway coach from Mao.[27]

The Worker's Party newspaper *Rodong Shinmun* extols the Kim cult especially in the Feb 16 and April 15 birthday issues. The political honorifics and titles for Kim Il-Sung and Dear Leader increase in mathematical proportion as their birthdays near. References to Kim have become a *sine qua non* of any DPRK speech, editorial, or pronouncement.

The DPRK's Marxist monarchy has its own numerology; on Kim Jong-Il's 51st birthday in 1993, Pyongyang city was bedecked with 2,160,000 flowers. During the loyalty Festival between 16 February and 15 April, North Koreans can savor life in the "Paradise on Earth" with special rations for food, soap, and toothpaste. The gaiety came amid world concern over Pyongyang pulling out of the Nuclear Non-Proliferation Treaty and amid a call by Supreme Military Commander Kim Jong-il, for a state of semi-war.

Bellicose tactics are not novel to the DPRK leadership. To shore up his power base with the military, Dear Leader regularly put the DPRK on a semi-war footing in response to the annual ROK/USA *Team Spirit* Defense exercises.

"The founder of the world's only communist dynasty, the Great Leader wanted to make the whole peninsula his legacy to his son, a graduate of an East German military academy in the times when East Germany was Europe's North Korea," opined Moscow's *New Times*. But as the author adds, "the interest of Soviet foreign policy is in breaking the useless military and economic alliance with the medieval monster whose teaching is the feudal variant of Stalinism…Kim Il-sung is *not worth* an alliance."

Seriously speaking Kim Il-sung was a greater phenomenon than he is portrayed in North Korea's funny propaganda intended for foreign consumption, "Those who have visited North Korea are shocked by the *Orwellian* character of the society that Kim created. In a society like this, people develop sincere and even exulted unanimity by the third generation. They love Big Brother."[28]

Following Kim Il-sung's death in 1994, his embalmed body was placed in Pyongyang's Kumsusan Memorial Palace. The Central Committee of the Worker's Party spoke of entombing the "Great Leader in a image of eternal life." As with Lenin and Mao, the dead dictator's tomb became a place of political pilgrimage. Despite his death, Kim Il-sung eternally retains the title of President of the Democratic People's Republic of Korea, in dynastic tradition.

Adulation of Jong-il was no less intense. "Today the Korean people are celebrating the birthday of our leader Kim Jong-il at a time when the entire Party, army, and people are accelerating the reconstruction of our country as a *Kangsong Taeguk*…Great Leader comrade Kim Jong-il's ideology is the noble, revolutionary mental food fueling our victorious march and the General's will is the guideline leading us to justice and truth," extolled a *Rodong Shinmun* editorial.[29]

At the time of Jong-il's death in December 2011, his son Kim Jong-un (28) assumed supreme power.

In life Kim had brilliantly combined the philosophical concepts of authoritarian Confucianism (respect), Marxism-Leninism (socialism/brute power), and traditional Korean rites of *Shamanism* (mysticism) into an arcane blend of political rule. In death he was mourned by his dour minions in the finest Orwellian tradition. Thus Big Brother had in a sense become a supra-natural figure, the grist of legend and double rainbows.

North Korea and the World; Diplomats, Guns, and Festivals

Until the early 1970's both China and North Korea proceeded along strikingly similar policy parameters. Both represented the communist side of the national divide, both were politically isolated, and both were ruled by cult/idol leaders who emerged from the cauldron of WWII resistance to the Japanese. The China of the "Great Helmsman" and the Korea of the "Great Leader" had been embarrassingly outshone economically and isolated politically by their free cousins.

Sino/American rapprochement and the subsequent admission of the People's Republic of China into the United Nations in 1971 changed the political atmosphere on the Korean peninsula and throughout East Asia. U.N. admission proved a diplomatic watershed for Beijing; for Pyongyang, the trickle down benefit would be a powerful ally on the Security Council and a hitherto unknown political legitimacy. In April 1973, for the first time in its twenty- five year history, the DPRK opened full diplomatic relations with several West European countries; Denmark, Finland, Iceland, Norway and Sweden. Likewise Pyongyang forged official links with Argentina and Iran. Equally important, the DPRK was accorded Observer Status in the U.N.[30]

Similar to Beijing's earlier efforts to expand diplomatic and trade ties in the early 1970's, the DPRK instituted a wide range of measures aimed at promoting Pyongyang's prestige. The reasons were manifold but stemmed from the need to nullify the ROK's socio-economic success, to *share or stop* the Seoul Olympics, and to keep the ROK out of the U.N. In all these central policy objectives, her diplomacy failed.

Nonetheless, North Korea had developed a community of ideological/military interests with much of the former East Bloc, the USSR, radical Third World states and "liberation movements." By the mid-1980's, Pyongyang maintained diplomatic ties with 100 countries (67 of whom cross recognize the ROK). Likewise in this period, Pyongyang stationed at least 8,000 military advisors in Africa through a series of bi-lateral security pacts. Pyongyang's *Juche* development model interested many observers. While North Koreans arrived in sub-Saharan Africa as early as 1965 to participate in agricultural and public works projects, by the 1970's African regimes were benefiting from DPRK security expertise, support to guerrillas, and forming elite "praetorian guards" detachments.

A multiplicity of military accords between the DPRK and Uganda, Ghana, Libya, and Ethiopia in the early 1980's became the order of the day. Following the independence of ex-Rhodesia in 1980, Zimbabwe's Premier Robert Mugabe appealed for military assistance; the DPRK sent an training unit of 106 advisors. By 1982, the elite 5th Brigade, shock troops infamous for ethnic genocide, was comprised of 750 North Koreans. DPRK units were active in a dozen countries.[31]

The Mediterranean island of Malta, illustrated a typical case of how a nominally non-aligned nation drifted into Pyongyang's diplomatic and defense sphere. The island's ruling Labour Party (Socialist), opened diplomatic ties with Pyongyang in 1972. Before long delegations from the tiny nation were regular pilgrims to Pyongyang; the visitors were feted in grand style in exchange for political tribute.[32]

In 1982, a secret defense agreement providing Malta with North Korean military advisors and weapons was signed. Also, the strategic Luqa airport was used by North Korean aircraft transiting to Africa. Malta's foreign policy began to parrot Pyongyang's until Labour was ousted in 1987 elections.

The DRPK's political isolation increased exponentially with the fall of the East Bloc/USSR and communist regimes worldwide. The once steady procession of solidarity delegations to Pyongyang to pay tribute to the Great Leader and Dear Leader dropped precipitously with only a smattering of official delegations from China, Cameroon or Cuba, fraternal groups such as the Communist Party of Greece, the Japan Socialist Party, or a motley gaggle of *political groupies* in *Juche* Study societies from Benin to Norway.

Diplomatically the DPRK is still widely recognized. Pyongyang maintained relations with 147 countries in 2001 although only 23 states maintain legations in the capital. Although cross recognition of the two *de facto* Korean states has been a reality for nearly two decades, the advent of *Nordpolitik* increased the quantity but not the quality of diplomatic posts in Pyongyang. This changed appreciably in 2000 when members of the European Union notably Italy, United Kingdom, and Germany opened diplomatic relations. By early 2001 Brazil and New Zealand established ties with North Korea.

Nonetheless, neither Washington nor Tokyo maintains *de jure* diplomatic relations with Pyongyang. Sweden provides consular services for the United States in North Korea. But while the U.S. has relaxed its trade embargo, Japan had been the North's major non-communist business partner with $375 million in trade in 2000, or less than ten percent of Tokyo's trade with the ROK.

Commerce between Tokyo and Pyongyang is channeled through the *Chongnyon*, the General Association of Korean residents in Japan, which actively lobbies to promote DPRK policy as well as represent the interests of a sizable minority of Korean residents. *Chongnyon* was founded in 1955, as one may expect, "thanks to the wise leadership of and kind assistance extended by the respected leader Kim Il-sung." In their heyday, the group supported 300 chapters, a University, and 154 schools. It also maintains companies and prints the English weekly *People's Korea*.

The group acts as a financial pipeline to the cash-strapped DPRK remitting more than $750 million annually until the mid-1990's. The organization which comprises 200,000 "patriotic Koreans" faces a decline in both ideological fervor and membership from second generation members. Cash flow from *Chongnyon businesses and rackets* to "support the socialist fatherland" has been in serious decline due to Japan's economic recession, police surveillance, and was estimated at $100 million annually in 2000.[33]

More ominously, North Korea has an expanding relationship with Islamic Iran. Rooted both in ideological hostility to the U.S., and a need to procure needed petroleum supplies on a barter basis, Pyongyang set up the Iranian oil link in 1989. The deal agreed to supply North Korea with one million tons of crude oil in exchange for $120 million in weapons, mostly Scud missiles, from North Korea's brimming arsenal. The drama has its roots in the eight year Iran/Iraq war. North Korea and Communist China were avid arms brokers to the Ayatollah. North Korea sold an estimated $1 billion in jets and tanks to Iran. At the end of the Iran/Iraq war about 300 North Korean military advisors were in the Islamic Republic.[34]

In December 1989, Tehran and Pyongyang quietly set up a Joint Defense Commission to "reinforce socialism and escalate joint struggles against U.S. imperialism." Since that signing there has been a consistent stream of military exchanges between Iran and North Korea, including a visit by Choe Gwang, Chief of the DPRK's General Staff. Delegations of Iranian Revolutionary Guards have regularly visited Pyongyang to discuss military cooperation. North Korea looks to Teheran as a natural market for SCUD missiles and possibly for nuclear weapons exports.[35]

Similar ideological ties bind Pyongyang with Havana. In 1986, a visit by Fidel Castro to his comrade Kim Il-sung produced both revolutionary rhetoric and a 20-year Friendship Treaty. The document commits the DPRK and Cuba to active support to the "peoples fighting imperialism and Zionism," (article 5) and offers Cuban support to Korean unification "on the principle of great national unity without foreign interference," (article 6). In a Pyongyang speech, Castro thanked "Comrade Kim Il-sung for having supplied our people with 100,000 automatic rifles and tens of millions of rounds...I assure you that I and my comrades will be as ever propagandists of the revolutionary cause of Korea."[36]

Even before the epic events in the East Bloc in 1989, leading to the collapse of communism in Eastern Europe and later the USSR, Pyongyang was decidedly on the diplomatic defensive. The inability to stop its ideological comrades from participating the Seoul Olympics proved a poignant political setback to Pyongyang's policy. The regime's consolation in a sense became the DPRK's 40th Anniversary Festival, a spectacular political rite staged in Pyongyang with a cast of millions of dutiful if dour participants. This celebration in veneration of the *Kim Cult*, classically chronicled by the Polish film, *The Parade*, represents a kind of contemporary "Triumph of the Will" where adulation of the Great Leader combines with a rhythmic succession of parades and pageant to evolve into a state of political pornography.

Pyongyang's policies towards its dwindling number of comrades remain constant but in a vacuum of increasingly rarefied ideological purity. Links with the former East Bloc/Soviet Union are severely strained and with People's China nervous and likely to become bitter. The DPRK's diplomacy with the West, however hesitant and uncoordinated, evokes a remarkable *deja vu* of China's hesitant "opening" in the early 1970's. North Korea, as in the twilight of China's Maoist era, was shadowed by impending factional strife between those supporting the elder Kim's dynastic succession, and an amorphous military/technocratic cadre, who may wish to see if a world exists beyond the Worker's Paradise.

Pyongyang Between Moscow and Beijing; Fishing in Two Ponds

The political lineage of North Korea rests in an eclectic mix of domestic Marxist-Leninist factions who came to prominence after liberation from Japan. Externally, a crucial test of Pyongyang's policies towards Moscow and Beijing emerged in the first decade of the Republic. Between 1948-1958, the war, intra-party disputes, and fallout from the 20th Party Congress in Moscow seriously tested the DPRK's mettle. The second period between 1984 until Gorbachev's diplomatic recognition of Seoul in 1990, brought the Kim clique intense disillusion.

Kim Il-sung's Partisan Faction, under Soviet patronage, the Yenan Faction, who had fought alongside Mao's communists in China, and the Soviet Faction of Koreans from the USSR, soon formed an uneasy coalition. After the first Congress of the Worker's Party in 1946, of the five men elected to the decision making Politburo were two Yenan Koreans, one Soviet, one native, and Kim Il-sung. The Central Committee included three Soviet returnees, four Yenan Koreans, and three native communists.[37]

The seeds of conflict, already present, began to germinate and grow during the Korean War. The DPRK depended on the USSR both economically and militarily, and drew up its policy jointly with Moscow. Josef Stalin probably believed that the unification of the North and South was quite possible especially after the victory of the 1949 Chinese revolution. Although Stalin played a key role in planning the war, it was Mao who offered fraternal aid to the North Koreans in the form of massive military deployments. The Soviets, who had promised Mao air cover for his troops reneged on the pledge on the eve of the Chinese deployment.

If the Korean War proved a cataclysmic event for the peninsula, the conflict provided a crucible for Kim Il-sung's purge of the Party. Kim's Yenan rivals were purged for military incompetence in late 1950, and later Soviet faction figures were dismissed for "defective organizational work." During the Korean War 450,000 party members from the original 600,000 were expelled.[38]

The other pivotal event triggering Kim's purges, was Nikita Khrushchev's speech denouncing Stalinism before the ideologically heretical 20th Party Congress in 1956. By demystifying the cult of Stalin, Khrushchev also shattered solidarity with Mao in Beijing and with Kim in Pyongyang thereby fostering the Sino/Soviet split. Khrushchev's enunciation of the principles of collective leadership and peaceful coexistence with the West contrasted with Kim's policies keeping North Korea under tight control in the Stalinist manner.

In December 1955, in a landmark speech "On Eradicating Dogmatism and firmly Establishing the *Juche*," Kim stressed his unique path, "The important thing is to master revolutionary truth, Marxist Leninist truth. We cannot have an imperative principle of doing everything as the Soviet Union does. Although some people say the Soviet way is best or the Chinese way is best, have we not now reached the point where we can construct our own way?" Reacting to rumblings in the wake of the 20th Congress, Kim brutally and effectively purged intra-party factions and domestic rivals. By 1958, North Korea had "completely rinsed itself of factionalism." The DPRK Worker's Party became a solidly single minded force around Kim.[39]

There was a political tug of war between Moscow and Beijing for the ideological heart of Pyongyang. In July 1961, not long after Park Chung Hee's coup in the ROK, Kim Il-sung was in the USSR to sign a "Treaty of Friendship, Cooperation, and Mutual Assistance." From Moscow, Kim proceeded to Beijing where he concluded a Treaty of "Friendship, Cooperation and Mutual Assistance" with China. Both treaties while regarding mutual defense and economic ties clearly implied that Pyongyang should remain neutral in the Sino/Soviet rift.[40]

During the long decades of the formal Sino/Soviet dispute between 1960-1989, Pyongyang played a precarious balancing act between the two communist giants. Mao's rule was likewise threatened by Soviet "revisionism" and it was no surprise that the PRC fostered the fraternal ideological links formed during the Korean War remained "as close as lips and teeth" to recall the graphic Maoist adage. Such political and ideological sentiments continued, despite some jolts, until a brief period early in the Gorbachev era. Despite massive military transfers to North Korea from the USSR, Gorbachev's *Glasnost* and *Perestroika* movements soon became anathema in Pyongyang. The PRC regime had redeemed itself in Tiananmen Square.

Former ROK Premier Minister Lho Shin-jung viewing the DPRK's dilemma stated, "North Korea has been fishing in both the ponds of Moscow and Peking. Sometimes the pendulum swings to Peking and other times to Moscow. Neither Moscow nor Peking enjoys the right to control North Korea. Whenever Peking or Moscow think they are in control of Pyongyang, then North Korea goes the other way."[41]

Kim's policy illustrated classic form, turning to Moscow for arms and e relying upon the Chinese to provide brokerage for economic links with Tokyo and diplomatic overtures to Washington. The North Korean leader was particularly furious of widening ROK/PRC trade and an overall Chinese rapprochement with the U.S. Thus the DPRK sought an obvious tilt towards the Russians. Sophisticated Soviet weapons poured into North Korea at the onset of the Gorbachev era reversing the Brezhnev policy of isolating the recalcitrant

Kim. A reaffirmation of the USSR/DPRK military links and a qualitative upgrade of the North Korean military with Soviet arms characterized the period. A spate of Soviet delegations visited North Korea to celebrate the 40th anniversary of Korean Liberation.[42]

Korea rated but a passing mention in Mikhail Gorbachev's July 1986, Vladivostok Far East policy statement, while China relations remained the crux of the address. Except for a brief rekindling of the Russian North Korean romance in mid-1980's, the ideological ties between the PRC and DPRK still remained the strongest.

After the USSR opened diplomatic recognition of the ROK in September 1990, it allowed *glasnost*-type criticism of North Korea in the Soviet press and cut back barter trade. Moscow had become an enemy. China despite its booming trade with South Korea, still remained ideologically supportive of North Korea. Thus the establishment of Beijing/Seoul diplomatic ties in August 1992, was yet another shock to Pyongyang. PRC Premier Li Peng's advice that "Korea/China normalization would promote the improvement of intra-Korean relations," was received with bitter remorse in Kim Il-sung's isolated capital.

Unification: Pyongyang's View

Although *de facto* national unity has been a consistent theme of the DPRK polity, it was not officially enshrined in the 1948 Constitution adopted at the creation of the Republic. While Article 1 enumerates that "Our state is the Democratic People's Republic of Korea," the document does not elaborate on state borders, nor offer even a historical definition of the nation.

While the original 1948 Constitution was an imitation of the 1936 Stalinist Soviet model, a Constitution promulgated in 1972 changed the state structures radically. This 1972 version departed from the Sino/Soviet state structure, created a strong Presidency and enshrined a *Juche* economic model.[43]

Significantly, Article 1 defines the "Democratic People's Republic is an independent socialist state representing the interests of all the Korean people." The document claims to speak for the nation. Article 2 states that the DPRK rests "on the political/ ideological unity of the entire people based on a worker/peasant alliance led by the working class." Article 3 reasserts that the DPRK is a revolutionary state; while Article 4 cites that society is guided in its activity by the "*Juche* idea of the Worker's Party of Korea, a creative application of Marxism/Leninism to the conditions of our country." On the issue of unification, Article 5 clearly outlines, "The DPRK strives to achieve the complete victory of socialism in the northern half, drive out foreign forces on a national scale, reunify the country peacefully on a democratic basis, and attain complete national independence."[44]

The concept of peaceful unification and national independence are thus legally enshrined goals of the Republic; so is the oft-stated goal to remove foreign forces (U.S. troops) from the peninsula. After his unsuccessful bid to unify Korea through military conquest, many political formulae had been put forth by Kim Il-sung to unify the country. He had presented a threefold plan; to strengthen the forces of socialism in North Korea, gather revolutionary forces in South Korea, and develop the international revolutionary movement.

In August 1960, the DPRK proposed national unification through a series of transitional stages. A North/South Korean Confederation plan was proposed. In June 1973, responding to ROK peace proposals, Kim again stressed the *confederal* concept. A Great National Congress was to convene and create a Confederal Republic of Koryo, recalling the unitary state which once existed (918-1392) and thus offering a historical framework. The founding of a *Confederal Republic of Koryo* would thus prevent a national split. Kim added that if the North and South wanted to enter the U.N. before reunification, they could join as a single state under the name *Confederal Republic of Koryo*. These remarks came shortly after the Security Council had approved the dual U.N. membership of both German states.[45]

Again in October 1980, Kim Il-sung proposed a unification plan based on a *confederal* state in which the differing social and economic systems of North and South would remain *unchanged*. Such a concept seemingly embodied political pragmatism and offered a confederation as a means to an end. Here too, the proposal was made during a period of considerable political upheaval and instability in the ROK.

In Kim's New Year's 1988 Address, the *Great Leader* stated, "We consider it the most reasonable settlement of the question of our country's reunification to establish a single *confederal* state, neutral, non-aligned, on the basis of north and south recognizing each other's existence." This was the first time that the North Korean leader recognized the need to offer *de facto* recognition of the opposite part of the divided country.[46]

Although the *confederal* concept was mentioned as early as 1960, its political evolution is based on the reality that the ROK will not mortgage its security to the North. It likewise reflects the PRC's influence of "one country, two systems," offered to the ROC on Taiwan in the early 1980's.

Kim's bellwether 1989 New Year's speech further honed the policy for the Democratic *Confederal Republic of Koryo* in which the *Great Leader* proposed a Pyongyang summit of "leadership level people" from the South. While not mentioning the ROK government, he invited its representatives from the ruling Democratic Justice Party (DJP), the Party for Peace and Democracy and both legal and proscribed opposition forces.[47]

Beijing's policy parameters are evident in DPRK's policy formation. On the eve of North Korea's unenthusiastic application for U.N. membership, Chinese Premier Li Peng during a visit to Pyongyang stressed to his comrades that a policy formula of "one people, one nation, two governments, two systems," should be applied to Korea.

This policy was echoed during an U.N. address by DPRK Foreign Minister Kim Yong Nam; "Both the North and South want a single unified state, not two states and look to achieve a reunification along the lines of confederation...based on one nation, one state, two systems, and two governments." The Minister elaborated, "the proposal for reunification is that the North and South form a unified national government to be represented by the north and the south on a equal basis under which the north and south exercise regional autonomy with equal rights and power. It will form a single state by uniting the two autonomous governments, maintaining the two systems intact...the homogeneous nationhood of the Korean people surpasses the difference of the systems of the North and South."[48]

In his 1993 New Year's Address, the *Great Leader* outlined "Our Party and government will make persistent efforts to reunify the country on the principle of national independence by forming a confederation based on one nation, one state, two systems, and two governments."[49]

As the rhetorical drumbeat for unification continued unabated, Pyongyang's policies while calling for the familiar *confederal* model, have also advanced a "Ten Point Program for Grand National Unity." Central to Pyongyang's political/military priorities rests the constitution's pivotal Article 5, the "national independence" clause calling for the withdrawal of U.S. forces from the peninsula and the suspension of the annual *Team Spirit* exercises.

"The DPRK government has subordinated everything to the goal of national unification," stressed Song Won-ho Pyongyang's Deputy Foreign Minister before the U.N. He advised that a *confederal* state outlined in Kim's Ten Point Program was the method to achieve national unity "within the 1990's."[50]

In his New Year 1994 Message, *his last*, Kim Il-sung reaffirmed "To reunify the country is the supreme task of our nation which must not be delayed. We must accomplish this cause of national reunification as soon as possible, so as to meet the unanimous, ardent desire of the entire nation to hand down the reunified country to our posterity." Kim again called for implementation of the Ten Point Program of Great National Unity...based on the Confederation of one nation, one state, two systems, and two governments. The destiny of the motherland is the destiny of the nation."[51]

Politically, Kim's confederation strategy rested on the time honored "united front" tactics in which government and more importantly and an amorphous alliance of dissidents and "revolutionary forces" in the South would form policy. The clarion calls for unification hark to Beijing's proposals across the Taiwan Straits. Despite its seemingly flexible tact, DPRK reunification policy exhibits a classic dialectic in which any political negotiation by the ROK government would inevitably compromise Seoul's security and sovereignty.

In September 1998 the DPRK constitution was revised yet again to pave the political path for the full accession of Kim Jong-il. While the Preface extols Kim Il-sung and his epochal achievements for reunification, Article 1 clearly states, "The DPRK is an independent socialist state representing the interests of *all the Korean people*." Article 9 adds, "The DPRK shall strive to achieve the complete victory of socialism in the northern half of Korea ...and reunify the country on the principle of independence, peaceful reunification, and great national unity."[52]

DPRK Foreign Minister Pak Nam Sun, speaking before the U.N. General Assembly, raised the familiar theme as late as 1999; "As long as Korea remains divided, the situation on the Korean peninsula and its surrounding areas will never be stable. The most reasonable way for reunification is the *confederal* formula, with which the north and south of Korea are able to realize national reunification fairly and smoothly on the basis of preserving each other's ideas and systems as they are." He added, "Any attempts of one side to change the other, making claims about the so-called "sunshine policy" and engagement while ignoring the reality that the systems are existing in the north and the south, will only entail confrontations and conflicts."[53]

Following the landmark June 2000 Summit, the DPRK began to trim its diplomatic sails and hinted at wider cooperation with the South but in the context "it is none other than the Korean nation that is responsible for Korea's reunification. Korea's reunification should be achieved independently by the concerted efforts of the Koreans in the North and the South, as stated in the North/South Joint Declaration."

The bellwether New Year 2001 Joint Editorial set the tone, "The credit for the great victory won last year which splendidly concluded the 20th century goes to leader Kim Jong-il's preeminent political ability and energetic activities…the momentous issue in achieving national reunification is to implement the June 15th North-South Joint Declaration to the letter. The north and the south will achieve reunification in an independent and peaceful way and through overall national unity, true to the spirit of the historic declaration."[54]

The Pyongyang leadership is striving to turn the anemic DPRK into the *Kangsong Taeguk* or Strong Prosperous Country. Yet, spirited hysteria and socialist ideology are not the solution but are actually the problem. Massive economic mismanagement, rigid ideological conformity, and the overbearing shadow of the Kim cult pose an insurmountable hurdle to any form of genuine.

Given these glaring economic and political realities now confronting the DPRK regime, it appears that Kim Jong-un can at best play for time before the clock runs out for North Korea.

ENDNOTES

1. Hak-Joon Kim, *The Unification Policy of South and North Korea; A Comparative Study*, (Seoul: Seoul National University Press, 1977), 42-45.
2. Lim Un, *The Founding of a Dynasty in North Korea; An Authentic Biography of Kim Il-sung*, (Tokyo: Jiyu-sha Press, 1982), 128-133.
3. Kim The Unification Policy, 44-45.
4. Jasper Becker, *Rogue Regime: Kim Jong-il and the Looming Threat of North Korea*, (Oxford: Oxford University Press, 2005), 45-49.
5. Ibid, 53.
6. Bruce Cumings, *Korea's Place in the Sun; A Modern History*, (New York: Norton, 1998), 195-196.
7. Vantage Point, April 1990, 13, 7.
8. Il-sung Kim, *For the Independent Peaceful Unification of Korea*, (New York: International Publishers, 1975), 32.
9. Vantage Point June 1990, 13, 8.
10. North Korea News, 22 October 1990, 4.
11. Becker Rogue Regime, 57-58.
12. Hy Sang Lee, "North Korea's Closed Economy." Asian Survey 28 (December 1988), 1265-1266.
13. Joseph Chung, "North Korea's Economic Development and Capabilities." *Asian Perspective* 11 (Spring/Summer 1987), 56-57.
14. Vantage Point March 1994, 17, 16-18.
15. Lee, North Korea's Closed Economy, pp. 1266-1267 and Vantage Point March 1994, 16.
16. Donald MacDonald, *The Koreans: Contemporary Politics and Society*, (Boulder, CO: Westview, 1990), 221-225
17. Vantage Point June 1995, 18, 14-15.
18. The Korean Peninsula in the 21st Century; Prospects for Stability and Cooperation, (Washington DC: Korean Economic Institute in America, 2001), 12-13, Bank of Korea (Seoul) 3 November 2011, 4.
19. William Brown, "Engaging and Transforming North Korea's Economy." Joint U.S.- Korea Academic Studies, Vol. 21, 2011, 141-142.
20. Kikwan Yoon, "Review of the Prospects for Inter-Korean Economic Exchange." *East Asian Review* 4 (Spring 1992), 74.
21. Bank of Korea (Seoul) 3 November 2011, 4.
22. Marcus Noland, "The Current State of the North Korean Economy." Korea's Economy 2012, 107.
23. Un, The Founding of a Dynasty, 19, 100.
24. Becker, Rogue Regime, 125.
25. Rogue Regime, 91.
26. Myers, The Cleanest Race, 49.
27. *New Times*/Moscow, 22/1991, 24-25.
28. *New Times*/Moscow, 41/1991, 26-27.
29. Vantage Point, March 2001, 54.
30. John J. Metzler, "The China Connection and North Korea's Emergence from Isolation." *The American Asian Review* 3 (Winter 1985), 115-116.
31. Pascal Chaigneau and Richard Sola, "La France face a la Subversion Nord-Coreene en Afrique, *Defense Nationale* 43 (Janvier 1987), 115-118.

32. *Pyongyang Times*, 21 and 28 August 1985.

33. North Korea Today #140, 31 May 2001.

34. *Insight*, 20 July 1987, 31.

35. *Pyongyang Times* 23 January 1993.

36. DPRK Press/UN 13 March 1986.

37. Koon Woo Nam, *The North Korean Communist Leadership 1945-1965; A Study of Factionalism and Political Consolidation*, (University of Alabama Press, 1974), 53.

38. Ibid, 88-90.

39. Ibid, 106-116.

40. Chin Chung, *Pyongyang Between Peking and Moscow: North Korea's Involvement in the Sino/Soviet Dispute 1958-75*, (University: University of Alabama Press, 1978), 55-56.

41. Premier Lho/Author Interview Seoul April 1985.

42. *People's Korea*, 24 August 1985.

43. William Simons/Editor, *The Constitutions of the Communist World*, (Alphen an den Rijn: Sijthoff & Noordhoff, 1980), 228-230.

44. Ibid., 232.

45. Kim Il-sung, For the Independent Peaceful Reunification of Korea, 205-206.

46. *People's Korea*, 10 December 1988.

47. DPRK Press/UN 1 January 1989.

48. DPRK Press/UN 29 September 1992.

49. DPRK Press/UN 1 January 1993.

50. DPRK Press/UN 5 October 1993.

51. DPRK Press/UN 1 January 1994.

52. *Handbook on North Korea*, (Seoul: Naewoe Press, 1998).

53. DPRK Press/UN 25 September 1999.

54. DPRK Press/UN 1 January 2001.

Korea

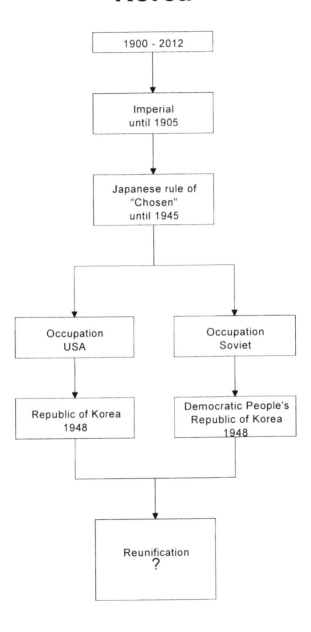

Chapter 6

Korean Unification/Prospects and Portents

An Introduction

Korea was first unified in 668 A.D. Unity through the Silla Kingdom, the Koryo Dynasty (936-1392), the Chosen/Yi Dynasty (1392-1910), and ensuing Japanese rule over Chosen lasted until 1945. Stated another way, adds Donald MacDonald, Koreans have been divided only three percent of their national lifetime; the three dynasties ruled a united country for a millennium.[1]

"Because of its geographic location in the proximity of China, it has existed as an autonomous state for most of its long history by virtue of control or intervention of its powerful neighbor. Whenever the power of China was not sufficient to protect the autonomy of Korea, another nation, generally Japan, would try to gain a foothold on the Korean peninsula. Since the first century B.C. the international status of Korea has been largely determined by either Chinese supremacy or by rivalry between China and Japan," related noted political scientist Hans Morgenthau

"The very unification of Korea in the 7th century was the result of Chinese intervention," adds Morgenthau. Later as a result of its victory in the Sino/Japanese war in 1895, the influence of Japan emerged. The defeat of Russia in the Russo/Japanese war of 1904-05, firmly established Japanese control of Korea. This was terminated with Tokyo's defeat in WWII. He added, "From then on, the United States replaced Japan as a check upon Moscow's ambitions in Korea. China by intervening in the Korean war, resumed its traditional interest in control of Korea. Thus, for more than two thousand years, the fate of Korea has been a function of either the predominance of one nation controlling Korea, or a balance of power between two nations competing for that control."[2]

Korea forms a nexus of competing and coinciding great power interests— China, Russia, Japan and the U.S. Thus, any change in the *status quo* touches on the vital geopolitical nerve of the neighbouring powers. The once glacial policy parameters between both Koreas encouraged by respective allies have somewhat thawed due to a meltdown of traditional Cold War military patterns of confrontation/ containment/support of the *status quo* through respective proxies, the disappearance of the USSR as a key regional player, and the re-emergence of China and to a lesser degree Japan as political brokers.

While a military component in preserving the *status quo* remains vital to any power equation, there is presently more political manoeuvre room between both North and South Korea. Although the divided peninsula remains in the vortex of great power interests, unification emerges as a realistic goal for both Korean governments. The spate of proposals reflects Pyongyang's plan to apply a *revolutionary* unification model: war, change through united front tactics, or a *confederal* compromise. Seoul supports a gradualist *evolutionary* model through rapprochement encouraging political and economic confidence building measures.

To ensure stability in the transition process, Washington must be willing to *keep close, credible and visible* military ties to Seoul. The U.S. in close concert with Japan must act as a political midwife to the rebirth of a united and independent Korea.

Economic Rapprochement

In a bitterly ironic way, the economic success of South Korea has widened the socio/industrial gap between both sides of the peninsula. Closing this socio/economic chasm will cost a staggering sum when unification occurs.

Following the euphoria of German unity, many Koreans assumed their country would *ipso facto* face a similar situation. Many pundits in the ROK realize that the unification bill may be smaller if commercial contacts exist prior to formal unity as was the intra-German trade case.

Economic interaction can be divided into two basic categories; direct and indirect trade and South Korean investment in northern joint ventures. Although the official ban was lifted in 1988, direct trade remains in the fledgling state; barter has existed between both sides in which southern rice and Goldstar Color TV sets were traded for northern anthracite coal since 1991.

Intra-Korean trade has been expanding steadily. Two-way trade began in the late 1980's and reached $100 million in 1991. By 2000 it totalled $425 million. While the original pattern saw an export advantage for North Korea, the pattern changed in 1998, and since then South Korea has run a surplus. Two thirds of ROK exports to the North were made on a non-commercial basis. According to Seoul's National Unification Board, South Korea and the KOTRA, trade in 2008 reached $1.8 billion but slipped to $1.7 billion in 2009 and $1.7 billion in 2011.[3]

There are basically two lines of thought regarding South/North trade and economic development. One views the unification cost as rising more rapidly if economic development is not promoted in the North. Likewise, the other sees the South as gaining a needed production foothold within a short distance of Seoul.

Since the South/North economies are reciprocally complementary, it may be more profitable for the ROK to relocate old sunset industries to North Korea than to Southeast Asia. Moreover there's a clear business logic to this plan as well as a parallel political incentive. A contrary view asserts that offering the DPRK economic aid only reinforces a regime about to collapse. Thus South Korea should wait for the fall and pick up the pieces rather than allowing economic cooperation to put the hardliners in Pyongyang on "life support" thus ensuing their durability and thereby hindering unification.

Given the realities that the DPRK will slowly adopt a "Chinese model" of economic openness amid tight political control, it may be prudent for South Korea to give active economic assistance to North Korea as to narrow the per capita GNP gap as well as the chasm separating the two economic systems in Korea. After repeated advice from China, it appears that the Kim dynasty made timid steps to modify the *Juche* ideology as to revive the DPRK's moribund Marxist economy.

Likewise the DPRK while North Korea's per capita GDP grew 4.7 percent in 2011, the DPRK income is estimated at $720, up from $688 a year earlier. Still the North's per capita GDP amounts to a mere 3 percent of that of the ROK according to Seoul's Hyundai Research Institute. South Korea's per capita income in 2011 reached $22,700.[4]

Significantly, socio/economic progress forces an inexorable wedge to open the political change. In the case of authoritarian systems such as South Korea prior to 1988, this proved the case; thus a totalitarian system such as Pyongyang's fears this political threat more than it does any experiment in "market socialism." Contrary to reinforcing isolation, and thus Pyongyang's propensity for reckless politico/military gambles, economic contacts likewise hasten political change. Joint ventures and investment by South Korean *chaebol* are crucial to co-development of North Korea; they may first be permitted in special economic zones.

Investments in Kaesong, North Korea by South Korean firms such as Goldstar, Daewoo, Hyundai and others would offer these companies an edge in competitive advantage fast disappearing in the South and often slipping to Southeast Asia and China. At the same time, such investment pries open socio/political doors in the North through economic empowerment of fellow Koreans. While *chaebols* are seeking a market and production base on the Chinese Mainland, these firms are likewise looking to open a backdoor to North Korea through joint ventures. As Seoul's *Korea Times* opines, "Since its establishment in 2004, the joint complex has weathered the storm of inter-Korean conflicts and North Korea's intermittent provocations. For Pyongyang, it is the goose that lays the golden eggs." Over 50,000 North Koreans are employed in 120 South Korean medium and small-sized companies. The complex provides the DPRK with more than $80 million in hard currency annually.[5]

Hyundai has invested $290 million in the North for the Kumgang tourist venture; the *chaebol* plans to bring a further $5 billion to develop the Kaesong industrial zone. Nonetheless looking at the poignant lessons of German unity, development throughout the DPRK will require massive capital from the Seoul government's North/South economic cooperation fund as well as international support from the World Bank and IMF. Despite huge challenges, the ROK stands to gain with a infrastructural renewal which can be channelled through firms such as Hyundai construction. The North may provide an opportunity to revive a moribund construction industry and gain new contracts in a place in dire need of development.

Currently, the ROK economic strategy towards the DPRK seeks to use trade and investment both to keep the north from collapsing as well as to gain as much political leverage as possible. The South views its trade to the DPRK as a form of economic aid and "political investment."

In terms of actual cost, one survey estimates, "unification cost estimated in this research turns out to be about 7 percent of the nation's GDP annually for ten years after reunification." Should unity come in the time frame 2020-2029, the analysis based on 2009 data would cost $1 trillion dollars and 6.86 percent of GDP. As Prof. Shinn Chang-min asserts, "The sooner reunification occurs, the lower the necessary costs will be; and the South alone will enjoy tremendous benefits from reunification, including 11.25 percent annual economic growth during the first decade following territorial unification."[6]

Realistically the cost of unification based on widening economic disparity between South/North production/population would be huge. While West Germany facing a far narrower economic gap with its East German cousins, was confronted by the unpleasant realities of even a deeper crisis than expected, the chasm between the Koreas is not only larger but even more opaque. The DPRK remains a closed political society equally lacking any genuine form of statistics and economic data. Statistical data has been filtered through a prism of propaganda.

The South's per capita income is approximately twelve times that of the communist North. Even should a foreign investment flow be opened, the DPRK suffers from a dilapidated infrastructure especially in the road, rail, and electric power grid. Investment in these sectors needs a minimum of $65 billion just to bring the North up the South's level in 1990. As a hypothetical model, using 2011 as a base, if reunification would be viewed as equalizing the per capita income between both sides of the peninsula, then to narrow the gap between a projected South Korean income of $22,500 and a $720 in North Korea would ensue a minimum cost of $1.2 trillion.[7]

As in Germany's case, Seoul's security links with Washington not only provide the climate for economic progress but permit political flexibility on the reunification issue. The ROK/U.S. Defense Treaty forms a *keystone of peninsular security* and also affords a foundation on which to build political structures.

Financially though, any currency equalization, as in Germany's landmark agreement to accept the GDR East Marks at near parity with the West's, would present a crucial challenge. While the ROK *Won* is internationally traded, the DPRK's *Won* is not part of any foreign exchange baskets. Parity reached for political purposes could prove financially disastrous for Seoul's Central Bank and future stability.

North Korea remains a distant economic frontier shrouded in a mist of misunderstanding and mistrust. A powerful sun of shared interests can quickly burn off the fog and reveal to South Korean *chaebol* both a production base, a market on their doorstep, and a boom for construction companies rebuilding infrastructure, especially road, rail and power networks.

There is an economic chasm to bridge too. When West and East Germany were united, GDP per capita in the East was less than half of that in the West. But North Korea is much farther behind. To attain the starting position as South Korea stands in 2012, the DPRK would need rapid and sustained growth. This is not possible given the strictures and structures of the North's economy. Sudden reunification could be highly destabilising for *both* the DPRK and the ROK. Uncontrolled population movement southwards, pressures on wage parity levels, and the crisis of economic expectations, could quickly cripple the united country.

Viewing the ROK/DPRK socio economic gap through the lens of the U.N. Human Development Report 1995, a global compendium of quality of life/health/education indicators, the ROK rated 31st out of 174 comparators. The DPRK stood at 83rd. By 2000, the ROK still ranked 31st but the DPRK no longer participated in the survey. By 2013, South Korea had soared to number 12 globally among 186 comparators, just behind Canada but ahead of Denmark, Singapore and France. The DPRK was not rated.[8]

At the time of unification, it is quite likely that North Korea will be discovered to be in far more dire straits than is even presumed today. Given the genuine paucity of reliable data, deciphering the DPRK economy emerges as an arcane art through which illusion, presumption, and disinformation create deliberate distortion thus making reliable analysis nearly impossible.

Political Conditions

The anxious transition following Kim Il-sung's passing (1994) and the death of *Dear Leader* Kim Jong-il (2011), has proven a tentative and unstable period for the DPRK Dynasty. While a *China Model* will eventually be adopted economically, it appears that the *Marxist Monarchy model* has been followed politically, thus allowing the elevation and rule of Kim Jong-un.

Any instability in the DPRK will naturally deter investment and will place North Korea ever farther behind its cousins in the South. It will also exponentially increase a propensity for Pyongyang to take a possible military gamble for unification.

Pyongyang's pullout from the Nuclear Non-Proliferation Treaty (NPT) raised poignant concerns. Intense pressures by the ROK, USA, and Japan have failed to satisfactorily resolve the murky issue of nuclear proliferation in North Korea's Yongbyon site. A tepid U.N. Security Council resolution, backed by China, called on North Korea to rejoin the NPT. After nearly another year of desultory diplomatic efforts to pressure Pyongyang, the Council issued an equally lukewarm "Statement," on the nuclear crisis.[9]

North Korea's nuclear program has impeded improvement in North/South relations and has created obstacles to normalization talks between the DPRK and Japan and the United States. The nuclear issue and likewise the evidence of Pyongyang's ballistic missile proliferation and exports to rogue states, moreover has deterred the DPRK's diplomatic rapprochement with Washington and as dangerously created a credible weapons potential facing the ROK, Japan, and the U.S.

The DPRK has discovered that even the prospect of obtaining nuclear weapons, let along testing them, has produced immediate concessions from its adversaries. As Myers opines, "For fifteen years the perception of a communist North Korea has sustained the U.S. government's hope that disarmament talks will work with Pyongyang as they did with Moscow. Only in 2009, after the Kim Jong-il regime defied the United Stares by launching a ballistic missile and conducting its second underground nuclear test, did a consensus begin to emerge that negotiations were unlikely ever to work."[10]

Some diplomats view Pyongyang's nuclear bid as less military and more political; namely to enhance the DPRK's status of being recognized as a major player in East Asia and more importantly as a gift to the military from Kim Jong-il, Supreme Commander of the People's Army, as a policy to assure its stature and sovereignty from *both* South Korea and China. Pyongyang's nascent nuclear capability, especially given the regime's bellicose and unpredictable nature, has proven to be variously a *wild card* and *bargaining chip*.

Playing such nuclear and missile cards offers Pyongyang the option to gain political standing, establish international space, and secure its cherished self-reliance. Cast as the unrepentant rogue regime and threat to the East Asian balance of power, Pyongyang's ruling elite gains a disproportionate influence through such presumably rash behavior.

Historically China held the fulcrum for the balance of power on the Korean peninsula. Reasserting traditional *Sino-suzereignty* over Korea, the PRC seeks to control both Korean states through a combination of diplomatic protection/ideological concurrence with the DPRK and of commercial/ political friendship with the ROK. In both cases China will try to keep both the U.S. and Japan from gaining a decisive advantage in Korea while keeping Russia *checkmated* in the regional balance.

Despite longstanding misgivings over the leadership, China is anxious to preserve stability on the peninsula. Such moves aim at correcting the imbalance sanctioned a century ago by the Treaty of Shimonoseki allowing Japan decisive political influence over Korea at Imperial China's humiliation and expense.

PRC policy whether seemingly defending the rogue DPRK or currying commercial favor with the ROK, aims at holding the key to peace and harmony on the peninsula, a contemporary recalibration of the traditional tribute status.

U.S./DPRK informal talks in Beijing, much like the U.S./PRC contacts in Warsaw in the 1950's and 1960's provide an opportunity for Washington to feel Pyongyang's political pulse. So do the informal talks between the U.S. and DPRK delegation at the United Nations.

While Washington has been at political loggerheads with Pyongyang over the nuclear proliferation/inspection issue, the U.S. was politically jolted by the DPRK first nuclear test in October 2006. The DPRK/U.S. nuclear crisis has assumed a dangerously cyclical nature; periodic confrontations between Pyongyang and Washington using the sounding board of the United Nations have reverberated rhetorically but could trigger a political miscalculation or military confrontation.

During a particularly dangerous June 1994 showdown concerning the IAEA inspections at the Yongbyon site, the U.S. proposed a weak economic sanctions package on Pyongyang which North Korea threatened would be a "declaration of war." The Clinton Administration came dangerously close to armed conflict with the DPRK. As Becker advises, "on 15 June 1994, Clinton had to make one of the most difficult decisions any American president had faced since the 1962 Cuban Missile Crisis."[11]

Washington lacking the support of China and Russia in the Security Council for even a mild draft resolution, allowed the move to wilt on the diplomatic vine. In parallel, a curious peace mission to Pyongyang by former President Jimmy Carter during the height of the crisis defused the immediate symptoms, and as importantly, saved face for Washington's stillborn sanctions initiative.

A false dawn in the DPRK/U.S. relationship which emerged after the Carter Mission was dashed by the death of Kim Il-sung in July 1994. American and DPRK negotiators later hammered out a controversial "nuclear framework agreement" which traded limited North Korean nuclear openness for an exchange of petroleum and provides two light water atomic reactors to meet the North's electric needs. As a corollary to the Geneva framework, the U.S./Japan and South Korea formed the Korean Energy Development Organization (KEDO), to administer the technical modalities of assistance to North Korea's energy production.[12]

Given the Clinton Administration's clumsy mishandling of the initial nuclear crisis and the subsequent Security Council *faux pas*, Washington and Seoul essentially decided upon a carrot and stick policy towards Pyongyang. The "Framework" was specifically designed not as a formal Treaty knowing it would not likely receive U.S. Senate approval. The deal would focus on curtailing the risk of nuclear weapons proliferation in North Korea in exchange for giving the DPRK *quid pro quo* benefits such as fuel oil and constructing two 1,000Mw "proliferation-proof" light water nuclear reactors at Kumho on the east coast.

The "Framework Agreement" garnered a deal which fit perfectly into Pyongyang's playbook favourites. By manipulating political see-saw emotions between military Armageddon and the prospects of peace, the new Kim Jong-il leadership was able to both gain short term rewards from the USA and the ROK as well as keep the clock running on its clandestine nuclear proliferation programs.

Shutting down the proliferation prone Yongbyon complex entailed an agreement to provide the difference in power for North Korea. Though the U.S., the ROK and Japan were among the original KEDO members, the multilateral organization has grown to include Australia, Canada, Chile, the European Atomic Energy Community, and New Zealand.

The ROK, Japan and the U.S. had contributed 90 percent of the $675 million raised between 1995 and 2000 with South Korea and Japan providing the loan funds for building the two reactors estimated to be $4.6 billion. By mid 2001, the site had been cleared for building of the plants. Until the atomic reactors would presumably come on line, the U.S. was obligated to provide North Korea with 150,000 tons of petroleum annually to offset fuel needs.[13]

North Korea never completed building power lines and the grid to be supplied by the Kumho Light-water Reactor. KEDO quietly expired in 2006.

Indeed the DPRK's entire infrastructure is dilapidated and operating on low power. Total energy in the North halved from 27 million tons of oil equivalence in 1990 to 14 million tons in 1998. Though coal is currently produces seventy percent of energy; between 1985 and 1997, coal production almost halved and this had an impact on the economy. In 1998 power generation capacity stood at less than ten percent of the South's 215 billion kilowatt hours. Railroads, roads and ports are in poor repair.[14]

Despite the dilapidated state of the DPRK's power grid and infrastructure, North Korea possesses a vast secret nuclear infrastructure at least a dozen sites of varying importance and capability. Moreover the medium range missiles *No-dong* 1 and 2 and *Taepo-dong* 1 such as was tested in perilous proximity to Japan in August 1998, allows the DPRK a delivery system for its weapons of mass destruction.

Given these realities, a multilateral diplomatic contact formula between ROK/DPRK on one side, and the U.S., Japan, PRC, and Russia on the other, could create interlocking patterns of political transparency as well as confidence building measures leading to greater peninsular security. What emerged as the *Six Party Talks*, a multilateral diplomatic formula with both Koreas as well as concerned regional powers, China, Japan, Russia and the USA allowed for serious denuclearization dialogue with the DPRK. The Six Party Talks which started in 2003, have provided a stop and start again process for the U.S. and its allies to test Pyongyang's political pulse and intensions as well as to allow for a transparent formula negotiate with the North.

UN Security Council resolutions concerning the DPRK nuclear weapons and missile systems have repeatedly called for Pyongyang to return to the Six Party Talks.

As importantly, the political ramifications of the 1994-1999 famine continues to plague North Korea. Because of the withdrawal of Soviet and Chinese food subsidies in the early 1990's, the cumulative effect of collective farming, food availability in North Korea declined steadily and then plummeted between 1995 and 1997, when flooding followed by drought struck the country.

A study, *The Politics of Famine in North Korea*, stated that from 1994 to 1998, between two and three million people died of starvation and hunger related illnesses. The food crisis did not begin with the floods in August 1995, as is commonly understood, but with the sharp reduction in heavily subsidized food and crude oil from the Soviet Union and China. Moreover though the international community mobilized to bring major food relief to North Korea, the Pyongyang rulers became deeply suspicious concerning access, and distribution on the part of donors. The vulnerable portions of the population died or were *triaged* by the authorities, especially in north Hamgyong province. Former Party ideologue and high ranking defector Hwang Jong-Yop estimated that death toll had reached 2.5 million people since 1995.[15]

As is often the case with such disasters, the regime was more concerned about foreigners seeing the effects of famine first-hand. The exposure of the hermetically sealed DPRK hermit kingdom to outside attention, made the ruling regime particularly nervous. Jasper Becker, analysing the famine mortality statistics argues that, "A death toll of three million would mean more victims than in Pol Pot's Cambodia...more deaths than in Ethiopia or Somalia."[16]

It is tragically ironic too, that the Kim Dynasty prefers neutrons for its nuclear program over nutrition for its people.

Nonetheless 2000 proved a watershed year for Pyongyang. Diplomatic ties were opened with Italy and other European Union members, the landmark June Sunshine Summit was held, and the visit of U.S. Secretary of State Madeleine Albright to North Korea, were all part of a wider policy of engagement. The Albright visit was as monumental as it was ill-timed. The Secretary of State found herself being *feted* by Kim Jong-il in the midst of grandiose propaganda celebrations commemorating the 55th anniversary of the founding of communist rule in North Korea and the 50th anniversary of the Korean War. Seeking standing and prestige, Kim Jong-il looked upon the Albright visit as both a boom for domestic consumption as well as a hugely legitimizing gesture from the USA, a country which after all, was the primary target of his ire. Secretary Albright was unwittingly manoeuvred into Jong-il's political narrative with little tangible U.S. policy gain.

While a visit by President Bill Clinton to Pyongyang was planned to apparently sign a deal on missile non-proliferation, it was shelved in the aftermath of the U.S. November 2000 elections. Many observers saw Clinton's planned visit as a classic style over substance venture which could guarantee only nebulous return. The Albright trip proved a profound embarrassment for the Clinton Administration's Korean legacy.

European countries have been quick to establish long severed links with North Korea. In a bid to explore a political *third way* in its policies towards Pyongyang, a European Union delegation led by the Swedish Prime Minister Goran Persson visited the DPRK in May 2001. Earlier the European Parliament passed a resolution calling for a better relationship between the EU and the DPRK. While the European Union had already opened the diplomatic and trade door to the DPRK; most EU states now have full diplomatic relations with Pyongyang, the move was a call to expedite wider relations.

Nonetheless the EU has played a leading humanitarian role in North Korea since the 1995 famine. Between 1995-2008 Brussels has provided 35 million Euros for long term nutrition and a further 124 million Euros via three channels: bilateral aid, World Food Programme humanitarian aid, NGO assistance. An additional 75 million Euros was been provided to KEDO.[17]

Once Jong-il had apparently established his credentials over the military and populace, the DPRK regime wished to engage in a more aggressive diplomatic game as did People's China in the wake of Taiwan's ouster from the U.N. in 1971. Nonetheless Pyongyang's playing the game of nations is set to the backdrop of continuing nuclear blackmail and creating insecurity especially in Japan and South Korea, thus posing new political and strategic questions in East Asia.

While DPRK regime stability is not assured; it remains precisely this enigma that causes most concerns over the intentions of not only Kim Jong-il but hardline elements in the People's Army. Nuclear weapons and even rudimentary means to deliver them, allows Pyongyang a disproportionate degree of political and psychological leverage in Northeast Asia. Thus despite its moribund economy, the DPRK holds a *Damoclean* sword over South Korea.

Whether unification comes from a slowly phased in Confederation, from a military gamble given that Pyongyang lives in a proletarian fantasyland, or the German model of absorption of a collapsed regime will be borne out in a decade. A Commonwealth pattern as envisaged by the ROK may provide a *transition model* for unity. Yet one must assume that given the very nature of Kim's closed society and economy, the DPRK's economic malaise is far deeper than Seoul presumes thus posing another formidable barrier to smooth reunification.

For example, the December 1991, "Basic Agreement" concluded after inter-Korean talks, produced a splendid theoretical document dealing with the political, social and economic aspects of national division. Mutual political respect, an ending of confrontation, a non-aggression pledge, and a plan to promote economic development are part of the 25 article pact. The Basic Agreement appears uncertain because it does not have binding force. It is a "gentleman's agreement;" there is no guarantee that either side will carry out its promises.

In Germany's case, the Basic Treaty was guaranteed by the Allies. In the final stages of unification, the "Two Plus Four" talks served as a binding force on the two German states. Both Bonn and East Berlin maintained firm security tires with their respective allies. Though Seoul is shielded by the ROK/U.S. Defence Treaty, Pyongyang presently lacks formal military ties with either Russia or China.

Value integration between the people in West and East Germany increased greatly after the 1972 Basic Treaty. Personal visits, a flow of information, and eased travel and cooperation changed the FRG/GDR relationship. An integration of values of the same nation was achieved through contact. Structural integration came after 1990, coming long after value integration. Conversely, both North and South

Korean leaders have long pursued their policies of national reunification in terms of top down structural integration, largely ignoring values integration.[18]

Value integration through promoting even simple contacts between the families separated by the divide has been nearly impossible. Even the most basic tourist links in which South Koreans travel through a Hyundai joint venture to North Korea's sacred, albeit isolated, Mt. Kumgang have been micromanaged. Tourists venturing by ship to the region, have a view of the hermetically safe region of the DPRK paradise before re-embarking on the ship to return to South Korea. The Hyundai enterprise has proven a financial disaster.

The South Korean TV and radio, which despite speaking the same language, are quite simply not seen nor heard in North Korea due to jamming and blocking. Thus while East Germans could easily, though illegally, tune in West German radio and often TV, prefixed radios in the North prohibit this practice. Choice is not possible. So total is the *totalitarianism* in the DPRK that Big Brother has even thought of pre-tuning the radios!

Though high-level contacts between ruling elites in Seoul and Pyongyang have proceeded apace in a quasi-Confucian format, there has been pitiful little contact between the divided families. While the historic June 2000 Summit addressed family reunification, and the ROK government has prided itself on family reunions in the post summit period, the numbers involved are miniscule. For example in mid-August, 100 individuals from each side were permitted to return to the "other side" of the DMZ to see their families; this out of an estimated ten million members of families torn asunder by the divide!

Long lost kin from the two Koreas met for the first time in fifty years. In December, another group family reunion of 100 North Koreans took place in the Seoul Central City complex; in Pyongyang a similar scene occurred at the Koryo Hotel. During the Korean War millions of family members were separated. Given the hostility between South and North Korea, most have not seen their family members since that time.

On the diplomatic front, both the ROK and DPRK delegations at the United Nations drafted a joint General Assembly resolution concerning the *Question of the Korean Peninsula*. The resolution stressing peace, security, and the reunification of Korea was adopted by consensus. The action was the first time the South and North formally worked together since separate U.N. memberships nine years earlier.

Presently, Pyongyang is experimenting with *controlled openness* and the Chinese model of *market socialism*. Nonetheless, the real hurdle remains political; transforming the DPRK *regime legitimacy* to the dynastic succession from Kim Jong-Il to his untested son Jong-un, is by no means assured over the medium term.

The combination of the military balance and a fear of an aggressive North Korea having tested nuclear weapons and ballistic missiles, has caused deep anxiety in Washington and in East Asia.

DPRK missile proliferation poses particular challenge both in light of conventional capacity and possible nuclear capabilities. The standard SCUD versions, the *Hwasong* 5 and 6 with a range of 500-600 kms are deployed and exported. North Korea's *Nodong* medium-range rockets with a range of 1,000 to 1,6000 kms have equally been exported to Iran and Pakistan. Not known for their accuracy, there are approximately 200 *Nodong's* in DPRK inventory. The *Taepongdong-1* medium range ballistic missile with a range of 1,500 to 2,500, has been a prototype for more presumably accurate and reliable rockets.

The *Musdan* intermediate range missile 2,500- 4,000 kms is still in development. But it is the *Taepongdong-2* intercontinental ballistic missile (ICBM) first tested in 2006 and again in 2012 which could theoretically reach the West coast of the USA which creates the most concern. The DPRK has not as of yet been able to miniaturize nuclear loads for the rockets. Still the missiles have South Korea, Japan and U.S. Pacific bases in range with conventional weapons.[19]

Even without nuclear arms the Korean People's Army (KPA) is terribly lethal and large, according to Nicholas Eberstadt writing in *Foreign Affairs*. East Germany and North Korea have roughly the same population 17 million versus 20 million—but Pyongyang's army is believed to be seven times larger than was East Germany's *Volksarmee* on the eve of German unification. Likewise since North Korea is not a direct political dependent as was the GDR, Seoul cannot hope to speed reunification via a well-placed bribe to an outside power as was the case between Bonn and Moscow.[20]

Russia has tried to renew its geopolitical role in on the peninsula. President Vladimir Putin has visited both North and South Korea in a bid to revive the strained Moscow/Pyongyang friendship and has gone to Seoul reinforce commercial ties. Given that Russia revoked the 1961 USSR/DPRK military treaty in 1995, relations with Pyongyang had been particularly poor.

Putin's July 2000 visit to the DPRK came in the wake of the North/South Summit and was in a sense an attempt to invigorate the once close relationship which had been allowed to drift for a decade. After being warmly received by Kim Jong-Il and party luminaries, Putin proceeded to pay his respects at the Kim Il-sung mausoleum. Visiting Seoul, President Putin again tried to wedge the Kremlin back into the Korean peninsular politics. A clear focus of the trip besides political posture was to find yet another platform on which to oppose Washington's plans for Theatre Missile Defence, a theme ironically but awkwardly echoed by the ROK government. Putin has focused on a *pro-active* Russian policy towards Korea to revive the Kremlin's role in the regional balance of power.

The DPRK's total armed forces stand at 1.2 million with one million in the Army. The DPRK maintains the world's fourth largest standing armed forces but according to the Military Balance 2012, "however equipment is in a poor state." North Korea relies on weight of numbers . Reserve components comprise 600,000 troops. Typically DPRK ordnance comprises numerous but vintage T-34 through T-62 main battle tanks, and Air Force squadrons top-heavy with Mig-17's, 19's, 21's, and fewer than 100 top flight Mig-29's. The ROK military has an active force of 655,000 troops with a massive reserve of 4.5 million. Most equipment is modern and well serviced. Naturally Seoul has its longstanding Mutual Defense Treaty with the USA dating from the 1950's and backed up the U.S. nuclear umbrella.[21]

Despite being technologically outclassed, the DPRK has developed into what is the most militarized country in the world today. The Korean People's Army numbers over one million active duty personnel of which 100,000 are organized into special operations units. A significant portion of the KPA forces are in an forward echelon attack posture. Similarly, the psychological blackmail balance favors the DPRK as a prosperous but exposed Seoul metropolitan region remains very vulnerable to Pyongyang's provocations short of war.

Given the realities of Korean history and the political predicament of Pyongyang, one cannot presume that unification will occur peacefully. Yet, even a phased-in program will likely lead to an era of unpredictably, Korea-wide socio/political discord, and economic instability. While South Korea has scored impressive economic gains, the depth of its political institutions has been achieved only recently.

Absorption of a totalitarian cousin, in a state of social shock and regime rejection, would usher in a period of serious disequilibrium. Equally the effective demobilization of the majority of the million member KPA and security police remains vital both to neutralize any effective northern power center and to cut the spiral of military spending. Money saved on the military must be reinvested back into the northern infrastructure to upgrade and harmonize the national road, rail, and power grid.

Contrary to the German model, unification will prove more costly to narrow the gap economically and the chasm psychologically. Commonwealth can ameliorate differences between the two societies and offer a balm to soothe political discord. A firm commitment by Seoul towards unification, a policy *sine qua non* in previous ROK administrations, proved nebulous both as time passed and Seoul's own democracy deepened. Given the prosperous and often narcissistic South Korean society, reunification has proved less of an emotional or nationalistic issue.

Partially to dampen unrealistic expectations, in the aftermath of the dramatic intra-Korean Summit, ROK Foreign Minister Lee Joung-bin addressing the UN General Assembly spoke of steering "intra-Korean relations away from tension and enmity, towards reconciliation, peaceful co-existence and co-prosperity, and eventual unification." While the modalities for better intra-Korean ties are being established, the cherished goal of unification seemed a distant glimmer.[22]

A prime motive behind President Kim Dae-jung's *Sunshine Policy* was to prevent the sudden collapse of North Korea, which has suffered from widespread famine and a deteriorating industrial base. Many estimates opine that it would cost South Korea more than $1 trillion to revive North Korea in a German-style unification against the $600 billion that a much richer Germany has spent over the past decade. Avoiding the DPRK's "hard landing" was a constant theme of ROK political and academic officials in the aftermath of German unity.

In 2011 President Lee Myung-bak did not mention Korean reunification in his address to the UN General Assembly. Equally in 2012, the ROK Foreign Minister Kim Sung-Hwan while calling for North Korean denuclearization, failed to mention even perfunctory words on reunification. Nonetheless, Seoul's position in the UN is admirable; the ROK has holds a two year term on the Security Council, the ROK remains a widely respected "global citizen," and a Korean, Ban Ki-moon is serving in his second term as UN Secretary General.[23]

When the UN Security Council passed a package of uncharacteristically tough sanctions on North Korea over the communist regime's nuclear weapons tests and missile proliferation, the Pyongyang leadership went rhetorically ballistic. Pyongyang's pro forma rants and raves towards South Korea and the United States were notched up in this "March Madness" to include scrapping the 1953 armistice which ended the Korean war. North Korea threatened to attack the USA with its newfound but happily not yet deliverable nuclear bombs.

Significantly the March 2013 Security Council resolution (2094) was unanimously passed after the DPRK third nuclear test and importantly included support from the People's Republic of China, the longtime but increasingly wary political mentor of the quaintly titled "Democratic People's Republic of Korea." The resolution stated the obvious; "reaffirming that proliferation of nuclear, chemical and biological weapons, as well as their means of delivery, constitute a threat to international peace and security." The lengthy ten page document equally "reaffirms its decision that the DPRK shall abandon all other existing weapons of mass destruction and ballistic programs in a complete, verifiable and irreversible manner." Specifically the resolution calls for tougher financial sanctions to the point of barring suitcases of bulk cash for various weapons deals.[24]

Even if the sanctions are selectively enforced by regional states such as China, the latest Security Council resolution underscores the unmistakable trend that the world community, even neighboring China and Russia, are weary and especially wary of North Korea upsetting East Asia's equilibrium. Japan was genuinely frightened, while prosperous South Korea kept a stoic calm.[25]

South Korea's new President Park Geun-hye has stated clearly, "We must deal strongly with a North Korean provocation." UN Secretary General Ban Ki-moon warned, "Nuclear threats are not a game. Aggressive rhetoric and military posturing only result in counter-actions, and fuel fear and instability."[26]

Ironically we see a contradictory situation where the UN Security Council slaps tough sanctions on the North, while at the same time United Nations humanitarian agencies are the major source of food and humanitarian assistance for at least a third of the North's population.

Though Kim Jong-un continues political tantrums in his fortified Pyongyang bunker, the reality remains that the land he rules stands as a neo-Stalinist totalitarian hell. The UN's latest Report on the "Situation of Human Rights in the Democratic People's Republic of Korea," documents "grave, systematic and widespread" human rights violations in North Korea. Interestingly this is the 22nd such report since 2003 and reflects 16 resolutions already passed on the DPRK dictatorship.

As in the past, the report outlines a terrifying totalitarian balance sheet where human rights and basic freedoms are stifled by a regime which would make Big Brother wince. The DPRK's communist rulers use widespread torture, gender discrimination and intimidation to control the populace. Those who have fallen afoul of the regime are part of what the UN human rights Rapporteur cites as many as 200,000 people in labor camps. The document cites use of "Torture and other cruel, inhuman and degrading treatment or punishment; public executions, extrajudicial and arbitrary detention; the imposition of the death penalty for political and religious reasons; the existence of a large number of prison camps, where serious violations of human rights are perpetuated."

The UN "strongly urges the government of the Democratic People's Republic of Korea to respect fully all human rights and fundamental freedoms and in this regard; to immediately put an end to the systematic, widespread and grave violations of human rights.[27]

Even in the midst of a peninsular crisis, the UN agencies continue to supply food aid to North Korea playing a vital role. In 2013, some $146 million is needed to respond to key humanitarian concerns such as the 1.6 million children needing regular assistance and access to nutritious food.[28]

Scenarios

Nightmare Scenario

Traditionally the Korean peninsula is viewed through the prism of geopolitics; the DMZ often described as one of the last frontiers of the Cold War still hosts a one million man standoff. Moreover, American forces, treaty bound to defend the ROK, are part of the "trip wire" in which any North Korean thrust across the de-militarized zone would at once involve U.S. troops in combat.

The DPRK maintains a hardened million man military backed by massive and numerically superior artillery and armor, stationed in forward echelons near the DMZ. More dangerous remains the 88,000 special forces which can be transported behind, under, and around the DMZ. While the DPRK's ordnance remains mostly vintage as compared with ROK and U.S. material, the fact remains that the North would likely attack first and with very little warning.

Equally North Korean SCUD missiles and an array of inaccurate but psychologically effective missiles and crude nuclear devices could put the South Korean capital Seoul at immediate risk and without doubt threaten Japan.

No-dong 1 (range 1,600kms) missiles are quite sufficient to reach Japan. *Taepo-dong* 1 (2,500km range) already in arsenal, pose a clear and present danger to the Japanese home islands as well as American military facilities on Okinawa.

While it is generally accepted that the South Korean forces and the U.S. would soon regain the advantage, this presumes that air re-supply and vital air superiority be maintained from early in the conflict. Though such a strategy would likely see Kim Jong-un desperate gamble for unification, it would likely trigger the devastation of the DPRK with tactical nuclear or neutron weapons providing a *Viking Funeral* for the Kim dynasty. Nonetheless during the particularly dangerous showdown in early 2013, the DRPK regularly threatened the winds of war would return to Korea and beyond to the shores of Japan and the USA.

During the "March Madness" showdown in which Kim Jong-un made daily military threats to both the ROK and regional powers, U.S. Secretary of Stare John Kerry visited the region to reassure allies. In Seoul Kerry stated clearly, "We will defend our allies. We will stand with South Korea, Japan and others against these threats. And we will defend ourselves. And Kim Jung-un needs to understand, as I think he probably does, what the outcome of the conflict would be. Our hope is that we can get back to talks."[29]

Speaking in Tokyo, Secretary Kerry elaborated, "The North has to understand, and I believe must by now, that its threats and its provocations are only going to isolate it further and impoverish its people even further....the United States will do what is necessary to defend our allies, Japan, Republic of Korea, and the region against these provocations. But our choice is to negotiate."[30]

"On the Korean Peninsula, the situation remains highly volatile," stated Secretary General Ban Ki-moon, "The international community has responded in a firm but measured way to the nuclear test, threats, and other provocative acts by the Democratic People's Republic of Korea. The recent developments have strengthened the international consensus that the DPRK will not be accepted as a nuclear weapons state." He added sternly, "I continue to urge the DPRK leadership to reverse course and return to the negotiating table."[31]

Dynastic Succession

Following the "Great Leader's" death in July 1994, Jong-il the "Dear Leader" inherited the dynastic mantle of the DPRK dictatorship. As envisaged by Kim Il-sung, the succession was smooth and the State remains *static/stable/Stalinist*. This theoretical plan remains problematic due to familial/ideological and military concerns. The DPRK's New Year 1995 address while traditionally delivered by the "Great Leader," was not bequeathed to "Dear Leader" but rather reflected a joint editorial of *Rodong Sinmun* and *Josonmingun*, the Party and People's Army papers respectively. Kim Il-sung's name was offered nineteen accolades and Jong-il's, a hardly-overwhelming twenty.

Since the passing of Kim Il-sung the New Years Address came in a form of a Joint Editorial of Party and People's Army papers rather than the ruler's traditional rambling speech. Despite having died in 1994, the Great Leader Kim Il-sung still serves *eternally* as DPRK President. Significantly the 2013 New Year Address was made by Kim Jong-un.

Military Matrix/Power Struggle

The million member People's Army will very likely determine the day in the long run; as the only organized force for stability, the military will serve as a force for continuity. It may also serve as kingmaker. The KPA fears, above all, being manoeuvred into a confrontation with the U.S./ROK by a bellicose Jong-un. A war of Unification, while patriotically inspiring, would likely see the DPRK's devastation. The military, many factions of which are unknown, and perhaps with China's support, would likely launch a *coup d'etat* to ensure Jong-un's ouster. A struggle *a la* Romania in the twilight of the Ceausceau era may erupt with the military opposed to Worker's Party and security police elements. The expanding influence of the military is clearly in evidence. Kim Jong-un, the newly crowned Marxist monarch, may owe his rule to a leadership dominated by the military.

Implosion/ROK Inheritance

Pyongyang's internal power struggle or misjudged military gamble could bring a quick collapse to the DPRK's house of cards. A massive refugee exodus from the North to South Korea, either contrived, managed, or unexpected, could confront the Republic with a crisis it cannot morally refuse. Should Jong-un employ the Castroite "Mariel Solution," large numbers of criminals, dissidents, infirm, or elderly people may be allowed to cross the DMZ flooding into the South prompting a serious security and humanitarian nightmare.

A refugee exodus would almost certainly follow the collapse of the DPRK, in which large numbers of North Koreans within a few days walk to the DMZ dividing line, will descend upon Panmunjom *en route* to Seoul and points south. Controlling the euphoria will be near impossible and a serious haemorrhage of North Korea's population could begin to move south. While the ROK would try to contain the situation, chaos would ensue, incidents would be staged by DPRK *agent provocateurs* for the world media witnessing the event, and the Seoul government would be hard pressed not to accept kith and kin despite nagging security and practical concerns.

Negotiated Settlement/Confederation

Such a scenario would emerge through ministerial and sub-ministerial government contacts. While a multiplicity of formulae are framed for confederations, commonwealth, and other political compendiums, the fact remains that both Seoul and Pyongyang must agree to a path which would monumentally alter the present power configuration. A phased-in plan is not likely unless one powerful party forces it on the weaker party, the ROK on the DPRK. Such an outcome is likely after a major political jolt such as a regime collapse in the North.

Visiting Berlin, Kim Young-sam stated, "As I passed through the wide-open Brandenberg Gate, I could not help but be reminded of the *Bridge of no Return* in Panmunjon, the Korean War truce village...The question of Korean Unification is no longer if it will happen but how and when it will happen."

Kim's budding optimism characterized Korean discussion for a brief but heady period in the aftermath of Germany's peaceful reunification. But Korean unity may be a more fragile flower. The ROK government while remaining theoretically wedded to the ideal, has through indecision, been tempted to slow down the actual process. Korea's neighbors, Japan, China, and Russia, are not anxious to have a bigger Korea on their doorstep. Seoul's subsequent *Sunshine Policies* were tinted by optimism too.

ROK President Park Geun-hye addressing a joint session of the U.S. Congress in Washington stressed, "Our chorus of freedom and peace, of future and hope, has not ceased to resonate over the last 60 years and will not cease to continue." President Park proposed a wider Seoul-Washington alliance, establishing an initiative for peace in Northeast Asia and laying the foundation for peace and reunification. She stated, "With the trust that gradually builds up, through exchange, through cooperation, we will cement the grounds for durable peace and eventually, peaceful reunification."[32]

That the Korean *nation* will be unified remains on the agenda of history; yet *the timing* will not likely fit the political agenda of whoever is in power in Seoul. Beyond the genuine patriotic euphoria of reunification, the ROK remains distinctly nervous concerning the economic price, social dislocation, and political ramifications of national unity.

Viewing unification from the perspective of the regional powers, all of them discreetly prefer the *status quo*. Japan above all fears a united Korea which in the medium term would likely emerge as a larger economic power and competitor. The USA would lose political leverage and likely face pressure to phase out its military bases. Russia would not easily be able to re-establish its former standing. Only China who looks to exercise its traditional political/economic hegemony over the peninsula, may stand to gain.

Since their separation, in both Korean states a kind of Confucian hierarchy became the foundation of leadership styles. In the South an appeal to traditional values and alliance patterns characterized governance, which later evolved into a fractious democracy. The South's economic empowerment path sharply contrasted with the North's Marxist/Leninist model.

South Korea has clearly won the battle of ideas, of socio/economic development, and the political legitimacy of a democratic state. One could say the South Korean model evokes Samsung, PSY, and software.

In the North a revolutionary model, a smashing of the *status quo* and the creation of a unique *Marxist monarchy* emerged as the bedrock of the regime. The

DPRK model evokes Stalinism, starvation and stagnation. Clearly the *raison d'etre* for the *Kim Dynasty* remains the defensive regime preservation in the shadow of China and the compelling socio/political challenge from Seoul.

Given the psychological trauma caused by a sanguinary century of colonial/communist rule in the North, one must imagine epic socio/political chasms to be surmounted in the best of circumstances. In the post-communist era, a psychological DMZ must not be encouraged to replace its military counterpart.

While reunification will ultimately be the supreme national task of the Koreans, given the peninsula's history and geography, its final political form will be influenced by the vortex of the great powers. Geopolitics will reassert itself. Historically, happy endings are never guaranteed.

ENDNOTES

1. Donald MacDonald, *The Koreans: Contemporary Politics and Society,* (Boulder, CO: Westview, 1990), 272.

2. Hans Morgenthau, *Politics Among Nations: The Struggle for Power and Peace,* (New York: McGraw Hill, 1993), 192-193.

3. Doowan Lee, "Estimating the Potential Size of Inter-Korean Economic Cooperation." Joint U.S. Korea Academic Studies Vol. 21, 2011, 155; Bank of Korea 9 July 2012.

4. *Korea Times* (Seoul) 26 February 2012 and Bank of Korea (Seoul) 9 July 2012.

5. *Korea Times*, "Absurd Threat," 1 April 2013.

6. Chang-min Shinn, "Korean Reunification: Costs, Gains and Taxes." *Korea Focus* 19 (Spring 2011), 82-84.

7. U.S. Korea Academic Studies 2001, 70 and Korea's Economy 2012, 109.

8. *United Nations Development Programme/*Human Development Report, 1995, 2000, 2013, 155-157 and 144 (2013).

9. UNSC/S 11 May 1993 and 31 March 1994.

10. Myers, The Cleanest Race, 9.

11. Becker, Rogue Regime, 165-166, and Don Oberdorfer, *The Two Koreas*, a Showdown over Nuclear Weapons, outlines how close the USA came to military conflict.

12. DPRK Press/UN "Framework Agreement," 22 October 1994; U.S. /UN 7 March 1995.

13. KEDO at Five/Annual Report 1999-2000.

14. Keun-wook Paik, "Energy Cooperation on the Korean Peninsula." *The World Today* 57 (February 2001), 22-24.

15. Andrew Natsios, "The Politics of Famine in North Korea." United States Institute of Peace/Special Report, (Washington DC: USIP, 1999),1-6.

16. Becker, "Rogue Regime," 210-211.

17. EU.com 30 April 2001 and Europa.eu 4 July 2011.

18. Kang-suk Rhee, "Korea's Unification: The Applicability of the German Experience" *Asian Survey* 33 (April 1993), 365-366.

19. *Profiles of Key North Korean Missiles*, (Washington, DC: National Committee on North Korea, 2013).

20. Nicholas Eberstadt, "Can the Two Koreas Be One?" *Foreign Affairs* 72(Winter 1992-93), 161-162.

21. *The Military Balance* 2012, 256-259.

22. ROK Press/UN 19 September 2000.

23. ROK Press/UN 21 September 2011 and 28 September 2012.

24. UNSC, Resolution #2094 (2013), 6 March 2013.

25. *Korea Times* "North Korea's March Madness," 19 March 2013.

26. UN Secretary General, "Statement on the Korean Peninsula delivered at the Press Conference in Andorra," 2 April 2013.

27. UNGA/A/C 3/67/L50, 9 November 2012, "Situation of Human Rights in the Democratic People's Republic of Korea," 1-5.

28. UN Press/Office of the UN Resident Coordinator in the Democratic People's Republic of Korea (DPRK), 29 April 2013, 1-2.

29. U.S. Department of State, Remarks with Republic of Korea Foreign Minister Yun Byung-se/ Remarks John Kerry Secretary of State, Seoul, South Korea, 12 April, 2013.

30. U.S. Department of State, Joint Press Availability with Japanese Foreign Minister Kishida After Their Meeting/John Kerry, Tokyo, Japan 14 April 2013, www.state.gov

31. UN Secretary General/Opening Remarks at Press Conference 17 April, 2013, 3.

32. "President Proposes Korea-U.S. Alliance a Global Partnership." 9 May 2013, Korea.net.

Germany. Courtesy of the University of Texas Libraries, The University of Texas at Austin.

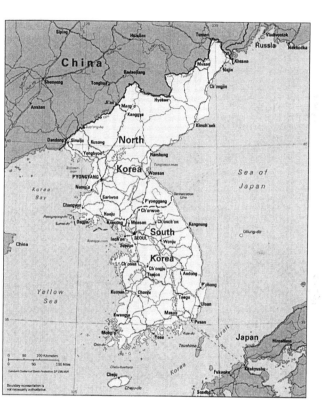

Korea. Courtesy of the University of Texas Libraries, The University of Texas at Austin.

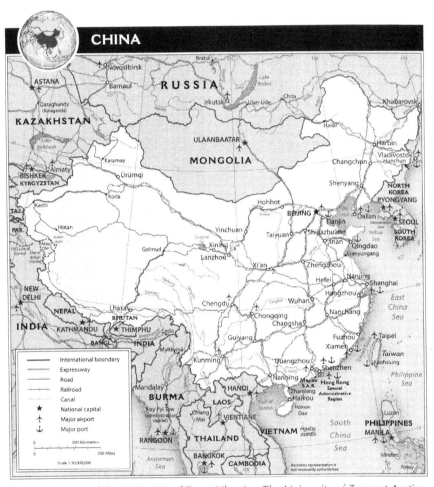

China. Courtesy of the University of Texas Libraries, The University of Texas at Austin.

Taiwan. Courtesy of the University of Texas Libraries, The University of Texas at Austin.

Chapter 7

People's Republic of China/The Mainland

An Introduction

Mao's conquest of the Mainland was the culmination of eighteen years of unmitigated trauma for the Chinese people. Having been battered by the ill winds of Japanese military aggression, occupation, and later the Nationalist/Communist civil war, all since 1931, the communist victory in 1949 seemed almost *anti-climactic*.

The proclamation of the People's Republic of China (PRC) in Tiananmen Square on 1 October 1949, not only ushered in another sanguinary chapter in China's long history, but brought about the first formal divide of the nation since the Ming Dynasty. Thus when Chiang Kai-shek's routed Nationalist armies fled to Formosa/Taiwan to establish an island exile for the Republic of China (ROC) government, the *de facto* division became formal.

Importantly, division of China into two governments claiming *de jure* control and legitimacy emerged from the carnage of a civil war, not a direct cartographical change by a foreign hand. Clearly while foreign powers were intimately concerned over the fate and status of China, the actual PRC/ROC separation was executed by the Chinese themselves. That differs from both Germany and Korea where *foreign powers* mandated the actual lines of division.

This case differed, too, in that it was the WWII Allied powers, of which China was one, who codified the return of Japanese occupied territories to the Nationalist government. The 1943 Cairo Declaration, clearly enumerated the return of "all the territories Japan has stolen from the Chinese, such as Manchuria, Formosa, and the Pescadores, shall be restored to the Republic of China."[1]

Notably, the Chinese Nationalists and French, two of the Big Five Allies, were excluded from the Yalta Conference in February 1945. As historian F.W. Marks relates, the Yalta Agreements conceded the *status quo* in Outer Mongolia, offered the Soviets use of the ports of Dairen and Port Arthur, and codified Moscow's controlling interests in the Manchurian railroads. Significantly, the details of the Yalta agreements regarding China were kept a secret; it was not until June that the Nationalists accidentally learned of the terms which included a Sino/ Soviet "friendship pact" foisted on an unwilling Chiang.[2]

Germans and Koreans could always rationalize that despite their respective regimes being the ideological antithesis of each other, national division resulted from foreign hands. Such was not the case in China where the foreign powers may have influenced the outcome of the civil war but did not dictate the *de facto* political formula in 1949. China's divide thus became more *personalistic* and thus intractable.

"On the eve of the proclamation of the People's Republic, Mao announced a state system of 'People's Democratic Dictatorship.' It would be a government of the 'broad masses' and would deny the most elementary civil and political rights to 'running dogs of imperialism.' " According to Professor James Gregor, the People's Republic "would be dominated by a dedicated cadre of the Chinese Communist Party, whose membership then constituted less than one percent of China's population."[3]

In his famous tract "On People's Democratic Dictatorship," Mao spelled out the policies which would permeate the new Chinese state. His priority was to establish an effective national government; success would bolster CCP claims to be representing the forces of a new order and prove the CCP had accomplished the reintegration of the huge country which had eluded Sun Yat-sen, Yuan Shi-kai, and Chiang Kai-shek. Power was divided power *among three elements;* the Communist party, the formal government structure, and the army.[4]

Standing with Stalin: 1950's Diplomacy

The creation of the People's Republic of China (PRC) and the evolution of the regime into an ideological scion of the Soviet Union, rocked the post-war world through its geopolitical reverberations. Mao's professed friendship, "It was through the Russians that the Chinese found Marxism," and his proclamation, "Internationally we belong to the anti-imperialist front headed by the Soviet Union," put the PRC in league with Josef Stalin.

Mao Tse-tung followed up his revolutionary rhetoric with a visit to the Soviet Union, his first sojourn abroad. But his experiences with the Soviets were baffling and contradictory; for several days Stalin did not even acknowledge his presence in Moscow. In a bitter blow, he was forced to acquiesce to an independent Mongolian People's Republic which was going to be under Soviet influence. Mao had claimed several times that Mongolia would come under Chinese dominance. He now had to abandon any idea that China would regain territories controlled by the Ching Dynasty.[5]

Yet, Mao's trip to Moscow produced the Sino/Soviet Treaty of Friendship, Alliance, and Mutual Assistance signed on 14 February 1950. The Treaty was hailed as "eternal and indestructible." Squadrons of Soviet aircraft soon arrived, along with advisors, and began constructing fifty model industrial units Stalin had pledged Mao. Some ten to twenty thousand Soviet advisors worked on more than a thousand industrial projects in China during the 1950's. According the Steven Mosher, a long duet with the Soviet 'elder brothers' followed in which Russian became a principal foreign language studied in schools, Chinese students went to the USSR, and Soviet-style centralized planning was adopted. The 1954 PRC Constitution was a copy of the 1936 Stalinist version. Even Chinese architecture adopted the blunt Stalinist features.[6]

Clearly the PRC's courtship with the USSR, despite its ideological logic, was one of *convenience or perhaps connivance*; nonetheless, for Western policy makers in the 1950's the chimera of Sino/Soviet *entente* evoked strategic nightmare scenarios not seen since the Axis threat during WWII.

During the Korean War, North Korean aggression was soon supported by Chinese communist "volunteers," offering convincing subjective proof of a Moscow/Beijing plot not only against South Korea but East Asia as a whole.

During those anxious days in 1950, the Nationalist Chinese redoubt of Taiwan, also known as Formosa or beautiful island owing to its Portuguese discovery, was expected to be Mao's next target. On 5 January 1950, President Harry Truman stated, "The U.S. government will not provide military aid or advice to the Chinese forces on Formosa." In the meantime, the State Department began drafting an official statement they would issue once Taiwan had fallen into communist hands.

The Far East policy was complicated by Dean Acheson's tragic misstatement, in which the Secretary of State *did not include* South Korea or Taiwan, among key American regional interests in East Asia.

Shortly after North Korean forces attacked South Korea on 25 June 1950, President Harry Truman, belatedly realizing the urgency of the situation, deployed the U.S. Seventh Fleet in the Formosa Straits between the Chinese Mainland and Taiwan. China's actions were indeed worth monitoring. PRC propaganda organs spoke of the "liberation" of all national territory, Taiwan and Tibet. On 2 September the Soviets had put a draft resolution before the U.N. Security Council calling for a withdrawal of U.S. forces from Taiwan; on 7 October, PRC troops attacked Tibet.

Again one recalls the Mao Telegram of October 1950, in which the Chinese communists, fully expecting fraternal Soviet assistance, prepared to enter the Korean War. Stalin did not deliver on his promises of air cover to the PRC "volunteers" despite Zhou Enlai's pleas for the promised Mig squadrons. This shortfall planted seeds of the Sino/Soviet dispute. Still the strategic fact remains that during the Korean conflict there was a large degree of Sino/Soviet coordination, logistical assistance, and "volunteers" to the cause of Kim Il-sung.[7]

On the diplomatic front, a U.S./U.K. Security Council initiative sought withdrawal of the Chinese "volunteers" from Korea. American delegate Warren Austin asked with his searingly sarcastic wit, "Did the Chinese communists go into Korea on a sentimental journey?" Regarding Formosa, Austin stated, there were no U.S. ground or air forces on the island; "the sole mission of the Seventh fleet was to prevent any attack from the Mainland on Formosa or from Formosa on the mainland."[8]

Although not a member of the U.N., the Beijing communists gained access to the Security Council proceedings under Article 32 of the U.N. Charter.

General Wu Hsiu-chuan, representative of the quaintly titled "Central People's Government of the People's Republic of China," took counterpoint with the American "criminal aggression against the territory of China; Taiwan." He also protested the ROC delegate having the "right to represent the people of China."

Wu warned ominously, "The irrevocable and immovable will of the 475 million people of China was to recover Taiwan and other territories belonging to China from the grip of the U.S. aggressors." The envoy stated that, in order to safeguard international peace and security and to uphold the sanctity of the Charter, it was the inalienable duty of the Council to apply sanctions against the United States for "criminal acts of armed aggression on the territory of China, Taiwan and its armed intervention in Korea." Ambassador Austin, exhibiting his sharp Yankee wit to puncture this *Orwellian* double-speak, stated sarcastically of Wu, "Glorifying peace, he sounded threatening!"[9]

Beyond its military and ideological portent, Mao's dispatch of troops to Korea helped wedge the issue of China's role at the U.N. into discussions. When the General Assembly's First Committee presented five principles for a cease fire in Korea, one significant paragraph opened a possibility that *following* a cease fire, the governments of the U.S., U.K., USSR, and the People's Republic of China would achieve a settlement of Far Eastern problems including Formosa (Taiwan), and of representation of China in the United Nations.

Philippine delegate Carlos Romulo stated sagely, "The Peking regime has ignored the proposals of the U.N. and shown it would not stop fighting until it recovered Formosa and a seat in the United Nations." Zhou Enlai in a cable to the U.N. called for a Korean settlement "by the Koreans themselves," and enjoined that "representatives of the People's Republic of China must assume their rightful place in the U.N."[10]

Despite its temporarily checkmated moves to gain China's United Nations seat, PRC diplomacy in the 1950's exhibited some remarkably successful achievements. Beyond fraternal ties with the USSR and perfunctory proletarian links with the East Bloc in October 1949, Burma was first to recognize the PRC in December; the Scandinavian states followed in January.[11]

The now legendary Bandung *Non-Aligned Conference* in 1955 provided a major diplomatic breakthrough for the PRC. Foreign Minister Zhou engineered Beijing's tilt from the confrontational "two camps policy" to a more flexible stance allowing relations with "feudal capitalist" but "anti-imperialist states." The *Spirit of Bandung* defined the non-aligned states for a generation.

The PRC abandoned its commitment of overt incitement of rebellion in newly independent states. The new policy became "Five Principles of Peaceful Coexistence;" respect for each nation's territorial integrity, non-aggression, non-interference in another nation's domestic affairs, equality among states, and peaceful coexistence. Beijing lobbied the Afro/Asian bloc, and by May 1956, Nasser's Egypt became the first Arab country to enter into diplomatic ties with the PRC, thus giving Beijing its first major diplomatic prize since 1950. In November after the ill-fated Suez Crisis, Egypt, Syria and Yemen, who had since also recognized Beijing, opposed American efforts to postpone debate on whether or not the PRC should be admitted into the U.N.[12]

Needless to say, the death of Stalin and Khrushchev's progressive de-Stalinization campaign launched at the 20th Party Congress in 1956, precipitated the Sino/Soviet schism. While both Stalin and Mao were subjects of cult-like political veneration, Khrushchev's heterodox speech, and its implications on communist icons, living and dead, caused anxious moments in both Beijing and Pyongyang. Diplomatically the decade ended with Beijing largely isolated from the West. Neither the U.S., Canada, nor any major European state established relations with People's China.

At the same time, the PRC was no closer to gaining China's U.N. seat from the ROC. Probing attacks on the Nationalist held isles of Quemoy and Matsu ensured that the PRC would remain in a confrontation mode with the United States. More significantly the subtle tensions between Beijing and Moscow starting from the Korean war, were to evolve into the shattering 1961 Sino/Soviet split.

China Courts the Third World/ The Cultural Revolution

PRC policy in the 1960's was built on the dual pillars of international revolutionary diplomacy towards Third World states and domestic mobilization to reinforce Chairman Mao's rule. Foreign policy witnessed a formal break with the Russian "revisionists" thus recalibrating national interests from a fraternal alliance with the Soviet Union to a revolutionary crusade defined by Lin Piao's "On People's War," an epistle to bellicosity.

Domestically the "Great Proletarian Cultural Revolution," a chaotic period launched in 1966 witnessed the PRC's socio/ideological cleansing and the elevation of dogma at the center of which was the thought of the idol, Chairman Mao. This ironically misnamed, Cultural Revolution, a riveting excess of *ideology over reason*, tradition, arts and education, has haunted and hampered the People's Republic for a generation.

African de-colonization provided an extraordinary opportunity for the PRC to prove its ideological credentials, to embarrass the Soviet "revisionists," and to gain new diplomatic support for Beijing's accession to the United Nations. Both a lack of Soviet "commitment" to the Egyptians during the Suez crisis, Moscow was busily suppressing the Hungarian revolution the same fateful weekend with China's tacit encouragement, and the Kremlin's unwillingness to recognize the Algerian/ FLN insurgents fighting France, cast Beijing into the role of revolutionary.

In the early 1960's a plethora of newly de-colonized African states set up diplomatic relations with the PRC. By 1965, a year before the Cultural Revolution, bilateral ties had already existed with twenty countries. Zhou Enlai's seven week African safari in 1963-64, illustrated China's aspiration to be a major player on the continent. Zhou's speeches were both highly rhetorical and pragmatic. His famous phrase, "An excellent revolutionary situation exists in Africa," was oft quoted.[13]

The proliferation of new African states afforded the PRC unbounded opportunities for diplomatic recognition, ideological footholds, and ultimate admission into the U.N. Africa was regarded as a major theater in the global struggle against Western "imperialism" and Soviet "hegemony" where China could enhance its revolutionary credentials by supporting "liberation movements."

China's professed aims were revolutionary, but its Africa policy like that of the Soviet Union was pragmatic. China placed a higher premium on African aid than did the USSR; such assistance was largely provided in the context of cold war and Sino/Soviet competition. In the early 1960's China dispatched arms to Zanzibar and Uganda. After the Cultural Revolution, military aid focused more specifically on "liberation movements" in southern Africa.[14]

Marshall Lin Piao's famous tract "On Peoples War" issued in 1965 stated, "The outcome of the world struggle hinges on the revolutionary struggles of the Asian, African and Latin American peoples." This ideological call to arms for global struggle against Western/Soviet interests ironically came as China was about to commence its own sanguinary struggle, the Great Proletarian Cultural Revolution. The Cultural Revolution's maelstrom created a Maoist frenzy domestically as well as a paralysis of the PRC's diplomacy internationally.

The Red Guards, the cutting edge of radicalism, sought to destroy Old Thought, Old Culture, Old Customs, Old Habits; violently replacing them with New Thought, New Culture, News Customs and New Habits, all dictated by quotations from Chairman Mao's *little red book.* After the Cultural Revolution began in earnest in 1966 much of China's normally active diplomacy was suspended. The period from 1966-69 was one in which China's policy makers marked time in African affairs. By mid-1969 diplomatic activity resumed and in 1970 Beijing opened relations with Ethiopia.[15]

Chinese technical aid emerged as an instrument of foreign policy serving a diverse series of objectives including promotion of the PRC's diplomatic standing, pursuit of its rivalry with the Soviets, and the propagation of revolution. Between 1954-1977 PRC aid to non-communist states was $4.27 billion, 58 percent of the total being directed to Africa. The main recipients included Tanzania and Zambia, locus of the Tazara railroad to the sea. Likewise, between 1961-1971 according to the U.S. Arms Control and Disarmament Agency, Beijing provided $1.14 billion in weapons to developing states. By the period 1967-76, the totals reached $2.15 billion globally, the majority being sent to Vietnam, North Korea, and to a smaller degree Tanzania. Military training was focused overwhelmingly on African states with 2,675 cadres trained between 1955-1976.[16]

The success and failures of the PRC invariably are judged through the proletarian prism of the Cultural Revolution. China's role in the world was emasculated by the excesses, foibles, and sheer terror of this period whose three core years 1966-69, signalled a decade of desultory inaction. Schools were closed and books burned; the ideological "soul engineers" had created a cultural desert. The Belgian diplomat Simon Leys in his riveting analysis *Chinese Shadows* recounts, "It is probable that the Cultural Revolution has left even deeper scars on the Chinese minds and feelings. It represented the climax of twenty years of periodic, sometimes violent purges, twenty years of systematic training in aggression, of legitimatizing violence and hatred."[17]

Opening to the World/The Nixon Visit and U.N. Admission

The July 1971 announcement that U.S. President Richard Nixon would travel to the People's Republic of China produced political shockwaves throughout East Asia. The Presidential visit in February 1972 opened what would be a geopolitical *Pandora's box* in America's Far East policy. The once-pariah People's Republic earned a surprising political legitimacy.

Nixon's road to Beijing was actually part of a dual desire by the U.S. to neutralize Chinese support for the North Vietnamese and to improve relations with the PRC. For Chairman Mao facing the still-turbulent aftershocks of the Cultural Revolution and the downfall of the "pro-Moscow traitor" Defense Minister Lin Piao, this tactical opening towards Washington was viewed as beneficial.

In his State of the World address in February 1970, President Nixon declared it would be in America's interest to improve relations with the People's Republic of China. In the following months, advises Gregor, Washington reduced restrictions on travel, trade, and contacts with China which had been in effect for two decades. A Presidential Commission recommended that the U.S. no longer oppose seating the PRC in the United Nations. On 15 July 1971, after a secret visit by Henry Kissinger to Beijing, Nixon announced that Zhou Enlai had invited him to China to pursue better relations.[18]

Interestingly, President Nixon's paving the path to Beijing dealt more in political style over policy substance. The President, himself an implacable anti-communist, had to convince the American public that a U.S. President would not be kowtowing before Mao's Marxist minions in the Forbidden City.

The first step was to stop calling the communist Chinese communists. Official press statements and public documents prefaced the word China with "People's Republic" and not "communist," "Red," or even "Mainland." "Mao Zetong and Zhou Enlai were now China's Chairman and Premier respectively not the Chinese Communist leaders," notes Sinologist Steven Mosher. In the State Department's official compendium of presidential statements toasts, and press conferences surrounding the China trip, the word communism appears not once. Clearly the word was taboo, and not because it would upset Maoist sensibilities. Ii was American sensibilities that such ellipses were intended to soothe," adds Mosher.

"During his week in China the old image of the People's Republic as a brutal dictatorship implacably hostile to America dissolved abruptly in a series of extraordinary *tableaux vivants;* Nixon applauding a revolutionary opera, Nixon at the Great Wall, Nixon offering a toast to Chairman Mao and the brilliant, witty Premier Zhou's exultation, 'Let us start a new Long March together,' " stresses Mosher.[19]

In the 1972 Shanghai Communiqué, the U.S. affirmed what it had considered a political/geographical truism, "The United States acknowledges that all Chinese on either side of the Taiwan Straits acknowledge there is but one China, and that Taiwan is part of China. The U.S. government does not challenge that position." The U.S. position stressed the "peaceful settlement of the Taiwan question by the Chinese themselves." The Shanghai Communiqué which was reached after what were described as "extensive, frank, and honest discussions," did not establish the legal status of Taiwan, nor did Washington accept Beijing's claims to sovereign jurisdiction over the island. Furthermore, bilateral communiqués are not considered legally binding in U.S. constitutional law, a point Beijing seems to have missed.

In the Communiqué, Beijing insisted; "the government of the People's Republic of China is the sole legal government of China; Taiwan is a province of China; the liberation of Taiwan is China's internal affair...the Chinese government firmly opposes all activities which aim at the creation of 'one China, one Taiwan,' 'one China, two governments,' 'two Chinas,' an 'independent Taiwan,' or to advocate that the status of Taiwan remains to be determined."[20]

"In the years between the Shanghai Communiqué in 1972 and the December 1978 announcement of the establishment of diplomatic relations, (beginning on 1 January 1979), the behavior of the leadership in Beijing tended to confirm initial U.S. expectations of immediate security benefits from the growing rapprochement," advises Prof. James Gregor. In effect, the U.S. no longer had to pursue a policy of containment. "For the first time in a generation, the United States no longer faced strategic challenges on two major fronts," Gregor added. "Peking ceased criticism of the U.S./Japan Security Treaty and supported the strengthening of the NATO alliance. By the mid-1970's Communist Chinese foreign policy in major parts of the world was generally compatible with that of the United States," Gregor opined, and as a result of the Sino/American relationship, Soviet strategic planning became more complex and uncertain.[21]

The *Nixon shock* of 1971, caused seismic political jolts worldwide. The reverberations reached from the Far East to the East River where the United Nations would soon commence a crucial session of the annual debate on China's admission. While the issue of Chinese representation had long shadowed Taipei's seat, during the 1950's the matter was routinely sidetracked by deft American diplomacy which precluded the matter from even reaching the U.N.'s agenda.

Between 1961 and 1970 an annual General Assembly debate had failed to gain the required two-thirds majority to pass a resolution ousting the ROC. Yet in 1970, though a resolution was adopted by 66 votes to 52 to keep Taipei in the Assembly, a political sea change was emerging.[22]

The 15 July 1971 Nixon announcement that he would visit the PRC tried to calm fears, "I want to put our policy in the clearest possible context. Our action in seeking a new relationship with the People's Republic of China will not be at the expense of old friends," nonetheless caused intense speculation and anxiety, most of all in Taipei and Tokyo.[23]

The political rapprochement and subsequent presidential visit was orchestrated by Dr. Henry Kissinger, the National Security Advisor and *grand vizier* to Richard Nixon.

As Kissinger extolled in his book *Diplomacy*, "Nixon was unique among American presidents this century by showing his preparedness to support a country with which the United States had had no diplomatic relations for twenty years, and with which his Administration had as yet had *no* contact whatsoever on any level; It marked America's return to the world of *Realpolitik.* "[24]

Later describing his secret mission to Beijing in July 1971, Kissinger opined "I could not have encountered a group of interlocutors more receptive to Nixon's style of diplomacy than the Chinese leaders. Like Nixon they considered the traditional agenda to be of secondary importance and were above all concerned with exploring whether cooperation on the basis of congruent interests was possible. This was why, later on, one of Mao's first remarks to Nixon was "The small issue is Taiwan; the big issue is the world." Kissinger added, "At Nixon's meeting with Mao, the Chinese leader wasted no time in assuring the President that China would not use force against Taiwan. 'We can do without them (Taiwan) for the time being, and let it come after 100 years."[25]

"When Henry Kissinger in 1971 flew from Pakistan into what he called the 'land of mystery,' on his first secret mission to the communist court in Peking, he also crossed from *realpolitik* into *romanticism*," advises Miriam London, "He cast moreover, a peculiar aura around the relationship between Washington and Peking that was to persist through several administrations to this day and degenerate into a kind of sentimentality."[26]

Thirty years to the day of the historic 1972 Nixon trip, President George W. Bush visited Beijing in 2002 albeit with a far less burdensome agenda.

On 2 August, Secretary of State William Rogers kept up the momentum by declaring that the U.S. "Will support action of the General Assembly this fall calling for seating the People's Republic of China. At the same time, the United States will oppose any action to expel the Republic of China or otherwise deprive it of representation in the United Nations...The Republic of China has played a loyal and conscientious role in the U.N. since the organization was founded."[27]

The diplomatic die was cast. Premier Zhou set the political stage, by stating that the PRC will only enter the UN under its formal name and without a two state formula. The 26th session of the United Nations General Assembly opened its annual consideration of the China seat on 18 October. Agenda item 93, "Restoration of the lawful rights of the People's Republic of China in the United Nations," would witness a week-long consideration of an Albanian draft resolution which would not only seat the PRC but likewise oust the ROC, a founder of the U.N., from membership.

The line of reasoning was starkly simplistic. Albania's delegate stressed at the opening of the debate, "It is more essential than ever to give that great and powerful socialist country its rightful place in this organization and to expel the Chiang Kai-shek clique." Somalia's delegate stated, "Taiwan is an integral part of the State of China...the question of the expulsion of a member state does not arise. The question is simply that of the withdrawal of U.N. recognition from a delegation which represents a government that is no longer in power."[28]

On Monday 25 October, the General Assembly heard closing arguments on what diplomats knew was a *fait accompli.* U.S. Ambassador George Bush stated Washington's case succinctly, "The issue is not the seating of the People's Republic of China in the U.N. In fact, for the first time in history there is something close to unanimity behind the proposition that it is time for the People's Republic to take its seat in the United Nations, including its seat as a permanent member of the Security Council. That is a major historic development. It is not at issue in the U.N. anymore."

Ambassador Bush, torn between traditional American political/ security support for Taipei and the dawn of a better relationship with Beijing, added, "This is the issue: shall we expel forthwith the Republic of China from the United Nations, or shall it continue to be represented here? That is the heart of the matter...the ROC should not and must not be expelled or deprived of its United Nations representation." The U.S. offered an alternative plan contained a draft resolution which would, as Bush said, "retain the ROC in the U.N., while seating the PRC in both the General Assembly and the Security Council. It reflects plain facts who governs in Taiwan and as well as who governs the Chinese Mainland."[29]

The Chinese representation was voted on at literally the eleventh hour. The expulsion draft was adopted by a weary General Assembly, by 76 votes to 35 with 17 abstentions. Along with the predictable assembly of East Bloc and Third World states, many close American allies such as Britain, Canada, and France supported expelling Taiwan. Key opponents of the resolution along with the U.S. included Australia, Japan, New Zealand, and the Philippines. Abstentions included Greece, Jordan and Spain.[30]

With the adoption of the Albanian resolution #2758 (XXVI), many Third World delegates such as Tanzania's Salim Salim literally danced in the aisles when the nine hour Assembly meeting ended at 11:35PM. The American draft resolution offering what amounted to Chinese dual representation was never voted on. The ROC delegation withdrew from the Assembly hall before the PRC was seated.

U.S. Secretary of State William Rogers in a policy overview admitted self-satisfyingly, "During 1971 we made a substantial adjustment of America's international role." Rogers recounted "striking progress" in China policy.[31]

The view from Far Eastern capitals, especially Taipei and Tokyo, was not quite so sanguine. Taiwan's unseating at the United Nations was the first of three major diplomatic setbacks for Taipei within a year. The U.N. debacle was soon followed by the Nixon trip to the PRC in February. Then came a stunning regional reversal; breaks in diplomatic ties with Japan in September, and Australia and New Zealand in December 1972. For the ROC, and especially President Chiang Kai- shek who exhibited a rare benevolence to the Japanese people after the Pacific War, Tokyo's policy switch was viewed as particularly perfidious.

For a restive and military weak Japan fearing an American disengagement from the Far East, the "Nixon Shock" provided a policy jolt to Tokyo. American Chinese *rapprochement* was viewed as a possible signal to "dump Japan" as Washington's chief ally in East Asia. Thus while the Foreign Ministry had wanted to recognize Beijing but refrained from doing so as to adhere to U.S. policy, the "Nixon Shock" produced a profound mistrust across the Pacific. Edwin Reischauer, former U.S. envoy to Tokyo, derided the thoughtless manner in which the Nixon Administration acted which frightened the Japanese and left lingering concerns about the value of American friendship and reliability.[32]

Foreign leaders, many of them implacable anti-communists, took the cue from Washington. The subliminal message was clear; U.S. policy did not consider it vital that Taiwan still hold the Chinese seat in the U.N. Moreover, in its judicious currying of the Chinese communists, the State Department had sent a less than subtle signal that an East wind was blowing. Even states such as Franco's Spain recognized Beijing. The PRC, still being jolted by the after-shocks of the Cultural Revolution gained a remarkable legitimacy in the assembly of nations. True to proletarian form, the PRC delegation demanded that a quotation of Confucius in the U.N. headquarters be removed, as it offended the "New China." Beijing was granted its wish.

China's Economy: Leaps, Slips, and Bounds

The economic achievements of proletarian China have been variously described with rapture, amazement and awe, only rarely leavened with a dose of sceptical reality. "Since liberation," the speaker will almost *religiously intone*, the production of just about anything and everything has leaped, bounded, and only seldom faltered. Since 1949 and the creation of a socialist state, China's economic development has been harnessed in varying degrees to official ideology. The rigid constraints and forced production goals of the traditional command economy, the *chaos* of the Cultural Revolution, and the *relative pragmatism* of the Deng Xiaoping era, have varyingly characterized China's economic landscape.

The communist conquest of the Mainland initiated a "socialist transformation" of China's economy. Land reform was expanded as the regime set out to nationalize production. During the First Five Year Plan (1953-1957) it was not uncommon to look at planning and the market as opposed to each other. By 1957, the great majority of peasants had joined farm cooperatives; agriculture soon accounted for 81 percent of the workforce. The role of the market was neglected resulting in a drop in output and quality, relate Lin Wei and Arnold Chao.

An economy in a rebuilding mode after WWII and the civil war would naturally offer some resounding statistical leaps. During the first Plan, industrial production increased 18 percent annually. Yet, "the peasants had to pay for heavy industrial growth mandated by the Soviet model."[33]

Inspired by his vainglorious enthusiasm, Mao launched *the Great Leap Forward* in 1958. Mao's answer to a dismal agricultural output was a strategy of heightened production goals, moral invectives, and mass mobilizations according to Sinologist Jonathan Spence. His plans were to boost productivity and industrial growth. Cooperative farms were merged into communes; dizzying grain production figures flowed forth. Reality soon shocked China as investment in heavy industry took precedence over farming. "The average amount of grain available to each person in China's countryside which had been 205 kilos in 1957 and 201 in 1958, dropped to a disastrous 183 in 1959, and a catastrophic 156 in 1960. The result was famine on a gigantic scale, that claimed 20 million lives between 1959-1962. Many others died shortly thereafter from the effects of the Great Leap, especially children, weakened by malnutrition."[34]

By 1962 the economy was in ruins, the Sino/Soviet rift a glaring reality, and China with little more to show than a list of purged officials, among them Liu Shao-chi and Deng Xiaoping. The Cultural Revolution lurched China into a political unknown and an educational chasm. The crusade by communist Red Guards against the "four olds" was to delete and purge the history, language and culture of China's ancient civilization.

Emerging from the constricting cocoon of the Cultural Revolution, the Chinese communists looked to the outside world, especially the capitalist countries, as a reservoir of riches which could be exploited by the pragmatic elements in the regime. The early 1970's witnessed a belated realization by the PRC's rulers that politics alone cannot produce food and sustenance. While "self-reliance" remained official doctrine, even before Deng's reform era, the PRC was already, albeit grudgingly, opening the long closed trade ties with the West.

The evolving economic policy was cautiously outlined by Deng Xiaoping in a little noticed address before the U.N. Sixth Special Session on Development, in which the newly rehabilitated Vice Premier asserted, "That self-reliance in no way means self-seclusion and a rejection of foreign aid. We have already considered it beneficial that countries should carry on economic and technical exchanges on the basis of respect for state sovereignty." Deng unabashedly stated, "China is a socialist country and a developing country as well. China belongs to the Third World."[35]

Deng's remarks, made two and a half years before Mao's death, served as the ideological preparation to justify reopening China's red doors to the world. The period 1973-1975 witnessed a new era in China's economic policy. Foreign trade was encouraged while at the same time large orders for factories and technology were placed abroad. In 1973, trade reached $10 billion up from $6 billion the previous year; by 1974 trade rose to $14 billion.[36]

By the mid-1970's more than 80 percent of China's trade was with the West, including the U.S. which officially opened its markets after the Nixon visit. In 1972, the first year of U.S./PRC direct trade, volume was $96 million; by 1973 due to a large shipment of American commodities to China, the amount rose to $800 million (exports of $740 million and imports of $64 million), by 1974 two-way trade rose to $935 million.[37]

In the sunset of the Maoist era, Deng had already begun to pave the way for a pragmatic path to restore economic viability, not because he deemed it ideologically correct but rather because for a nation of 850 million people there was no alternative short of famine. The new "open door" policy adopted in the late 1970's ended nearly two decades of social, economic, and technological isolation from socio/scientific trends. The *Four Modernizations Program* was launched to upgrade the areas of agriculture, industry, science and technology, and defense.

In shifting the focus from *class struggle* to the *Four Modernizations* after the landmark Third Plenum in December 1978, the Chinese Communist Party criticized its earlier policies as extreme and unrealistic and took the unprecedented approach of encouraging private business and creating conditions conducive to it. In effect the CCP wanted to use private business to fill a number of gaps caused by shortcomings of the state sector. China's unique Maoist experiment had created serious problems beyond those inherent in other socialist economies.[38]

One of Deng's tenets was that it is permissible that some people get rich as a stimulating effect for the rest, states Dr. Thomas Gold adding, "As a part of the shift from class struggle to modernization, the party removed labels from many former class enemies." Private business boomed. At the time of the Third Plenum there existed only 100,000 individual enterprises; by 1981 the number had reached 1.8 million and by 1988, the total exceeded 14 million.[39]

China's state sector remained formidable, comprising the classic "iron rice bowl" smokestack industries employing three out of four urban workers. This control of the old polluting industrial economy would be slow to change.

In 1980, the PRC commenced arms sales to the world. Military aid, previously free, began to be replaced by sales at cost. China's arms trade is conducted through two networks, the defense industry and the People's Liberation Army. China North Industry Corporation (NORINCO) emerged as a conduit for weapons shipments. Beyond traditional military sales, the People's Liberation Army (PLA) evolved into an *enterprise* in itself; military business ventures managed and directed and managed by officers in the provincial commands became the order of the day.

"The PLA's involvement in the money-making businesses surged in the eighties, at the direction of Deng, who wanted to focus budget spending on economic development," writes Richard McGregor. Before the central government has cracked down on "*PLA Inc*," the armed forces played an key commercial role in the Mainland economy. In July 1998, Jiang Zemin ordered the PLA to divest itself of business interests, a decision both political and economic. In fact the military was involved in widespread smuggling, corruption and a parallel economy. The process of dismantling the PLA's business empire began in December 1998. PLA firms were involved in everything from luxury hotels, to cell phones, pharmaceuticals, and smuggling of Mercedes Benz via trading companies.

Although it gathered steam as economic reforms began in 1978, the PLA's move into business really took off in 1984. At its peak in the late eighties, the PLA-run empire included more than 20,000 companies employing over 500,000 people in a host of endeavours. "More secretive tan even the Party itself, the military developed into a state within a state," advises McGregor. In fact reliance from cash from these commercial operations actually "distorted the management of the military budget."[40]

While economic activity was permitted on an unprecedented scale, albeit still involving relatively small numbers of China's billion people, the CCP maintained tight political/ideological control.

The agricultural reforms that commenced in 1978 contributed to the rapid expansion of the food supply. In 1978, 790 million Chinese or 82 percent of the population were living in rural areas. Rural non-agricultural activities were also encouraged to create off-farm employment for farmers. The agricultural reforms, export incentives and price/ market reforms, became one of the most dynamic sectors in China. So too did changes in the state sector where the government would lay off 50 million workers in state firms; the three 'irons'; the 'iron chair' of a lifelong job, the 'iron rice bowl' of the promise of employment and the 'iron wage' of guaranteed income, were according to McGregor, "all dismantled."[41]

With his economic reforms, Deng was pursing one goal writes German author Uli Frantz, "to build China into the strongest socialist system in the world. The great battle inside the Party leadership is constantly rekindled by the so-called cage politics. Reformers and orthodox alike agree that the social system—allegorically a bird—belongs in a cage. Their differences arise over the dimensions of the cage. Deng has no desire to give the bird its freedom, just room enough to spread its wings."[42]

PRC officials alluding to the *birdcage allegory* assert "the door to the cage is open, but the bird does not want to fly out." This claim is highly disputable.

Prison labor from a vast network of detention camps makes a handsome profit for the socialist state. All China's prisoners, political and criminal, live in a network of camps known as *Lao Gai* meaning "reform through labor." To put the matter into poignant perspective, this penal force serves not only to *reform* offenders, but to *create commercial pr*ofits for the PRC through a lucrative network of export outlets selling *Lao Gai* produced products.

Harry Wu, former *Lao Gai* inmate and respected researcher on the system comments, "China is a bird with two wings: politics and economy. The bird cannot fly with either of its two wings tied. The former Soviet Union, with its economic wing bound, desperately flapped its political wing only to crash."

What about China? He adds, "The economic wing capitalism moves unflaggingly ahead, yet the country continues to struggle...as long as the Chinese communists continue a policy of crushing all forms of dissent, the two wings will resist cooperation, and the bird will die of exhaustion." Wu advises, "In political terms the China of today is not so different from the Nazi Germany of the 1930's or the 'Evil Empire' of the USSR condemned by Ronald Reagan. Reagan based his concept of the 'Evil Empire' on its Gulag. It is common knowledge that tyrannical systems need a method of suppression to maintain power; Hitler had his concentration camps, Stalin had his Gulag. Similarly since the dawn of the People's Republic, Chinese authorities have never hesitated to use the *Lao Gai* in their efforts to maintain domestic political control."[43]

Lao Gai has come to stand for the regime's vast system of politically imposed slavery. It merits painfully little attention from the majority of China specialists and is overwhelmingly disregarded by the foreign business community. In a rare criticism from the international community, Mary Robinson, United Nations High Commissioner for Human Rights urged China to consider ending its use of "re-education labor camps," a practice she described as running counter to international principles banning forced. work. Speaking in Beijing, Robinson, a former Irish President, acknowledged the PRC's long history of using the labor camps, but added "that attitudes towards the administration of justice have changed both in the world at large and here in China too."[44]

While concern about China's human rights record has been widespread in Western countries, formal censure of the PRC's record has been rare indeed. Though the U.S. and European governments have long tried to pass a resolution in the UN Human Rights Commission in Geneva, Beijing has always adroitly stifled discussion through its support from developing nations, many of whom have the same sort of wretched records on human, civil, and religious rights as does China.

The PRC's continuing *cultural genocide* in Tibet continues to capture the attention and ire of the West. Yet, while Tibet has become a *boutique cause celebre* for the West Coast, the *Rive Gauche*, and the *chic classes* everywhere, there's painfully less concern for the wider issue of human rights and religious rights for *all Chinese*.

A key element in opening China's economy has been to induce foreign investment and technology to stimulate the export sector. The policy involved establishing Special Economic Zones (SEZ) in 1979-1980, a far more ambitious plan than export processing zones. SEZ's such as Shenzhen near Hong Kong were tasked to be laboratories experimenting with market reforms. By 1984, such policies were extended to fourteen coastal cities; and by 1990 to Shanghai.[45]

The year 1978 marked the end of an era of chaos and socialist stagnation of China's economy. "Since 1978, central planning has largely given way to market forces," states a Survey of the China-United States Exchange Foundation which adds that China's GDP grew from $341 billion in 1978 to $8.2 trillion in 2012. "Between 1978 and 2012, Chinese per capita income grew from $354 to $6,102." In the same period , Chinese international trade surged from $20 billion to $4.3 trillion to become the second largest trading nation in the world.[46]

The fast pace of economic reform in China has invariably fuelled socio/political tensions such as inflation, corruption, and income disparities. Likewise, socialist shock therapy, especially in the Maoist era, caused irreparable environmental damage. "Environmental challenges have increased dramatically in the past 30 years as China has accelerated its economic growth," writes Dr. Junjie Zhang, adding, "the deterioration of the overall state of China's environment has drawn global concern." Measured by the Environmental Performance Index by researchers at Yale, "China ranks 116 out of 132 countries." Seven river systems are polluted and China is the world's largest greenhouse gas (GHG) emitter.[47]

In 2000 growth was officially put at 8%. Naturally Hong Kong and increasingly Shanghai, after all the favored city of the CPP's ruling elite, have profited from the economic reforms. Hong Kong has traditionally been the locus of an extraordinary economic experiment in entrepreneurialism. Whether as a British Crown Colony or as a Special Administrative Region of the PRC, Hong Kong has followed the mantra of free markets allowed the vision of enterprise to turn this once sleepy coastal city into a dynamic global player. It has prospered despite Beijing's creeping efforts to erode the political and press freedoms guaranteed for fifty years.

But the nervous optimism which followed the 1997 Hong Kong Hand-over to China soon disappeared almost as quickly as the stunningly spectacular fireworks over Victoria Peak on that July evening. The cause of the economic malaise had less to do with Beijing's politics, than with the reverberations of the East Asian economic crisis. Thus while China has been exceedingly cautious not to cause any alarm in Hong Kong as not to kill the proverbial golden goose, the wider East Asian markets were not so thoughtful.

Chris Patten, last British Governor of Hong Kong opines with searing analysis, "From Manchuria to Canton, from fertile coast to arid central Asian hinterland, China's present social and economic state contains examples of most of the centuries of the last millennium. It all encompasses too, most known economic models from clapped-out public ownership to sweatshop capitalism, from peasant agriculture in village markets to trading in derivatives in futures markets. Its government is manned by Stalinist hacks and smart Stanford Business School graduates. Its prevailing political ethos, market Leninism, market socialism, capitalism with Chinese characteristics, Shanghai-style socialism, call it what you will, is intellectually incoherent but infused with an iron determination to hold on to power and a barely controlled nationalist rage."

Governor Patten added, "Add this to the extraordinary mix of 1997 Hong Kong, the worldly-wise and modern capital of the overseas Chinese, with its regulated markets, common law, attractiveness for overseas investors, native managerial skills, competent administration and experienced entrepreneurs, now *that* produces a real spark of combustion."[48]

Despite the social uneasiness throughout the land, it's unlikely that China's leaders think that social instability is yet serious enough to threaten their rule. The countryside protests appear to be reactions not against central rule but against he arbitrary powers of local officials. Even though protests have grown in cities by people laid off from state enterprises, they do not yet challenge party rule; rather they seek to redress grievances. Even the CCP has jumped on bandwagon and regularly offers up the sacrificial lambs of disgraced party cadre to prove the CCP's commitment to anti-corruption efforts.

Economic reforms are the balm to soothe people's grievances. grievances. Strong economic growth has proven the elixir to revive the PRC's socio/political stagnancy. From 2003 to 2007, China's exports increased on average by 29 percent a year and amounted to $1.2 trillion, During the same time imports increased on average by 23 percent annually to reach $956 billion. Major trading partners included the USA, Japan, South Korea and Germany.[49]

In parallel to robust trade, the PRC attracted formidable foreign investment flows. China gained $106 billion FDI in 2010 almost replacing the 2008 level. FDI flows into Hong Kong reached $66 billion. While Mainland China remains the largest FDI recipient, most of the investment comes from Hong Kong, Japan, South Korea and Taiwan.[50]

"China's economy grew at 9.9 percent during the 1979-2009 period, and 10.7 percent during 2001-2009." Indeed and despite being buffeted by the winds of global recession, China was able to reach a strong 10.3 percent growth for 2010. By mid-2010, Beijing's reserves reached an amazing $2.5 trillion.[51]

Part of this culture of corruption certainly concerns the likely statistical falsehoods which underwrite the system. As in the Maoist part, when production figures were part of the proletarian folklore, today's impressive growth statistics are likely driven by political imperatives more than economic realities.

Furthermore, and most dangerous politically, development is uneven fuelling regionalism. The pace of reform does not address the socio/political needs of the people since naturally all depends on political stability, a classic Catch 22-scenario in which political freedom may fuel disincentives to development. Clearly the archaic Maoist banners about the glory of work for the party have been supplanted by slick new slogans, "To Get Rich is Glorious."

Tiananmen: Crisis and Aftershocks

The communist crackdown in Tiananmen Square represented a watershed in the relations between the PRC and the West. While the systematic use of coercion and terror was not in itself unusual in the People's Republic, even many Chinese had assumed that such sanguinary tactics had disappeared with the passing of Mao and the final purge of the Gang of Four. For the West, most especially the U.S. and Canada seduced by the paradigm of a "changed China" in the post-Mao era, the political class was shocked and the people sickened by this grim reality.

It appeared the ghost of the dead dictator Mao had returned in the surrealistic shadows and among the crackle of gunfire that warm June night in Beijing. To be sure, the heady days of May-June 1989 seemed to herald almost politically cosmic events never before seen in the People's Republic. Mikhail Gorbachev, leader of a reformist and once reviled Soviet Union, was being courted in the Forbidden City. Throngs of students, many infused by an eclectic political philosophy, were streaming to the very nerve center of the Middle Kingdom, Tiananmen Square. Before long students were taking the unprecedented tact of questioning and chastising the CCP authorities.

In the article *China: The Romance of Realpolitik*, Miriam London advises that what began in the Spring of 1989 in China's capital as "a peaceful student demonstration for 'dialogue' with the government on democratic rights and reforms swiftly turned into a popular movement, much like that sparked by Solidarity in Poland eight years earlier. It was also the realization of the regime's worst fears. Deng and his aged cohorts had long shown an obsession with Poland's Solidarity movement and recognized the potential for a similar development in China." She added "Within China in the late seventies, the full realization that three decades of sacrifice and turmoil had gone for nothing, that China was still a beggar among modern nations, produced a "crisis of confidence" in the Communist Party's ability to lead. The new notion that China was 'going our way' and that Deng's economic reforms would of necessity lead to a democratised political system, reflected Western wishfulness, not Chinese reality."[52]

Deng's intolerance of political openness and any direct challenges to Communist Party political hegemony contrasted with his desire to loosen the Party's control over China's economy.

The popular earthquake of Tiananmen was long in coming. In China for most of the population the immediate causes of dissatisfaction relate not only to vague yearnings for democracy but more importantly to profound economic frustration and disgust over social inequalities and corruption. During the past ten years, the average income in China has more than doubled, but the expectations of Chinese had risen even more resulting in dissatisfaction and anger mixed with bitterness at the advantage enjoyed by high officials.

During the six weeks of Tiananmen, the students were in the vanguard of the demonstrations. The protests which began as a politically charged mourning for the deceased reformist party secretary Hu Yao-bang, went on from 17 April to the blood soaked night of June 4-5, a total of fifty days, writes historian John Woodruff. By 26 April, an editorial in the CCP newspaper *People's Daily* declared that the demonstrations were a "planned conspiracy" and that they caused "*great chaos,*" watchwords in communist parlance for an impending crackdown.

Hardline Premier Li Peng had won Deng Xiaoping over to the logic that the disorders were part of a conspiracy to overthrow communist party rule. "Yet the CCP itself was divided and actually in danger of implosion from its failure at crisis management in the heart of the Chinese capital," says Woodruff. Martial Law was seemingly useless as the throng of students scoffed at the edicts and at the old men who issued them. Worse yet, in the minds of the ruling circle including Deng, was the attempt of Zhao Ziyang to deal with the demonstrators. Woodruff added, "The crisis within the Communist party itself, not the struggle in the streets, produced the bloody crackdown. For Deng Xiaoping and those who favored imposing a Leninist hard line, this loss of *party control* was the core question. Deng viewed the issue as life and death of the party."[53]

"For Deng, the demonstrations represented a direct threat to the survival of the CCP and the PRC," writes Sinologist David Shambaugh adding, "To save the Party/State required firm and intimidating action. At first Deng watched as his designated successors factionalized and proved indecisive. Then he took matters into his own hands. He rallied remnants of the Old Guard, mobilized reliable units of the PLA, and called in the tanks."[54]

Units in the Beijing capital garrison were likely considered perhaps too close to the students in the square; while the troops would perform passive security duties, they could not be relied on to crackdown on command with brute force. So while the protesters and West *assumed* the military was *paralysed* from action, the CCP was marshalling provincial units to move on Beijing to deal with the protesters the old fashioned way.

As in Budapest in 1956 what *appeared* to be a Soviet pullback, turned out to be a brief and foreboding lull before a massive counterattack with *untainted* rural troops who cared nothing for firing on the people and re-imposing order.

Simon Leys, the Belgian authority, stressed to *Le Point* that the Tiananmen massacre was orchestrated by "a regime of ferocious stupidity." He added that the "leaders of the party always consider that a massacre and bloodletting are indispensable for the good health of their power...this has been used since even before the founding of the regime in 1949." French Sinologist Richard Sola advised, "The myth of the People's Army was broken on the barricades, the students are not victims of simple repression, but of the power struggle inside the Communist Party...an old fascination with the Stalinist system and a dream of a return to the Maoist era."[55]

Tiananmen produced searingly poignant images; the imposing Goddess of Democracy statue which graced the Square, the man whose stoic heroism held back a column of tanks, and the jarring images of Western Friday evening TV programs being interrupted to bring a special news bulletin from Peking showing police officials barging into the transmission trailers and shutting down the satellite feed to the world outside the new walls of China.

Yet for all their purported moral revulsion and pious pronouncements on the Chinese carnage, few Western governments, except France, had the courage to offer more than perfunctory condemnations of the crackdown, only to offer quiet obeisance to the octogenarians who committed it. It was no coincidence that the Federation for a Democratic China was founded at the Sorbonne in Paris soon after the massacre to coordinate the large dissident student movement.

Revulsion soon turned to *realpolitik* and then to arcane rationalization. Somehow the Chinese rulers were magically exempt from the political and moral code applied to the East Bloc or South Africa. "Since the establishment of relations with the People's Republic of China, each U.S. administration has refrained from using whatever real leverage it might have had to inhibit Peking's repressive policies. This policy of 'sparing the sensitivities' of the communist court in Peking was not only unwise but unnecessary," London adds.[56]

Aside from a verbal rebuke and a timid set of sanctions regarding high technology transfer to the PRC, the United States did little to signal its disgust over the Tiananmen events. As summer moved into autumn, the white heat of human rights concern over Tiananmen had become tepid. In the U.N. General Assembly, the global forum resounding with endless discussions on rights and freedoms the world over, few states cared to raise the spectre of the incident. Britain's John Major nonetheless warned the PRC, "No government can survive indefinitely by the suppression of peaceful dissent."[57]

Alain Peyrefitte of the French Academy queried, "So is China an empire forever immobile? What is so discouraging in China is the eternal going backward. After the pendulum moves towards progress it then swings towards reaction. Was China as traumatized as the West by the Spring of 1989? It was the first time the West discovered in China a cruel world, not only to denounce it but to be compassionate for it. It is also the first time that the West's compassion has moved the Chinese."[58]

Publication of the politically explosive Tiananmen Papers in 2001, reopened the controversy. The documents, minutes of Politburo meetings during the crisis, illustrate the decision making process between hard-line and reform factions. The documents illustrate how the Chinese leadership argued fiercely over whether they should establish martial law to crush the student protests. According McGregor many military units balked including the commander of the legendary 38th Army Lt. General Xu Qinxian reportedly said, "No matter what charges are laid against me, I will absolutely not lead the troops myself." General Xu was court- marshalled for his action. "The siege mentality in Beijing lasted for at least six months after the crackdown," advised McGregor. In fact the modern PLA which has 2.3 million troops, has an astounding 90,000 party cells operating inside it, about one for every twenty-five people attached to the forces. As in the old Soviet military the political commissar tradition lives on.[59]

Unification: Beijing's View

Since the creation of the People's Republic in 1949, four Constitutions have been promulgated; in 1954, 1975, 1978, and 1982. Concerning the central issues of the nature of the state and unification, each of the documents has exhibited an evolving political line, both starkly clear in the nature of the source of power, and increasingly focused regarding Taiwan.

Typically, the constitutions in communist states are not intended to be enduring documents but rather transitional thematic instruments written to serve the purpose of the state. For example, in the 1954 Constitution Article 1 states, "The People's Republic of China is a people's democratic state led by the working class and based on the alliance of workers and peasants." Article 2 adds, "All power in the People's Republic of China belongs to the people."[60]

The 1975 document reeks of the Cultural Revolutionary rhetoric, while the 1978 Constitution in Article 1 states, "The People's Republic of China is a socialist state of the dictatorship of the Proletariat led by the working class and based on the alliance of the workers and peasants." Article 2 adds clearly, "The Communist Party of China is the core leadership of the whole of the Chinese people. The working class exercises its leadership over the state through its vanguard the Communist Party of China. The guiding ideology of the PRC is Marxism Leninism/Mao Tse-tung thought."[61]

The 1982 document reaffirms in Article 1, "The People's Republic of China is a socialist state under the People's democratic dictatorship led by the working class and based on an alliance of the workers and peasants. The socialist system is the basic system of the People's Republic of China."[62]

While the Chinese communists had long called for unification of the motherland, in both bellicose and conciliatory terms, such aspirations were not specifically ensconced in the earlier PRC Constitutions. Commenting on the draft 1954 Constitution, Liu Shao-shi candidly asserted that the document need not enumerate China's borders; "Those who have proposed that an article be added concerning territorial boundaries have done so with the idea of affirming in the Constitution that Taiwan is an unalienable part of Chinese territory. This shows a good intention. But the constitution does not need articles to be added for this purpose. That Taiwan is China's inviolable territory has never been questioned. It is the task of the Chinese people, and they are certain to carry it out, to liberate Taiwan from the rule of U.S. imperialism and the traitorous Chiang Kai-shek clique and complete the unification of our country."[63]

By 1978 in the aftermath of the Cultural Revolution, a profound sea change had affected juridical relations across the Formosa Straits. The Preamble to the 1978 Constitution adopted by the Fifth National People's Congress, states, that there is a call to "consolidate and expand the revolutionary united front" with our compatriots in Taiwan, Hong Kong and Macao. More importantly the Preamble asserts, "Taiwan is China's sacred territory. We are determined to liberate Taiwan and accomplish the great cause of unifying our motherland." The only specific reference in the 1978 document *vis-a-vis* unity comes in Article 56 in which citizens are called on "to support the leadership of the Communist Party of China, support the socialist system, and safeguard the unification of the motherland."[64]

The Preamble to the 1982 Constitution reaffirms, "Taiwan is part of the sacred territory of the People's Republic of China. It is the inviolable duty of all Chinese people, including our compatriots in Taiwan to accomplish the great task of reunifying the motherland." The Constitution does not specifically address reunification.[65]

The Taiwan issue has long been a political and emotional sounding board for the PRC. Premier Zhou Enlai in his famous 1956 speech "Oppose the U.S. Occupation of Taiwan," stressed candidly, "The Chinese people are determined to liberate Taiwan. This is the unshakable common will of the 600 million people of China. The Chinese government has repeatedly pointed out that there are two ways for the Chinese people to liberate Taiwan, that is by war or peaceful means." Such statements seemed echoed across the Formosa Straits.[66]

Not since the bellicose rhetoric of the 1950's have the PRC's rulers renounced the use of force as an option to "liberate" *Jiefang* Taiwan. Although Beijing has increasingly offered the choice between carrot and stick diplomacy to Taipei, the stark reality remains that the military option, that of a classic, if difficult, cross-straits invasion has never been ruled out.

Yet in late 1978 and early 1979, an extraordinary series of domestic and geopolitical events coincided which in effect encouraged pragmatism. In 1978 the Third Plenum of the Chinese Communist Party Eleventh Central Committee decided that reunification would be better achieved by a "peaceful united front." That famous Plenary session likewise set the stage for sweeping economic reforms. On 1 January 1979, coincidentally the day that Washington opened full diplomatic ties with Beijing, the National People's Congress issued a "Message to Our Taiwan Compatriots." The statement proclaimed a policy to reunify the motherland peacefully, *heping tongyi.*[67]

Significantly the seemingly conciliatory Message to the Taiwan Compatriots also coincided with a series of geopolitical jolts for the PRC. Vietnam sensing a Sino/U.S. strategic rapprochement following the Carter diplomatic recognition, attacked and ousted Cambodia's Beijing-backed Pol Pot regime. Less than a month after the normalization of Washington/Beijing political ties, an emboldened PRC fought a border war to "teach Vietnam a lesson."

In April 1979, the PRC announced that it would not extend the 1950 Treaty of Friendship with the USSR whose thirty-year term expired in April 1980. The perceptions of Sino/American *entente* were also very likely to have served as a impetus to Soviet aligned-Vietnam to invade Chinese-aligned Cambodia to oust the *Khmer Rouge* regime. The attack came days after the Carter White House announced diplomatic ties with Peking.[68]

Later Beijing and Washington, along with most of Southeast Asia, were aligned together in opposing Vietnam's occupation of Cambodia; a dubious diplomatic benefit of the new détente with the PRC.

On the eve of PRC National Day 1981, the National People's Congress sent greeting to the "Taiwan compatriots" and offered clarification of the Nine Point Plan for peaceful reunification. The salient points were talks between the ruling parties of the PRC and ROC, namely the Communist Party and Kuomintang. The statement added "this would be the third time CCP/KMT talks would cooperate in the cause of great national unity." Most significantly, the statement promised Taiwan a "special administrative region that can retain its armed forces...Taiwan's current socio/economic system will remain unchanged...people in authority in Taiwan may take up leadership posts in national bodies....Taiwan investment is welcome on the mainland with legal rights and profits guaranteed...visits, mail, and trade between both sides are encouraged."[69]

In September 1982, Deng Xiaoping presented the landmark concept of "one country/two systems," *yiguo liangzhi*. Furthermore, article 31 of the PRC's 1982 Constitution provides that "the country will establish special administrative regions when necessary. The system adopted in this special administrative region will be stipulated according to the specific conditions in form of law by the National People's Congress." This provided for a basic legal framework of one country/two systems.[70]

Such "guarantees" were nervously spurned by the ROC government on Taiwan who viewed this latest *entente* as a unpleasantly ironic reminder of the two earlier periods of CCP/KMT cooperation in the 1920's and during the Sino/Japanese war.

"Taiwan is a sacred part of Chinese territory" stated Deng Yingchao in an New Year 1984 appeal which equally added a subtle threat to "Taiwan independence" activities which could "forebode fortune or disaster for the future." Reunification, she said, was one of China's three major tasks for the 1980's.[71]

While visiting the U.S., PRC Premier Zhao Ziyang rhetorically boasted, "Is it not an important point common to the two sides that they both believe there is only one China? Moreover, China's peaceful reunification has come to be the common language for both the Kuomintang and the Communist Party." Later Premier Zhao, pressed for the concept of "one country, two systems" to be put into place after unification which would take into account the interests of the state and the nation as well as the current state of affairs in Taiwan." As long as the KMT and the Communist Party share a common language on peaceful reunification, everything else can be negotiated."[72]

During this period momentum seemed to favor rapprochement. When the British government raised questions with China over the future status of Hong Kong, Beijing made it clear it would not renew the lease on the New Territories in 1997. A series of Sino/British negotiations ensued; a formal accord ratified in September 1984 provided for the Crown Colony to revert to the PRC in 1997 as a "special administrative region" presumably in which Hong Kong's free wheeling commerce and way of life would be unchanged for fifty years.[73]

The "changed" China played a hard game with Britain over the Crown Colony's future. Prime Minister Thatcher recalled that Deng had warned her that "China could walk in and take Hong Kong back later today if they wanted to."

Thatcher retorted that they could indeed do so, but this could bring about Hong Kong's collapse, "The world would see what followed a change from British to Chinese rule." Thatcher recalled, "For the first time he (Deng) seemed taken aback: his mood became more accommodating." The nervous countdown to PRC control in 1997 commenced; "confidence in the Colony was fragile," and the Prime Minister admitted, "I felt depressed."[74]

The concept of one country/two systems accorded Hong Kong thus put increasing political pressures on Taipei. Despite the smiling diplomacy of Beijing's Marxist mandarins and the notable political achievement of the Sino/British accords, the PRC has *never renounced the use of force* against Taiwan. The nature of the threat is usually couched in the caveat that any manifestation of "independence," or "separatism," would invite attack. While stressing one country/two systems, both CCP and government officials openly warn that "Taiwan independence" would provide a *causus belli*.

Qimao Chen, of the relatively liberal Shanghai Institute for International Studies warns, "The sovereignty problem is very sensitive; no Chinese leaders can be regarded as cowards in protecting sovereignty. If China's sovereignty is seriously harmed, e.g., if certain countries support Taiwanese or Tibetan independence and try to separate Taiwan or Tibet from the PRC; China has no choice but to adopt all necessary means to protect its sacred sovereignty."[75]

In his New Year's 1995 Address, PRC President Jiang Zemin raised the tone against Taiwan separatism but offered a recalibrated plan for reunification of the motherland. Jiang put forth an eight-point plan stressing the principle of "One China," but allowing a subtle breathing space for Taipei's development of economic and cultural ties worldwide. Still its tenor is crystal clear; the PRC refuses to refute the option of force. "Our not undertaking to give up the use of force is not directed against our compatriots in Taiwan, but against the schemes of forces to interfere with China's reunification and to bring about Taiwan independence."[76]

Such statements should invite no misperceptions. The March 1996 crisis across the Straits coinciding with Taiwan's democratic Presidential elections refocused the reality of the PRC's military options against an *errant* Taiwan. A clear, consistent, and proportionate U.S. defense response, prompted by Congress and supported by the While House, defused the most serious armed confrontation between Beijing and Taipei since the 1950's.

The PRC can be expected to use the Taiwan issue both as a nationalist rallying point and as a political lightning rod to test the fortunes of the emerging Mainland leadership. The historic Hong Kong handover in 1997 provided Beijing with another rhetorical platform. So did the Macao transfer in 1999.

China has renewed calls for Taiwan to follow Hong Kong's example and return to Mainland rule under a similar deal. Yet Taipei government officials have firmly rejected PRC pressure to adopt the Hong Kong style "one country-two systems" formula that returned the former British colony to Chinese rule, even though Hong Kong's fortunes have not substantially declined under PRC rule.

As PRC President Jiang Zemin stated triumphantly on the first day of China's rule over Hong Kong, "The prospect of complete unification is now in sight; the 'one country, two systems' formula for Hong Kong and Macao would set an example for the final solution to the Taiwan question." Taiwan's Premier Lien Chan, retorted that Hong Kong after all, was a British colony, whereas the ROC remains a sovereign state and democratic country. Taipei's nervous confidence reflected the experience of living in the shadow of the dragon, even if protected by the Taiwan Straits.[77]

The period leading up to Taiwan's 2000 Presidential elections witnessed another simmering confrontation between the PRC and the ROC. Again the perceptions and misperceptions regarding the three major candidates offered the PRC the chance to both bully and cajole. Given that a major contender was the *separatist-inclined* Democratic Progressive Party (DPP), there was no shortage of rhetoric nor lack of suspense. Indeed following a narrow DPP victory, and after the first anxious months of Chen Shui-bian's Presidency, a calm soon emerged between Beijing and Taipei. Cool tempers prevailed in Taipei political circles; few serious politicians wished to alter the *status quo* and tamper with the time-bomb phraseology of "Taiwan" or the "Republic of China."

Since the mid-2000's, the cross-straits relations have evolved into a mixture of relative clam punctuated with political melodrama usually focused on the outcome of Taiwan's hotly contested elections. Economic, tourist, and family exchanges have grown dramatically. Importantly the PRC is facing the challenges of growing social unrest and rampant corruption which seriously threaten stability of the regime, as well as the aftermath of the fractious the 18th Communist Party Congress in 2012. While China's communists laboriously selected a leader, Xi Jingping, Taiwan's spirited voters democratically re-elected President Ma in 2012.

The reverberations of the September 11th 2001 terrorist attacks on the U.S. were felt in the Far East. The PRC quickly aligned its policies with Washington and joined the "war on terror" against "fundamentalism and separatism." For Beijing there was the clear political advantage of being able to crackdown on the Muslim minority in western Xinjiang under the banner of opposing "terrorism." It also neatly dovetailed with the PRC's demonization of Tibet and Taiwan "separatism."

Since 1949, the PRC has endured the political gyrations of the communist revolution, the cult of Mao and the Cultural Revolution, and the amazing socio/economic changes following the Deng Xiaoping era. Contemporary China attempts to project a *soft power* image globally. The establishment of Confucius Institutes as a bridge to promote Chinese language and culture internationally seems richly ironic, given that the CCP once waged a furious anti-Confucius campaign. Starting in 2004, the program has grown exponentially to 350 university affiliated Confucius Institutes and 430 additional Confucius classrooms at secondary schools by 2011. More than 1,000 Chinese language teaches have been sent to the USA under the program. Under Beijing's official sponsorship Confucius, the 5th century BC sage, has now gained new attention from Australia, to Canada, Europe and the USA promoting the Middle Kingdom's *soft power*.[78]

Under the assertive authoritarianism of PRC President/ CCP Party leader Xi Jinping, the ruling communists have re-calibrated their domestic message: the *Chinese Dream*. The Dream has four components: *"Strong China; Civilized China; Harmonious China ; Beautiful China."* According to economist Robert Lawrence Kuhn, the Dream stresses the "need to legitimize one-party rule," and adds that "Xi is putting nationalism at the core of his leadership; his nationalism is proactive, riding the high road of patriotism and pride."[79]

The *Chinese Dream* focuses on building the PRC as an economic and military power, with the CCP serving as a paternalistic force promoting the political narrative of social tranquillity, fairness and a cleaner environment.

Yet, the PRC's socio/economic modernization is confronted by the contradictions of a still authoritarian political and civil arena not to mention stunning levels of corruption, much of it inside the CCP.

Dissident Liu Xiaobao, though imprisoned for his pro-democracy activities, won the 2010 Nobel Peace Prize. Prof. Liu's efforts towards political openess and a working civil society pose a direct long-term challenge to the government; that of a more open and democratic China.

ENDNOTES

1. USDS, "In Quest of Peace and Security: Selected Documents on American Foreign Policy 1941-1951, (Washington DC: GPO, 1951), 10.

2. Frederick W. Marks, *Wind Over Sand; The Diplomacy of Franklin Roosevelt*, (Athens: University of Georgia Press, 1988), 181, 188-189.

3. James A. Gregor, *The China Connection; U.S. Policy and the People's Republic of China*, (Stanford: Hoover Institution, 1986), 28.

4. Jonathan Spence, *The Search for Modern China*, (New York: Norton, 1990), 514-519.

5. Ibid, 524.

6. Steven Mosher, *China Misperceived American Illusions and Chinese Reality*, (New York: Basic Books, 1990), 80-81.

7. Charles Kraus, "Zhou Enlai and China's Response to the Korean War," Wilson International Center for Scholars/North Korea International Documentation Project E dossier #9, June 2012.

8. United Nations Bulletin/UNB, December 1950, 9: 659-660.

9. UNB/December 9, 661-663.

10. UNB/February 1951 10, 106, 130-131.

11. Spence, Search for Modern China, 525.

12. Gregor, The China Connection, 61-62

13. Bruce Larkin, *China and Africa 1949-1970: The Foreign Policy of the People's Republic of China*, (Berkeley: University of California Press, 1971), 38-39, 64-70.

14. Warren Weinstein, and Thomas Henriksen/Editors, *Soviet and Chinese Aid to African Nations*, (New York: Praeger, 1980), 102-104.

15. Larkin, China in Africa, 88.

16. Weinstein and Henriksen, 104-107, 119-120.

17. Simon Leys, *Chinese Shadows*, (New York: Viking Press, 1977), 41-47.

18. Gregor, The China Connection, 78.

19. Mosher, China Misperceived, 140-143.

20. USDS Bulletin 1972, 66, 431-438.

21. Gregor, China Connection, 90-92.

22. UNGA/Plenery 20 November 1970.

23. USDS/Bulletin, 1971, 65, 121.

24. Henry Kissinger, *Diplomacy*, (New York: Simon & Schuster, 1994), 724.

25. Ibid, 726-727.

26. Miriam London, "China: The Romance of R*ealpolitik*, " *Freedom at Issue* no. 10 (September/October 1989), 10.

27. USDS/Bulletin 1971, 65, 193.

28. UNGA/Plenary 18 October 1971, 1-3.

29. UNGA/Plenary 25 October 1971, 11-14.

30. UNGA/Plenary 25 October 1971, 41.

31. USDS/Bulletin 1972, 66, 462.

32. Edwin Reischauer, *Japan: The Story of a Nation*, (New York: McGraw Hill, 1990), 267-268.

33. Lin Wei and Arnold Chao/Editors, China's Economic Reforms, (Philadelphia: University of Pennsylvania Press, 1982), 94-96, 242.

34. Spence, The Search for Modern China, 553.

35. *Peking Review*, April 1974, 17, 10-11.

36. Mike Mansfield, *Charting a New Course/Mike Mansfield and U.S. Asian Policy*, (Rutland, VT: Tuttle, 1978), 122.

37. USDS/Trade with the PRC, 1975.

38. Spence, *Search for Modern China*, 621.

39. Ramon H. Myers/Editor, *Two Societies in Opposition: The Republic of China and the People's Republic of China after Forty Years*, (Stanford: Hoover Institution, 1991), 159-160.

40. Richard McGregor, *The Party: The Secret World of China's Communist Rulers*, (New York: Harper Perennial, 2012), 113-1114.

41. *World Economic Survey 2000*, (New York: United Nations, 2000), 144-145 and Richard McGregor, *The Party*, 42-43.

42. Uli Frantz, *Deng Xiaoping*, (New York: Harcourt, Brace, Jovanovich, 1988), 86.

43. Harry Wu, "China's Gulag; Suppressing Dissent Though the Lao Gai, " *Harvard International Review* 20 (Winter 1997/ 98), 21-22.

44. Un.org, 26 February 2001.

45. *IMF Survey* 19 April 1993, 114-115.

46. "U.S. China Economic Relations in the Next Ten Years: Towards Deeper Engagement and Mutual Benefit," Hong Kong: China-United States Exchange Foundation, 2013, 18-20.

47. Junjie Zhang, "Delivering Environmentally Sustainable Economic Growth: The Case of China," Asia Society/New York, September 2012, 4-7.

48. Christopher Patten, *East and West: China, Power and the Future of Asia*, (New York: Times Books, 1998), 77.

49. *International Trade Statistics Yearbook 2008/Trade by Country*, (New York: United Nations, 2009), 124-125.

50. *Asia-Pacific Trade and Investment Report 2011*, Economic and Social Commission for Asia and the Pacific, (New York: United Nations, 2011), 47-51.

51. John Wong, "China's Economy 2010," *East Asian Policy* 3 (Jan/-March 2011), 13.

52. London, "China" 9-13.

53. John Woodruff, *China in Search of Its Future: Reform vs. Repression 1982-1989*, (New York: Lyle Stuart, 1990), 191-192, 219-220.

54. David Shambaugh, "Deng Xiaoping: The Politician, " *China Quarterly* Vol. 135 (September 1993): 457.

55. Author Interview/Prof. Richard Sola, Paris August 1989.

56. London, "China" 13.

57. UNGA/PV 28 September 1989, 47.

58. Alain Peyrefitte, *La Tragedie Chinoise*, (Paris: Fayard, 1990), 313.

59. McGregor, *The Party*, 110.

60. PRC Draft Constitution/1954 (Peking: Foreign Languages Press, 1954), 73-74.

61. Constitutions of the People's Republic of China: 1978 (Peking: Foreign Languages Press, 1978), 6-7.

62. Constitution of the People's Republic of China: 1982 (Peking: Foreign Languages Press, 1982), 11-13.

63. PRC Draft Constitution/1954, 60-61.

64. PRC Constitution/1978, 6, 14.

65. PRC Constitution/1982, 5.

66. Winberg Chai, Editor, *The Foreign Relations of the People's Republic of China*, (New York: Putnam, 1972),292.

67. PRC Press/UN January 1984, 1-2.

68. USSR Press/UN April 1979, 1-3.

69. PRC Press/UN 30 September 1981, 1-2.

70. Qimao Chen, "The Taiwan Issue and Sino-U.S. Relations, " *Asian Survey* 27 (November 1987), 1170-1171.

71. PRC Press/UN January 1984, 1-3.

72. PRC Press/UN January and May 1984, 1-2.

73. *Sino/British Declaration on the Question of Hong Kong,* (Beijing: Foreign Languages Press, 1984), 29-34.

74. Margaret Thatcher, *The Downing Street Years,* (New York: Harper Collins, 1993), 261-262 and 490.

75. Qimao Chen, "New Approaches in China's Foreign Policy, " *Asian Survey* 33 (March 1993), 249.

76. PRC Press/UN February 1995, 2-7.

77. "The Future of Taiwan," *Washington Times,* 11 August 1997.

78. "Confucius Lives," *China Daily* (China Watch supplement), 27 October 2011, C.1-2.

79. Robert Lawrence Kuhn, "Xi Jinping's Chinese Dream," *International Herald Tribune,* 5 June 2013, 6.

Chapter 8

Republic of China/on Taiwan

Formosa in the 1950's: Strong Friends/Good Diplomacy

The reverberations of the Chinese civil war continued to send political shock waves across the Formosa Straits even after the Nationalist government went into exile on Taiwan in 1949. The ominous shadow of Mao's People's Republic darkened the skies over Taiwan until well into the early 1950's when a formal Mutual Defense Treaty was signed between Washington and Taipei.

Nonetheless, in the early chaotic period of withdrawal to Taiwan, the ROC government had hardly found a refuge as much as a last-ditch redoubt. Only a fortuitous combination of tenacity, fortitude, and the ironic "good fortune" of the Korean war, allowed Chiang Kai-shek's forces to secure a tenuous foothold in that pivotal year, 1950.

Following the Second World War, Formosa had been returned to the ROC government under the terms of the Cairo Agreement of 1943, signed by President Franklin D. Roosevelt, British Prime Minister Winston Churchill, and Chinese President Chiang Kai-shek. The declaration clearly stated that territories Japan had stolen from China, such as Formosa and the Pescadores, be *restored to the Republic of China.* The U.S. was also a signatory to the Potsdam Declaration of July 1945 which reaffirmed that the terms of the Cairo Declaration should be implemented.[1]

The 1951 San Francisco Peace Treaty between the Allies and Japan clearly stated in Article 2, "Japan renounces all rights, title, and claim to Formosa and the Pescadores." Later the 1952 Sino/Japan Peace Treaty concluded between Taipei and Tokyo reaffirmed the terms of San Francisco and added that Japan similarly renounces rights to the Spratly and Paracel Islands."[2]

Thus while Nationalist forces already occupied Formosa at the end of WWII, the flight of the ROC government from Nanking to Taipei presented U.S. policy with a crucial choice, would Washington help defend the beleaguered island against an imminent invasion by the Chinese communists?

In the early days of January 1950, with communist forces about to attack Hainan island and then possibly Formosa, the State Department recommended that President Truman should not offer military aid or advice to the Chinese Nationalists. A draft of a Presidential policy statement, said in part, "Nor do we have any intention of utilizing the armed forces of the U.S. for the defense of Formosa or the detachment of Formosa from China. The U.S. government will not pursue a course which will lead to involvement in the civil conflict in China." A follow-up draft, sharpened the message, "The U.S. government will not provide military aid or advice to Chinese forces on Formosa."[3]

President Truman's statement on 5 January 1950 advised that U.S. forces would not become involved in the existing situation and "The U.S. government will not pursue a course which will lead to involvement in the civil conflict in China. Similarly, the U.S. government will not provide military aid or advice to the Chinese forces on Formosa." Truman stated, however, that Washington would continue to provide economic aid to Taipei.

Headlines screamed "Truman Bars Military Help for Defense of Formosa; British end Nationalist Tie." At the same time, America's hands-off policy on Formosa was interpreted as leaving Washington free to accept the transfer of China's U.N. seat to the communists. Such action was regarded as inevitable, given Britain's impending recognition of the PRC. Less noticed amid the chaos in the Far East, was the violation of American consular property in Beijing as well as the recall order for U.S. foreign service officials in China.

On 12 January, Secretary of State Dean Acheson, in his famous discourse before the National Press Club, omitted Korea and Formosa from the U.S. security sphere in East Asia. Stating that the "defensive perimeter runs from the Ryukus to the Philippine Islands," he added, "So far as the military security of other areas in the Pacific is concerned, it must be clear that no person can guarantee these areas against military attack."

In April a bleak CIA risk assessment cautioned "fall of Taiwan before the end of 1950 seems the most likely course of future developments."[4]

Less than a month before the outbreak of hostilities in Korea, a *Top Secret* State Department memorandum discussing Assistant Secretary of State for Far Eastern Affairs Dean Rusk's China policy options spoke of "packaging" three points: Formosa, Recognition of Communist China and seating China in the U.N. Later Rusk told Secretary Acheson that "The Gimo would be approached, probably by Dulles...with word that (a) the Fall of Formosa was probably inevitable (b) the U.S. would do nothing to assist Gimo in preventing this (c) the only course open to the Gimo to prevent bloodshed was to request U.N. trusteeship. The U.S. would be prepared to back such a move for trusteeship and would ready the fleet to prevent any armed attack on Formosa while the move for trusteeship was pending."[5]

In a separate action, Rusk outlined plans to depose Chiang Kia-shek by General Sun Li-jen. In May a curious chain of events led Dean Rusk to propose an American-sponsored *coup d'etat* in Taiwan and led Dean Acheson to believe there was no viable alternative. An entirely different scenario would shape President Truman's response that fateful Spring.[6]

Clearly in the early part of 1950, and despite the oft-heralded Truman Doctrine in Europe and the Near East, the United States government had made a clearly determined decision to distance or detach itself from the ROC. But events on the Korean peninsula were to provide a bittersweet reversal in the swing of the policy pendulum.

North Korea's attack across the DMZ into South Korea in the early morning hours of Sunday, 25 June 1950, triggered a prompt *volteface* in American East Asian policy. Quick and determined action through the U.N. Security Council, fortuitously being boycotted by the USSR over the non-seating of the PRC, brought together the multinational forces for Korea.

The Truman Administration ordered the Seventh Fleet into the Formosa Straits to "prevent any attack on Formosa...as a corollary of this action, I am calling upon the Chinese government on Formosa to cease all air and sea operations against the Mainland. The determination of the future status of Formosa must await the restoration of security in the Pacific, a peace settlement with Japan, or consideration by the United Nations."[7]

Yet even after the arrival of Chinese "volunteers" in Korea in October, thereby illustrating the nature of Mao's "internationalist commitment" the State Department still held to a policy of neutralizing Formosa. Beyond the oft-stated paradigm of "unleashing Chiang's forces" or letting Formosa pose a flanking threat to the Mainland, Dean Rusk stressed that Taiwan "should be militarily neutralized while the Korean action is in progress."

On the political front, in November the Administration pressed for a U.N. agenda item, "Question of Formosa," which had its heart a preservation of the perilous peace but within a multinational framework. While its status was studied by a U.N. commission, hostilities were unlikely; the tactic would buy time for the U.S. Shortly after a draft resolution was written, State dropped the initiative. The Joint Chiefs of Staff advised "it might be undesirable to proceed with the Formosa item in the General Assembly." John Foster Dulles conceded that "it would be unwise to seek U.N. General Assembly directives which could not be adequately flexible."[8]

Nonetheless, while Truman's strategy towards Taiwan remained static, the tactics changed in light of the Korean War. A Mutual Defense Agreement between the U.S. and ROC went into effect in February 1951 providing defensive weapons and American advisors to Chiang's forces.

While Formosa's fortunes had already brightened, a new administration in Washington in January 1953, and a subsequent move to a cease-fire in Korea, signalled a profound sea change towards Taipei.

In his first State of the Union address, President Dwight D. Eisenhower declared that U.S./China policy would be strengthened. Referring to Truman's orders to the Seventh fleet which had in effect *both protected and neutralized* Formosa, Eisenhower said wryly: "There is no longer any logic or sense in a condition that required the U.S. Navy to assume defensive responsibilities on behalf of the Chinese communists...the Seventh Fleet will no longer be employed to shield communist China."[9]

During 1954-55, the Communists initiated a series of artillery attacks on the offshore islands of Quemoy and Matsu, Nationalist held fortresses on the China coast. Nationalist nervousness against being restrained from their stated mission of re-conquering the Mainland prompted the ROC's U.N. Delegate T.F. Tsiang to implore his American counterpart Henry Cabot Lodge, to keep the U.N. out of cease-fire discussions in the Formosa Straits.

Tsiang feared that "what was in the making was an arrangement similar to the 38th parallel in Korea and similar to the Indochina settlement, to put a line between Formosa and the Mainland, and if that is done it will be the beginning of the end as far as the nationalists are concerned." Ambassador Lodge related Dr. Tsiang's concerns that the ROC would "be sold down the river."[10]

It was against this background that the U.S. and the Republic of China concluded their negotiations for a Mutual Defense Treaty, signed in December 1954. The Treaty clearly stipulated defense of Taiwan and the Pescadores islands, but *significantly not* Quemoy and Matsu. As importantly, Congress passed the "Formosa Resolution" on 29 January 1955, authorizing the President to "employ the armed forces of the United States as he deems necessary for the specific purpose of security and protecting Formosa and the Pescadores against armed attack, this authority to include the securing and protection of such related positions and territories of that area now in friendly hands."[11]

Despite some wrangling with ROC officials, Dulles insisted that his priority was the passage of the Formosa Resolution. On 25 January, the resolution passed the House by a margin of 410-3, and within days the Senate by a vote of 83-3. Dulles deliberately ambiguous towards Quemoy, had based his tact on safeguarding Congressional support for the Mutual Defense Treaty and Formosa Resolution by denying the opposition any serious ground for contention.[12]

Diplomatic historian F.W. Marks asserts, "Both the Defense Treaty and the Congressional resolution were the work of the able and adroit Secretary of State John Foster Dulles, whose measured response came amid repeated, but spurned, offers of political concessions to the Chinese communists. The Treaty came with a classic set of caveats since the Secretary felt that if Washington was going to commit itself to a military link with Taipei, it should exercise more control on the ground. Chiang had expected an American guarantee on Quemoy and Matsu to be explicit while Dulles, preferred to remain vague."[13]

Flexible realism characterized the Dulles approach. During a news conference concerning a cease fire arrangement on Quemoy, he stated, "We do not expect the parties to this struggle whether the Chinese Nationalists or the Chinese Communists to renounce their ambitions. We don't expect that to be done any more than we expect that to happen in the case of Germany or Korea or Vietnam. But even though they retain their ambitions, they might renounce the use of force."[14]

Beijing regarded diplomatic recognition as the pearl which Dulles never ruled out basing his policy not upon traditional moral factors or equally traditional ground of *de facto* control, but rather on national interest. Since he envisaged recognition as inevitable in the long run, it all came down to a matter of timing. Talks with PRC diplomats were initiated in Geneva and later Warsaw; American prisoners from the Korean war were released and a partial cease fire achieved in the Formosa Straits. Historian F.W. Marks recounts that in fact, Dulles was always open to the possibility of a two China policy with Peking to assume Taipei's place in the U.N. Security Council and to occupy a separate seat in the General Assembly.[15]

A new confrontation broke suddenly and explosively on Quemoy in the summer of 1958. The PRC precipitated the conflict probably for its own internal political reasons to create a crisis, to start an anti-rightist campaign, and to launch its vainglorious "Great Leap Forward."

Perhaps the need was external, equally to thwart any Washington/Moscow detente. The U.S. responded with a massive show of military power and a display of diplomatic resourcefulness. The crucial factors in the outcome of the crisis were the collapse of Communist China's blockade of the islands and the nullification of Beijing's power by Chinese Nationalist/American defensive tactics. The U.S. display of force along with simultaneous use of diplomacy succeeded. Throughout the crisis from 23 August 6 October, the two major themes of force and diplomacy alternated in world headlines.[16]

The Quemoy crisis ended anti-climatically. On 6 October PRC Marshall Peng issued a dramatic and curiously composed appeal to the "Compatriots on Taiwan, Penghu, Quemoy and Matsu" in which he announced that "of all choices peace is the best," and that for "humanitarian reasons" bombardment would stop

for one week. Whether this cease-fire was the fruit of the U.S./PRC ambassadorial talks in Warsaw or the fact that the PRC forces had been badly mauled by the defending Nationalists under General Yu Ta-wei is another issue.

Dulles went to Taipei and in a meeting with Chiang, convinced the Gimo to reject the use of force if at all possible in seeking a return to the mainland. The Dulles/Chiang communiqué stated that the mission of the ROC "resided in the minds and hearts of the Chinese people" and the "principal means of achieving that mission would be the implantation of the three principles of Dr. Sun Yat Sen--nationalism, democracy and social welfare--and not necessarily the use of force."[17]

Soon after Dulles left Taipei, Beijing declared a *de-facto* ceasefire. Marshall Peng in a second message to Taiwan ordered "troops at the Fukien front not to shell Quemoy...on even days of the calendar." He admonished that the document issued after the Chiang-Dulles talks was "only a communiqué devoid of legal force. There is only one China, not two. All Chinese will not allow the American plot forcibly to create two Chinas to come true."[18]

Mao's *pseudo-victory* in the Quemoy crisis was glorified at the China Youth Art Theatre, on 28 October the play "The Paper Tiger" opened in Beijing. A satire about "the men in the White House who dream of annexing Taiwan...the play ends with the collapse of the White House and defeat of the war maniacs."

Quemoy remained in the news and regained center stage during the 1960 Nixon/ Kennedy Presidential debates. The even day/odd day artillery barrages battering Quemoy and Matsu lasted until the mid 1970's, albeit in later years with near-harmless propaganda shells.

Washington Recognizes Beijing

In inverse proportion to the strong American commitment to Taiwan's security and diplomatic standing were an ongoing series of confidential discussions between the U.S. and PRC. Contacts initiated in 1955, while not formally aimed at opening ambassadorial ties, provided a direct "hot line" between the antagonistic governments. Thus despite non-recognition, Washington had an established, working, and expandable clear channel open for communication with Beijing.

During the Eisenhower years U.S./PRC talks opened in Geneva in August 1955 and were conducted there until December 1957. Seventy-three sub-ministerial rounds took place at Geneva's *Palais des Nations*. Following the departure of Ambassador Johnson, the talks resumed in Warsaw in the fall of 1958 at the height of the Quemoy crisis. Fifty-eight sessions were held in Warsaw during 1958-1966 on such issues as Taiwan, exchange of newsmen, and Vietnam. The U.S. side did not realize it, but the discussions deepened the wedge in Sino/Soviet relations. Beijing deduced from the crisis that Moscow would limit its intervention where the U.S. was involved and would exclude Taiwan from any military confrontation. The triangular relationship was never the same since the Quemoy crisis.[19]

Although the discussions often seemed an exercise in diplomatic tedium, Ambassador Johnson had stressed that the talks produced a window through which both sides could pass messages, detect changes in nuance quickly, and build up a reservoir of experience in dealing with each other. Since Western embassies in Beijing were kept in strict isolation, the U.S. in fact had more contact with the PRC government during the period of the talks than any other Western country having formal diplomatic relations with the Chinese communists.[20]

Despite the *de facto* if often non-dramatic contact between Washington and Beijing, strong pressures in the U.S. favored some form of rapprochement with People's China. Beyond the polemic that "we can't ignore China" and thus should offer recognition, a formal two-China policy was nonetheless wisely avoided by successive administrations.

Assistant Secretary of State J. Graham Parsons told a lawyers forum in the waning days of the Eisenhower era, "To propose as a serious basis for negotiations with Peiping a concept which it has repeatedly rejected and to which our ally the Republic of China is bitterly opposed, is merely to expose ourselves to ridicule by the Communists and to mistrust by our ally. Despite the disparity of its components, China is a divided country just as are Vietnam, Korea and Germany. Do we wish to advocate a similar solution repugnant to these allies too?"[21]

"It is accurate to say that no other non-communist nation has had such extensive contact with the Peiping regime as we have had," later advised Lyndon B. Johnson's Secretary of State Dean Rusk, "The problem is not lack of contact...it is what, with contact, the Peiping regime says and does."

Speaking in 1966, Secretary Rusk outlined a ten point plan for China policy. Key points included "honoring commitments to the ROC and to the people of Taiwan...we will continue to assist in their defense and try to persuade the Chinese communists to join us in renouncing the use of force in the area of Taiwan."

Rusk also reiterated efforts to prevent expulsion of the ROC from the United Nations. At the same time he opened the door for further unofficial contacts with the PRC, encouraged the Warsaw talks, and did not close the door on improved relations when "Peiping abandons the aggressive use of force and proves it is not irrevocably hostile to the U.S."[22]

The Vietnam War brought Americans face to face with a communist Chinese-supplied enemy. It also gave rise to a series of diplomatic contacts which culminated in the Kissinger initiative to the People's Republic.

In 1972, Marshall Green, Assistant Secretary for East Asian Affairs told Congress, "We would welcome an improvement in our bilateral relations with Peking." While offering *de jure* support for Taiwan, Green stressed that the world has rightly viewed the 1972 Nixon trip to China as a policy watershed. "It is not however a sudden shift in policy. The meeting was a culmination of a long series of carefully planned and executed steps which were initiated as soon as President Nixon took office."[23]

The Nixon visit, a masterful piece of political choreography coinciding with the commencement of the 1972 Presidential election campaign, did not offer formal recognition to the Marxist Middle Kingdom but rather placed Washington on an inexorable policy course, fuelled by speculation of economic and strategic gain, pulled by the personal magnetism of the brilliant Zhou Enlai, and bound by the perceptions of the Shanghai Communiqué.

For Taiwan, already uneasy over the likely ramifications of the Nixon trip, Secretary of State William Rogers offered formal solace, "In seeking a new relationship with the PRC we have constantly kept in mind the interests of our friends. We have not negotiated behind their backs. We stand firmly by all our treaty commitments"[24]

During the Ford Administration (1974-76) Washington reaffirmed its security ties with the ROC with at least fifty formal pronouncements. Indisputably the inertia favored the PRC. A succession of official, academic, and media delegations visited China and spoke with near unanimous rapture of this Asian giant fuelling "China fever" in the U.S. Despite People's China still being pulled by the undertow of the Cultural Revolution and the other sanguinary ravages of Maoist rule, the PRC basked in a near *golden haze* of policy euphoria.

The 15 December 1978 decision by President Jimmy Carter to circumvent Congressional consultation and offer *de jure* diplomatic recognition to the PRC, and to abrogate the 1954 U.S./ROC Mutual Security Treaty, effective 1 January 1979, thus became a logical policy outcome of the process started by Nixon's "long march" to Beijing.

Ambassador U. Alexis Johnson, the initial point man for Washington's contacts with China commented, "The concessions for normalization came almost entirely from us. It was the President of the United States who paid the first tribute-bearing pilgrimage to the throne of the Middle Kingdom. Peking had obtained full recognition from the Carter administration without agreeing to renounce force against Taiwan. This sort of weakness was not a good note on which to begin our formal ties with a people as proud and face conscious as the Chinese."[25]

Perhaps more poignant was a *New York Times* article which prophesied, "Trade with China; High Hopes in U.S." At the time of Carter's announcement, two-way U.S./Taiwan trade was $7.2 billion and U.S./PRC trade $1.2 billion.[26]

Despite Carter's severing diplomatic ties and unilaterally abrogating the military treaty without prior consultation with the Senate, the U.S. Congress passed, by a considerable bi-partisan margin, the model "Taiwan Relations Act" (PL 96-8) which offered both a *de facto* formula for government-to-government dealings, and allowed for the U.S. to provide weapons necessary for Taiwan's self defense. The TRA stipulates that the President cannot alter these guarantees "without the consent of Congress."[27]

The ROC's former consular facilities in the U.S. were nebulously renamed the Coordination Council for North American Affairs (CCNAA); the U.S. legation in Taipei became the American Institute on Taiwan (AIT). In 1994, during the Clinton Administration, the ROC was permitted to upgrade its status in the U.S. with the more obvious name Taipei Economic and Cultural Office (TECO).

Predictably Beijing balked at the TRA. Foreign Minister Huang Hua met with U.S. Ambassador Leonard Woodcock and warned that the Congressional move constituted an attempt "to interfere in China's internal affairs...and give official status to U.S./Taiwan relations." He chided the U.S. government that "great harm will be done to the new relationship."[28]

Huang Hua's remonstration carried little weight in Washington. In April the TRA passed the House and Senate by an overwhelming vote showing strong bi-partisan support. Members of Congress were determined to ensure ROC security, not only because the U.S. had made a formal commitment to protect the island but because U.S. credibility would suffer if such a commitment appeared to be nothing more than a tactical posture assumed by a particular administration. The TRA serving as a surrogate for the abrogated Defense Treaty, mandated that the U.S. make available "arms of a defensive character" to "enable Taiwan to maintain a sufficient self-defense capability."[29]

Despite strong sympathy for Taiwan, the strategically seductive "China Card" policy, that of PRC facing off the Soviets power, began to gain currency even among traditional supporters of the ROC. Soviet/Vietnamese aggression in

Afghanistan and Cambodia respectively had shaken the Carter White House out of strategic slumber and emboldened Dr. Zbigniew Brzezinski, the President's Polish-born national Security Advisor, to tilt the U.S. towards strategic harmony with Beijing against Moscow.

The advent of the Reagan Administration, despite initial misgivings in Beijing over the President's strong friendship for Taiwan, continued to build upon the "China Card" logic. Early in the new Administration, Undersecretary of State for Political Affairs Walter Stoessel stressed; "Our policies towards Soviet expansion and hegemonism run on parallel tracks."[30]

Yet, while the U.S. increasingly plied its favors the Communist Chinese sought to distance themselves from any strategic connection with Washington. By October 1981, China was referring to the U.S. as a "hegemonistic" power. Before long, the strategy was evident; the PRC would maintain a carefully calculated distance between itself and the U.S.[31]

At the same time, China was equally adamant to stop the flow of defensive weapons being sold to the ROC. The August 1982 Communiqué on U.S. Arms Sales to Taiwan, cites the policy "gradually to reduce sales of arms to Taiwan, leading over a period of time, to a final resolution." While the communiqué did not specify an exact timeframe, nor quantitative or qualitative means in which weapons sales to Taiwan would be phased out, the intent was unmistakably lucid, to hinder and possibly *neutralize ROC defensive force modernization.*[32]

Less transparent was the juridical nature of a Communiqué; such are statements of *intended policy*, not Executive Agreements, nor treaties, and thus do not entail specific legal obligations. The Clinton Administration removed the cap on defensive arms sales to Taiwan in 1994.

Engine of Self Reliance; The Economy--1951-2001

Taiwan's socio/economic success story remains nearly unrivalled in East Asia. A small, war-ravished, resource-poor, ex-Japanese colony, threatened by imminent attack, pulled the proverbial rose from the dragon's jaw and turned the island into a resounding success story. A judicious combination of private incentives, keen perseverance and a spirit of self-reliance brought Taiwan the envied status of a Dragon of the Far East.

At the onset of Nationalist rule, Taiwan was an overwhelmingly agrarian economy with sixty-one percent of Formosans involved in farming. The yeoman *"land to the tiller"* program transformed the labor force landscape into an island of owners whose output increased exponentially. Land reform between 1949-1953 was a key factor in improving income distribution. The proportion of tenant farmers fell from 38 percent in 1950 to 15 percent in 1960. By 1957, 83 percent of farmers were part owners/cultivators.[33]

The success of the agricultural transformation was made possible by a combination of private incentives and public action. Agriculture was a prime mover of Taiwan's development in the early stages. In 1952 farming generated 56 percent of the labor force and 32 percent of the GDP. But by 2009, the farm sector accounted for only 5 percent of employment and 1.6 percent of GDP. In the 1960's and 1970's the island hosted labor intensive light-industries. By the 1980's manufacturing shifted to a high-tech focus and a widening service sector.[34]

Taiwan's post-war development can be divided into two phases with 1961 as the demarcation year. The first phase was characterised by import substitution/land reform, the second period saw outward oriented export expansion. The percentage of exports in the GNP jumped from 9 percent in 1952 to 49 percent in 1980. Yet, the 1950's were an era of trade deficits with American aid relied upon to finance imports. U.S. aid was terminated in 1965.[35]

Guiding plans for both agricultural reform and industrial development rested in Sun Yat Sen's Principle of People's Livelihood, a unique concept which contrary to communism preserves the market price and encourages enterprise to take full advantage of the merits of a free economy. In short, the Principle of Livelihood calls for a planned free economy. In Taiwan, initial emphasis was placed on achieving stability and later towards agricultural and industrial production aimed towards foreign trade. To illustrate the point, in 1952 the private manufacturing sector contributed 35 percent to total production and the public 65 percent; by the end of the 1960's the ratio had been reversed to 70 percent private and 30 percent public. While the initial response by investors towards the export strategy was tepid, firms soon realized the climate of opportunity.[36]

Importantly, the phase-out of American assistance provided the impetus for local entrepreneurs to look to market forces, not a foreign friend, to provide economic stimulus. In 1966, the government set up the Kaoshiung Export Processing Zone (EPZ), a concept emerging as a global model for developing states, including the Mainland.

At the close of WWII, Taiwan's per capita income stood at a paltry $70; by 1980 the figure had reached $2,280. In the first three decades, annual GNP growth rates soared meteorically by 8.2 percent in the 1950's, 9.4 percent in the 1960's, and 9.9 percent in the 1970's. Average growth over the period reached a formidable 9.2 percent. One of the key elements in Taiwan's growth pattern is the equitable distribution of wealth. In the 1950's, income distribution was a not very different from the levels exhibited in most Least Developed Countries; the situation soon changed with a considerable narrowing of income disparity. Taiwan joined South Korea as East Asian examples of minimal income inequality.[37]

Adhering to a committed policy of self-reliance, the ROC government strive to make the "Taiwan Miracle." Between 1963 and 1980, the island witnessed rapid economic development with an average annual growth of 10 percent. As the island further industrialized between 1981 and 1995, growth still kept an impressive pace at 7.6 percent annually. The economic performance outshone some stunning political setbacks on the international stage.[38]

"The government's role in the process of economic growth has been to maintain a stable environment for development and to encourage the private sector," stated Dr. K.T. Li, the driving force behind Taiwan's transformation to an economic power. Over the period 1952-1988 its role gradually shifted from being a leading one to a recommending one. Since 1970, exports have made the greatest contribution to growth. The government took steps to refocus investment from labor intensive industries to technology intensive ones.[39]

By the 1980's Taiwan was making a dramatic shift from textile production and switching over to high tech industries. This was a direct result of high wages on the island and the comparative advantage found by Taiwan firms in Southeast Asia and later in Mainland China. The high-tech focused Hsinchu Science Industrial park provided the leading edge of Taiwan's drive to upgrade traditional industries and nurture high technology firms. Hsinchu has evolved into Taiwan's Silicon Valley.

Interestingly ROC development patterns differ considerably from South Korea's. Though the Korean *chaebol* have been centralized and hierarchical by design, Taiwan firms are typically decentralized. Taiwan firms likewise have made major investments on the Mainland while few ROK companies beyond Hyundai have invested in North Korea.

The ROC's growth patterns also differ from that of the PRC. Taiwan has opted for a pragmatic, evolutionary approach rather than a politicized, revolutionary one chosen by the PRC, and has retained many of its traditional cultural values instead of destroying them as in the PRC. As Prof. John C.H. Fei at Yale observes, the ROC became a laboratory which tested the compatibility of traditional values with modernization. The findings have been quite conclusive; traditional Chinese cultural values make a positive contribution to modernization, rather than obstructing the process.[40]

The following table lists the ROC, PRC, and Hong Kong's GDP growth rates in the past decade as to illustrate the dynamism of the three Chinese economies.

	ROC	PRC	HK
1991	7.6	9.2	2.3
1992	6.8	14.2	6.3
1993	6.3	13.5	6.1
1994	6.5	12.6	5.3
1995	6.1	10.5	4.7
1996	5.6	9.6	4.8
1997	6.8	8.8	5.2
1998	4.6	7.8	-5.1
1999	5.7	7.1	3.0
2000	6.5	8.0	10.5

(World Economic Survey; 2000, 248).

2010	10.8	10.4	6.8
2011	4.1	9.3	4.9
2012	1.3	7.8	1.4

(IMF Regional Economic Outlook Asia /Pacific 2013, 6)

By the 1990's Taiwan's people had tasted, and then indulged upon, the fruits of socio/economic success, political liberalization, and yes, social selfishness. Taiwan's experience is typical of poor countries which have become rich. Prosperity has grown and income has risen from $145 in 1951 to $16,353 in 2009. Living costs have skyrocketed and Taipei has become one of the world's most expensive cities.

Until the late 1980's Taipei was a stopover for those visiting the spectacular National Palace Museum and staying at the equally splendid *Grand Hotel*. By the 1990's Taipei evoked other East Asian capitals on the business circuit, with expensive hotels, pricey boutiques, and a glittering World Trade Center. The juxtaposition of the Japanese-era colonial architecture, the monumental Chiang Kai-shek Memorial, and the glass and brass buildings seen globally, set a new tone.

Diplomacy by Trade; 1982-2002

Domestically energized by a high growth export oriented economy, but internationally ostracized by near-total diplomatic isolation, Taiwan in the 1980's and early 1990's began to reappraise its world standing. Clearly the island's 21 million people had reached a level of prosperity unknown in China's long dynastic history. At the same time PRC efforts to isolate the ROC, especially in the wake of the U.N. ouster and the Nixon visit, proved devastatingly effective.

Even in the early 1960's the ROC led the Mainland in diplomatic recognition; in 1963 Taipei led in the political contest by a significant margin 58 to 42. The major shift came in 1970 when both Canada and Italy recognized the Mainland but Taipei still remained ahead in the recognition race with 60 to 53. This was soon to change.

The U.N. jolt and the ensuing ramifications of the Nixon visit put ROC diplomacy into a tailspin. By 1973 the ROC had ties with only 39 countries as against the PRC's 85. In 1977 Taipei maintained ties with 23 states versus the PRC's 111. While many states recognized the PRC, few acceded to Beijing's claim that Taiwan was China's territory. Most simply "took note" of the claim.[41]

The severance of Washington's relations had a profound psychological and practical effect on an increasingly isolated ROC. While losing its closest Western ally and friend, Taipei likewise lost its last Permanent member on the U.N. Security Council. The other two Council members, the U.K. and France, had already recognized the PRC in 1950 and 1964 respectively.

Yet even after Washington switched its *de jure* ties across the Straits to Beijing, the U.S. maintained a large *de facto* presence in Taipei via the American Institute in Taiwan (AIT). It became an ironic truism that both the AIT as well as the Coordination Council on North American Affairs (CCNAA), and subsequent TECO establishments in respective countries became larger than the former embassy and consulates.

Significantly they have channelled an exponentially larger trade volume. In 1985 two-way U.S./ROC trade stood at $21 billion, by 1991 the sum reached $36 billion, in 2002 $50 billion, and in 2012 , $63 billion.[42]

The same could be said of Canada. When Prime Minister Pierre Trudeau severed Sino/Canadian diplomatic ties in 1970, Ottawa responded with a particularly vain shunning of the ROC. Despite a campaign by official Ottawa to treat Taiwan just short of a hostile nation, trade with Taiwan actually grew. In 1986 an unofficial Canadian Trade Office was established in Taipei to oversee booming commerce between Canada and Taiwan. In 1986, two-way trade stood at nearly $2 billion; by 2000 it had reached $3 billion. By 2011, trade reached $6.6 billion.[43]

While the U.S., Japan, and Germany kept strong commercial links with Taiwan despite the lack of political ties, the United Kingdom, fearing ramifications for Hong Kong in the twilight of British rule, assumed an ambivalent attitude towards Taipei.

The Foreign Office forbade any direct association with Taipei; no meetings were permitted with government officialdom. The ROC's representative in London was however, upgraded in 1992 from the Free Chinese Centre to the Taipei Representative Office in the UK. Thus when former Prime Minister Margaret Thatcher visited the ROC to exclaim, "*Thatcherism* is clearly alive and well and living in Taiwan," her trip was sponsored by American Citibank and decidedly *not* the Foreign Office. Britain's representative office in Taiwan is now known as the "British Trade and Cultural Office." Raymond Tai, Taiwan's former diplomatic representative in London recalled that Lady Thatcher was a "very pragmatic and very patriotic" figure. When she visited Taipei, "she required a British Jaguar as her official car instead of the more commonly used American Cadillac during her visit to Taiwan."[44]

Germany is Taiwan's largest trade partner in Europe. Despite lacking diplomatic relations since 1972, commercial links have grown dramatically. In 1972 two-way trade stood at $227 million; by 1990 it reached $5.9 billion. By 2010 two way trade reached $14.7 billion.

Taiwan's international trade volume in 1950-52 was nearly $300 million, with exports approximately $100 million and imports $200 million. By 1992 trade amounted to $150 billion, with exports reaching $80 billion and imports $70 billion, and by 1999 reached $233 billion with exports at $122 and imports totalling $111 billion. By 2009 even in the midst of global recession, Taiwan's trade stood at $378 billion with exports at $204 billion and imports at $174 billion. Taipei's major trade partner ironically remains the PRC with Mainland/Hong Kong trade comprising 29 percent of Taiwan's global commerce. USA trade has slipped to 11 percent of Taiwan's commerce.[45]

Taiwan's trade boom in the 1980's, as well as the islands brimming foreign exchange coffers, put the ROC into the international limelight. Taiwan's $111 billion in foreign exchange reserves, more than Tokyo's, has also softened the political tone of many past critics. Thus the ROC operates in a unique, if novel, setting of a paucity of *de jure* diplomatic ties but a plethora of *de facto* trade links.

Though the Republic of China maintains diplomatic ties with 22 countries, Taipei hosts only fourteen resident embassy legations. Nonetheless there are forty-two trade representative offices ranging from such obvious appellations as the Belgian Trade Association, the Canadian Trade Office, and the German Trade Office, to the more vague, Brazil Business Center, Manila Economic and Cultural Office, and the Malaysian Friendship/ Trade Center. Likewise fifteen American states maintain commercial offices in Taipei.

Trade with Eastern Europe was in an expansion mode even before the collapse of communism. In 1979, the ROC quietly opened trade links with the former East Bloc. Despite a sputtering start, commerce with Poland, Hungary, and Czechoslovakia grew steadily. By 1989, bilateral trade between the ROC and the Central and Eastern European countries stood at $288 million; by 1997, the figure had jumped to $910 million. In 2012, two-way trade between Taiwan and Hungary reached $1.2 billion; the region has become an important outlet for Taiwan exports.[46]

A politically ironic but perfectly logical trade relationship exists between the ROC on Taiwan and the Socialist Republic of Vietnam. Taiwan emerged as Vietnam's major investor with over $4.3 billion invested in the Indo-Chinese land by 1997. The reasons remain complex but the logic is compellingly simple, growing labor costs have forced ROC firms to look offshore to Southeast Asia. A sizable ethnic-Chinese community in former South Vietnam has provided a logical base of investment and trade. The China External Trade Development Council has overseen a meteoric growth in commerce from a paltry $1.6 million in 1988, $40 million in 1989, to $650 million in 1993.[47]

The ROC has looked to diversify its once predominant trade links with the U.S. While American trade still remains the cornerstone of its commercial relationships, both growing pressure from Washington to reduce once-lopsided deficits and a realization by Taipei that true self-reliance means market diversity, has reduced the once solid ties. Equally the lure of the Mainland as a production base and market has served to diversify and refocus Taiwan firms in an important but politically entangling market.

Parallel to its commercial efforts, Taipei has continued to expand its traditional agricultural and technical assistance missions. Rooted in a series of successful agricultural missions in Africa in the 1960's, efforts aim at brining the "Taiwan experience" to needy nations and its 22 diplomatic allies.

Currently the International Cooperation and Development Fund (ICDF) manages 32 technical missions operating in 28 partner countries in Africa, the Caribbean, and Central America. As of 2011, some 81 lending projects had been signed entailing $550 million. Taiwan allocates approximately 0.14% of its GDP for global development assistance. Projects are focused in agriculture, micro and small enterprises, emergency relief, public health and credit guarantees. Taiwan's ICDF teams operate through Central America, the Caribbean, in Africa and the South Pacific. Taiwan has about 200 aid experts overseas.[48]

Strait Talks: Taiwan in the 1990's

Socio/economic realities have encouraged a subtle but certain political rapprochement between the ROC and the PRC. While political contact between Taipei and Beijing has been hesitatingly cautious, Taiwan businessmen have been bold to the point of brashness in their trade and investments with their mainland counterparts. It remains a poignant truism that Taiwan's socio/ economic success story, the need of markets and a pool of reasonable labor, has no farther to look than to its Chinese cousins across the once-forbidding Formosa Straits.

Thus while the ROC government has wisely spurned the PRC's sugar-coated political offers of *"one country, two systems"* Taiwan has nonetheless encouraged commercial links to flourish between the estranged members of the Chinese family. Equally, the PRC communists have allowed the spirit of commerce to transcend dealing with an "errant province."

Building bridges across the Taiwan Straits thus has been a delicate but deliberate endeavor, carefully choreographing events to "save political face" while at the same time cultivating commercial ties to gain an economic advantage. Indirect trade between Taiwan and mainland China via Hong Kong was worth a mere $78 million in 1979; by 1991 the figure had risen to $5.8 billion, accounting for four percent of Taiwan's total foreign trade.[49]

By 1994, two-way trade totalled $16.5 billion or 9.3 percent of Taiwan's total trade. In 1995, Mainland trade reached $20 billion, 9.6 percent of Taipei's trade. Hong Kong remains the *entrepot* for this commerce. Some economists fear that the growing ROC/PRC trade relationship could make Taiwan "hostage" economically to the PRC.[50]

Naturally trade does not exist in a political vacuum. The lessening of cross-straits tensions, encouraged a trade trickle to reach a torrent. In 1979 "smuggling" best described cross-straits trade, the ROC government fighting a losing battle against such privateers. From 1987-89 allowing a "semi-legal" trade, Taipei adopted a policy of "no contact, no encouragement and no interference." In 1987, the ROC government legalized commerce and started a boom with mainland products. Investment on the mainland became substantial. Before the mid-1980's there was none. By 1988, Taiwan businessmen had invested $294 million which soared to $2 billion by 1990. Coastal provinces were major recipients.[51]

Indirect Taiwan investment on the Mainland has continued to grow. By 1991 there were 3,800 projects valued at $3.4 billion; in 1992 the number had reached 10,230 with an accumulated value of $9 billion. Analysis of such investments shows that 70 percent were located in Fukien and Kwangtung. Originally, most firms went to Fukien but since 1990 the trend has been to the Pearl River Delta. Most firms are labor intensive projects aimed at exports.[52]

Naturally such a significant commercial movement could not take place without at least the grudging acquiescence of the Taipei government and a willingness in Beijing to shelve socialist principles thus allowing a potentially destabilizing contact with the prosperous Taiwan cousins. Taiwan became a major overseas investor; from 1981 to 2009, the cumulative outflow of FDI from Taiwan amounted to $117 billion, much of the investment going to the Mainland.[53]

In November 1987, as part of President Chiang Ching-kuo's wider democratizations, the ROC lifted its 38 year ban barring residents from visiting the Mainland. Remaining restrictions on certain categories of civil servants and military personal were relaxed. Before 1979, many Taiwan residents had secretly travelled to the mainland via third countries; Beijing allowed the visits and Taipei, for humanitarian reasons, did not prosecute them.

Between 1979 and 1987, about 10,000 people illegally visited the PRC. Ironically, the flood of families from Taiwan visiting their home provinces on the Mainland caused a backlash; the more these people saw of the once forbidden China, the less they were enchanted with it. Having relieved their profound homesickness, the visitors saw that backwardness on the mainland actually made them more attached to Taiwan. Viewing how different the two societies had become, Taiwan residents became less optimistic about reunification.[54]

The tourist and humanitarian nature of the original visits, some 470,000 in the first two years alone, soon translated into business trips. Statistics from the ROC's Mainland Affairs Council (MAC) show that between 1984 and 1992, Taiwan residents made some 4.2 million visits to China. Some sent remittances to relatives and others to buy property.

A flood of mail and telephone calls continue to cross the Straits too. Letters were traditionally routed through Hong Kong, the postal volume reaching 57 million pieces. In June 1989, indirect telecommunications were permitted. In 1992, 18 million letters were exchanged, 12 million from the Mainland and 6 million from Taiwan. Telephone links were almost in the opposite number; Taiwan people prefer to call, and mainlanders to write.[55]

In May 1991, when President Lee Tung-hui announced the "end of the communist rebellion" thus officially ending the Chinese civil war, the ROC entered a new political and economic milieu. The practical effect was to treat the PRC as a "political entity." A delegation of the semi-official Straits Exchange Foundation (SEF), went to Beijing on a courtesy visit. Taiwan had recognized the existence, if not the legitimacy of the PRC state.[56]

Economic interaction grew exponentially despite the Taipei government's calls to damper Mainland fever as well as to formally ban investments in high-end sectors of information technology.

Taiwan investment on Mainland China represents levels of high risk commerce lacking a formal legal and consular structure through which to operate. Furthermore, it exists on a territory not formally recognized by the ROC government. In essence it evokes classic Chinese entrepreneurism, doing profitable business in a risky environment. Yet beyond business, cross-straits commerce has proven a significant commercial wedge, not without inherent dangers, of the ROC's modernization model for the Mainland. The scales of commerce are causing what politics had dared not dream of.

Political institutions did not engender the economic spillover, rather economic interaction brought about institutions. Prior to 1991, there were no formal structures for cross-straits ties. In 1991, Taiwan established the semi-official Straits Exchange Foundation (SEF) to deal with the mainland in civil disputes. In response, Beijing set up the nominally "unofficial" Association for Relations Across the Taiwan Straits (ARATS). In other words, economics brought about political formulae and institutions.[57]

Evocative of Adam Smith's *invisible hand* guiding economic interests, the private sectors of the various economies joined together to move across political boundaries to form an integrated regional economy outside the direct purview of government.

In South Korea's case, despite the formal political structures between the ROK and DPRK, commerce between Seoul and Pyongyang is nearly nil, exchange of family visits, mail and telephone calls, virtually nonexistent. In the ROC case, a firm foundation of commercial, cultural and tourist ties are well established and operational despite being in a legal limbo. Such links are unofficially but effectively managed by the SEF and ARATS. The ROC/PRC formula nonetheless remains far short of the earlier FRG/GDR socio/ economic contacts.

The government-funded SEF was created as a private body to bypass the national policy of no official contact with Beijing. The need for such contact, however, has grown dramatically due to disputes arising from the growing exchanges of people and commerce across the Straits. Taipei's cabinet-level Mainland Affairs Council, (MAC) the official policy planner for Mainland affairs, was established in 1991. The Taiwan government's Mainland policy can be summarized in three points; Stabilization, maintaining peace across the Taiwan Straits; Institutionalization, steadily promoting policy measures for cross-straits economic and trade contacts; Globalization, establishing an open environment for Taiwan to link to the world.[58]

After a series of desultory discussions between both groups, the SEF and the ARATS conducted their first formal meeting in Singapore to discuss essentially consular matters. The talks focused on the establishment of effective communication channels, protection of rights and benefits of Taiwan businessmen in Mainland China, safeguards for freedom and property, and exchange of private visits. Later SEF Chairman C.F. Koo, stressed, "From now on Chinese on both sides of the Straits should renounce the zero-sum logic and champion the win-win concept instead."[59] Interestingly both billionaire businessman C.F. Koo and Wang Daohan are close to their respective chiefs of state. Thus the "non-governmental, economic and functional" discussions had an official blessing. "Two enemy brothers," opined *Le Monde* of Paris.

Despite pressures on the SEF side not to stray from the tight MAC- imposed negotiating script, the Singapore talks established a mechanism for ROC/PRC contact. Taipei insists that relations with the mainland evolve along the three phase National Unification Guidelines, the first stage envisaging that private contact between both sides be conducted indirectly.

According to John Chang, Taipei's former Minister for Overseas Chinese Affairs, during the past forty years, the Taiwan Straits have witnessed three basic phases of confrontation between the PRC and ROC--the first phase 1949-1959 military confrontation; the second phase 1959-1987, peaceful confrontation; and from 1987 to the present, a separation eased by growing commercial and family ties across the Straits.[60]

The SEF tends to be aggressive and seek accelerated contacts with the Mainland while the MAC, being an official policy maker, takes a more cautious approach. By June 2010, the SEF and the ARATS signed the Economic Cooperation Framework Agreement (ECFA) which seeks fair treatment on Taiwan products in the Mainland market. The cross-straits commerce is amazing; trade with the Mainland amounted to $153 billion in 2010, or 29 percent of Taiwan's total. Taiwan moreover enjoyed a $77 billion surplus with the PRC. Mainland China has become Taiwan's largest export market with 42 percent of total and the second largest source of imports. Such commerce between two rival governments echo what Wang Yi, director of the PRC's Taiwan Affairs Office stated, "We need to closely follow this key objective for winning hearts and minds of the Taiwanese people."[61]

Clearly the road to rapprochement will prove exceedingly difficult--with political curves often challenging the SEF and ARATS to swerve from their seemingly non-political formulae and to enter the realm of rhetoric and confrontation. The SEF and ARATS are merely mechanisms *for managing relations*, not solving the intractable political issues, and thus remain transitory albeit crucial players.

Establishing a Joint Secretariat for the SEF and ARATS consultations, with rotating meetings between Gulangyu island alongside Xiamen/Amoy and Quemoy would be a practical and prudent step towards managing relations, especially the consular functions needed for the burgeoning business ties.

The concept would begin to formalize the relationship as well as demonstrate a willingness to work with counterparts on essentially consular functions. The Joint Secretariat, providing the *modus vivendi* for cross-straits relations, would furthermore serve to manage what will emerge as direct transportation links between Taiwan and the Mainland. The setting would equally allow for a un-official social and economic sounding board for both sides to gauge unexpected situations which will inevitably arise in the relationship between the Chinese states.

Unification: Taipei's View

The ROC's traditional unification policy rested on a militant and unambiguous formula of militarily re-conquering the Mainland *Guangfu Dalu*; in other words ousting Mao's regime and restoring the Nationalist government.

In the early days of Chiang Kai-shek's refuge on Taiwan, despite the impending communist attack on the island, the ROC, at least rhetorically, posed an equally bellicose threat. "Zero sum politics dominated the conflict between the communists and the Nationalists from October 1949 to early 1955; both sides vowed to conquer the other," advised Zhan. Negotiation was shelved in favor of militancy. It is widely believed that were it not for the sudden outbreak of the Korean war and the immediate U.S. intervention in the Taiwan Straits, the PLA would have crossed the Straits and captured Taiwan, although at very heavy cost," Zhan surmises.[62]

To be sure, in the early 1950's during and after the Korean War, Chiang Kai-shek seriously contemplated such an action but was kept on a tight tether by President Truman and ironically the presence of the Seventh Fleet. As the State Department's Robert Murphy recounted, "The Nationalists' dream to return to the Mainland, this ultimate hope of which buoyed them up, was often expressed to visiting American officials. The morale of the troops on Taiwan, could scarcely be maintained lest there be an incentive of anticipated return to their homeland."[63]

Militant national unification policy, not unlike South Korea's Rhee, was considered as a serious option by the ROC and ROK governments, but warily viewed by the U.S. State Department. During the Formosa Straits crisis of 1958, a sea change emerged in the policy due to the dogged but prudent diplomatic skills of the U.S. Secretary of State. Addressing the U.N. General Assembly, John Foster Dulles advised, "We believe a peaceful solution can be found. Talks are going on between the U.S. and the Chinese Communist ambassadors in Warsaw. We seek a prompt cease-fire and equitable conditions that will eliminate provocations and leave for peaceful resolution the different claims and counter-claims that are involved."[64]

Focusing on the desirability of a cease-fire in the Straits, and firing a carefully calculated diplomatic salvo in the Warsaw Talks, Dulles suggested sagely that a renunciation of the use of force by Beijing apply equally to Taipei, "because it would be quite impractical and wrong" to ask Beijing alone to abandon the use of force. In any event the Nationalists could not return to China because he did not feel that "by their own steam they are going to get there."[65]

When visiting Taipei in October John Foster Dulles extracted promises from the Gimo that unification policy would be better served by implementing Sun Yat-sen's Three Principle's of the People, *San Min Chu I*, to the PRC rather than the more bellicose Re-conquer the Mainland, *Guangfu Dalu*.

By 1962 when the Mainland was reeling from the socio/economic after shocks of the Great Leap Forward, Chiang viewed this Year of the Dragon, as a propitious time for liberation. He stated, "We can no longer vacillate or hesitate to perform our duty to deliver our people, our nation, and the whole world from catastrophe." At the Warsaw talks Washington assured the Peking delegation that the U.S. would not back Chiang's military moves.[66]

Despite policy rhetoric, by the early 1960's a riveting reality was emerging. With no probable return to the Mainland, the ROC's refuge on Taiwan was going to be more than temporary and thus the government's socio/economic policy should turn the island into a thriving and prosperous place serving as a model for all China. "Build up Taiwan, Re-conquer the Mainland," offered hope, albeit through tempered realism. President Chiang called for Taiwan's development as an "invincible bastion for national recovery...let us recover the Mainland and continue to build a new China on the basis of the Three Principles of the People."[67]

Curiously the ROC Constitution while adopted in 1946 before the division of China, had never been amended to call for national unity. Nonetheless, Article 1 sets the philosophical foundation for unification--the ROC's *raison d'etre* as well as what can be interpreted as a call to Mainland recovery. "The Republic of China, founded on the Three Principles of the People, shall be a democratic Republic of the people, to be governed by the people, and for the people." Article 4 adds, "The territory of the ROC according to its existing national boundaries (1946) *shall not be altered* except by a resolution of the National Assembly."[68]

Sun Yat-sen's Three Principles of the People: *Min Chuan*/ Democracy, *Min Sheng*/People's Livelihood, *Min Tsu*/Nationalism remained the ideological foundation of ROC recovery policy. Such policy dated to the founding of the Republic of China, Asia's first Republic.

Only in 1991 was the Constitution amended to reflect the *de jure* status of national division. Article 10 of the Additional Articles, authorizes a law recognizing "one country, two areas, two political entities." Thus the most significant piece of legislation concerning the PRC's status remains the "Statute Regarding Relations Between the People of Taiwan and the Mainland Area," adopted in 1992.[69]

In 1979, despite being buffeted by a barrage of PRC peace overtures, the ROC countered with the "three no's" for Mainland policy—no negotiations, no compromise, and no contacts.

During the 1970's passengers arriving at Taipei's Sungshan Airport were greeted by billboards calling for national recovery but by the early 1980's a less militant mainland policy was obvious even on the popular level. New signs advertising electronic shows had replaced the earlier political message, a practical reflection of "*Taiwan, Inc.*" Ironically today the downtown Sungshan airport hosts a stream of flights to the Mainland and is a hub for Chinese tourists.

The ROC, while officially upholding the "Three No's" principle politically, demonstrated growing tolerance in its practices towards economic exchanges across the Straits. Taipei gradually relaxed restrictions on such contacts, less in response to Beijing's appeal for wider ties than in recognition of fast evolving reality shaped by the economic initiatives of its citizens. By 1990, according to Chong-pin Lin, Taipei's commercial policy of the "Three No's" (no direct shipping, no direct communications, not direct trade) existed in name only.[70]

On an equally practical level, the lifting of martial law in 1987 and the removal of the ban on Mainland travel soon created a dynamic of its own. The passing of President Chiang Ching-kuo and the orderly transfer of power to Lee Tung-hui, a Taiwanese, likewise changed the tenor if not the spirit of unification policy. During this period of political fermentation, the KMT's 13th Party Congress reflected a major shift in Mainland policy--the rhetoric of recovery was couched in socio/economic not military terms. As Maria Hsia Chang stresses, "the present ROC mainland policy is pragmatic, and driven by constituency pressures in an increasingly democratic and pluralistic political system."[71]

Taipei's fundamental policies towards Bejing can be summed up as "One China Two Political Entities," *Yigou Liangqu*. Under the 1946 Constitution, the ROC regards itself as the legal government of all China, and Beijing is a political entity that controls the Chinese mainland.

The ROC government has established a three tier structure of government and private institutions to deal with the PRC.

In September 1990, the National Unification Council was created as an advisory board to the President. In January 1991, the Executive Yuan (Cabinet) established the Mainland Affairs Council, a formal administrative agency under the Premier to manage Mainland/Taiwan political relations. In February, MAC approved the semi-private Straits Exchange Foundation (SEF) to handle commercial/technical relations with the Mainland.[72]

The Guidelines for National Reunification were adopted by the National Unification Council; the blueprint laid down the principles and pattern for peaceful unity. With a clearly stated goal to "establish a democratic, free and equitably prosperous China," the Guidelines envisage a three step process:

1. *Short term*: Phase of Exchanges and Reciprocity. Encourage exchanges; set up a mechanism for exchanges (SEF); improve people's welfare on both sides.

2. *Medium Term*: Phase of Mutual Trust and Cooperation. Establish official communication; direct postal, transport and communications links. Mutual visits by high-ranking officials; both sides taking part in international organizations and activities.

3. *Long Term*: Phase of Consultation. Empower a consultative organization for unification through which both sides discuss the grand task of unification and map out a constitutional system to establish a democratic free, and equitably prosperous China.[73]

The Guidelines are based on the recognition that there need not be a fixed time frame in which to achieve unification. Instead the three-phased process allows both parties to gradually acclimate themselves to a unification framework and a political model that meets their needs. The ROC and PRC *remain* in the first phase.

Naturally unification momentum is pushed by growing cross Straits trade ties as much as pulled by DPP opposition counter-pressures. President Lee had to maintain a precarious balance between KMT intra-party rivalry as much as to watch the DPP on his political flank. In his first State of the Nation Address in 1993, Lee reaffirmed that, "Taiwan and the Mainland are integral parts of China, and all Chinese have blood links."

Yet under Lee's leadership the traditional iconography of the Republic of China took an increasingly *Taiwanese* leaning. The MAC accepted cartographic changes on ROC official maps reflecting the PRC names. The capital was no longer referred to as Peiping the KMT's name for the city meaning northern peace, but rather Beijing. Taiwan also accepted the once shunned PRC provincial names.

More obviously ROC political holidays and the design of the national currency and passports have been in flux. Commemoration of the 28 February incident, long *taboo* on Taiwan under the Nationalists, became official in 1997 during Lee's tenure. The day commemorates inter-communal riots between native Taiwanese and the newly arrived Mainlanders in 1947.

Since the election of Chen Shui-bian, ROC government publications have taken a distinctly less Chinese flavor; the *Free China Journal* has become *Taipei Journal*; *Free China Review* has become *Taipei Review.*

The once ubiquitous presence of Dr. Sun Yat-sen and Chiang Kai-shek has been diluted. Though new currency bears Dr. Sun and Chiang on the 100 and 200 NT notes respectively, higher denominations have been de-politicised with pictures of Little Leaguers, Students and Satellite dishes as well as flora and fauna. Significantly the Republic of China Passports, will now *also* carry the name Taiwan.

While Lee's own controversial *Two State Theory* caused thunderclouds to form over the Straits in July 1999, it was the bitter 2000 Presidential election campaign leading to the narrow victory of the separatist-inclined DPP party, which roiled the waters. After a tough three-way race, the DPP's Chen Shui-bian was elected President of the Republic of China with a plurality. The long ruling KMT was out of the Presidential Office but retained its legislative majority.

Given the DPP's past political rhetoric, the PRC viewed the political change in Taipei with white heat emotion tempered only by a "wait and see" policy encouraged by pragmatists in Beijing's ruling circles. Chen's new Administration had to defuse a ticking political time-bomb. Fortunately it did.

Acting with alacrity and aplomb, President Chen pledged that if the PRC regime *did not use force*, Taipei's new government would *refrain* from declaring Taiwan independence, changing the government name, placing the concept of state-to-state relations in the ROC constitution, holding a referendum to establish an independent Taiwan, abolishing the National Unification Guidelines.Chen extended the olive branch of peace and promised cooperation with the PRC.[74]

On Taiwan itself, the election triggered continuing stock market tremors, a loss of local business confidence, and an outflow of investment. The problems were compounded domestically by government infighting, percolating political schisms inside the DPP, and factionalism inside the KMT.

Viewed in the East Asian context, a slowdown in some of Taiwan's leading computer and information related industries, had seriously impacted on the island's economy. Between 1953 and 2000, under KMT administrations, the Taiwan economy grew an average of 8 percent per year. Incomes jumped from $50 to $14,111. The "Taiwan Miracle" dimmed from 2000 to 2004 where growth slowed to 2.7 percent while incomes remained static.[75]

The political gyrations and sea-saw policy of the DPP's years ended with the election of KMT President Ma Ying-jeou in a 2008 landslide. Yet the reverberations of the global recession later in the year saw GDP growth dip to a seven year low of 1.87 percent.

Since Ma assumed office there's been a "fundamental shift in cross straits policy, which redefines the relationship between Mainland China and Taiwan," asserts Man-jung Chan, of the National Security Council who adds, "The goal of our Cross-Straits Policy is to achieve peace and stability across the Straits, and to ensure Taiwan's prosperity and security." President Ma has stressed the "3 Nos" and the 3 Yeses." The "3 Nos" affirm "No Unification, No independence, and No use of Force." The "3 Yeses" desires "Prosperity, Security and Dignity."[76]

"Cross Straits *rapprochement* are a signature of President Ma's tenure; a diplomatic truce, the ECFA Trade Pact, cross-straits tourism," stated Prof. Jacques de Lisle, Professor of Law at the University of Pennsylvania.[77]

Significantly ROC unification policy while a *sine qua non* since 1949 has reflected the ruling Nationalist Party's (KMT) goals. The ever changing nuances of unification policy, reflect shifts in the ROC's political landscape. Given Taiwan's greater political democratization and working, if often fractious three-party system, balancing the separatist-inclined DPP, the pro-unification New Party, and the faction ridden KMT, poses crucial challenges to the *Unification vision*. The ROC's Unification policy, after all, reflects the agenda of the party in power.

ENDNOTES

1. U.S. Department of State (USDS) "In Quest of Peace and Security: Selected Documents on American Foreign Policy 1941-1951, " (Washington DC: GPO, 1951), 10.

2. USDS, "American Foreign Policy 1950-1955: Basic Documents, (Washington DC: GPO, 1957), 425-426.

3. USDS *Memorandums* 3-4 January 1950, 1-3.

4. Foreign Relations of the United States (FRUS)1976, 6, 330.

5. USDS Memorandum (Top Secret) 31 May 1950.

6. Ronald McGlothlen, *Controlling the Waves; Dean Acheson and U.S. Foreign Policy in Asia*, (New York: Norton, 1993), 122-125.

7. USDS, "American Foreign Policy," 2:2468.

8. USDS "American Foreign Policy," 2: 2469, United States Delegation to the General Assembly/Draft Resolution on the *Question of Formosa* (Secret) US/A/C, 1/2266 13 November 1950; U.S. Delegation to the General Assembly *Memorandum* of Telephone Conversation/Subject Formosa (Secret) US/A/C, 1/2289 24 November 1950.

9. USDS "Far Eastern Series," 1959, 55-56.

10. USDS/USUN 19 October 1954.

11. USDS "American Foreign Policy," 1957, 2 2486-2487.

12. Frederick W. Marks, *Power and Peace: The Diplomacy of John Foster Dulles,* (Westport, CT: Praeger, 1993), 81-82.

13. Ibid, 81-84.

14. USDS, "American Foreign Policy," 2502-2503.

15. Marks, Power and Peace, 79-80.

16. Kenneth Young, *Negotiating with the Chinese Communists: The American Experience 1953-1967,* (New York: McGraw Hill, 1968), 137-138.

17. Ibid, 197-198.

18. *Peking Review,* 28 October 1958, 5.

19. Young, "Negotiating with the Chinese Communists, " 7-15.

20. U. Alexis Johnson, *The Right Hand of Power: Memoirs of an American Diplomat,* (Englewood Cliffs, NJ: Prentice Hall, 1984), 261-262.

21. Graham J. Parsons, *The American Role in Pacific Asian Affairs,* (Washington DC: GPO, 1960), 14-15.

22. Dean Rusk, *U.S. Policy Towards Communist China,* U.S. Department of State (Washington, DC: GPO, 1966), 3-10.

23. USDS/Bulletin 1972, 66, 741-742.

24. USDS/Bulletin 1972, 66, 463.

25. Johnson, "The Right Hand of Power," 264-265.

26. *New York Times,* 19 December 1978.

27. U.S. Code/96th Congress, 1980, 93.

28. PRC Press/UN, March 1979, 1.

29. James A. Gregor, *Arming the Dragon: U.S. Security Ties with the People's Republic of China,* (Washington, DC: Ethics and Policy Center, 1987), 14.

30. Walter J. Stoessel, *Foreign Policy Priorities in Asia,* U.S. Department of State, Current Policy Series no. 274, April 1981, 2.

31. Gregor, "Arming the Dragon," 59-60.

32. PRC Press/UN August 1982, 1.

33. Shirley Kuo, Gustav Ranis and John C.H. Fei, *The Taiwan Success Story; Rapid*

Growth with Improved Distribution in the Republic of China, 1952-1979, (Boulder, CO: Westview, 1981), pp. 46-52 and Yu Tzong-shian, *The Story of Taiwan/Economy*, (Taipei: GIO, 1998), 19.

34. "Economic Development of the ROC/Taiwan," Council for Economic Planning and Development Executive Yuan/Taiwan ROC, 2010, 20.

35. Kuo, "The Taiwan Success Story," 6, 25.

36. K.T. Li, *Economic Transformation of Taiwan, ROC*, (London: Shepheard-Walwyn, 1988), 29, 85.

37. Kuo, "The Taiwan Success Story," 7, 30-34.

38. Yu, "The Story of Taiwan," 11, 19.

39. K. T. Li, "Sources of Rapid Economic Growth: The Case of Taiwan, "*Journal of Economic Growth* 3 (Summer 1989), 7-11.

40. Myers, "Two Societies in Opposition, " 98.

41. John Copper, "Taiwan's Diplomatic Isolation: How Serious a Problem?" *The Journal of East Asian Affairs* 6 (Winter/Spring 1992), 205-207.

42. *Census.gov* Foreign Trade Statistics by Country.

43. *Financial Post* 26 October 1987, and Canadian Trade Office in Taipei.

44. *China Post*, 10 April 2013, 4.

45. "The Development of International Trade in the Republic of China (Taiwan), " Bureau of Foreign Trade/Ministry of Economic Affairs/Taipei, 2011, 11 and German Trade Office/Taipei.

46. *ROC Yearbook* 1999, 153 and Taipei Representative Office, Budapest, Hungary.

47. *China Post* 22 April 1994.

48. Author visit/data collection, International Cooperation and Development Fund/(ICDF), Taipei/June 2011.

49. Charng Kao, "A Greater China Economic Sphere: Reality and Prospects, " *Issues & Studies* 28 (November 1992), 55.

50. *Free China Journal*, 6 January 1996.

51. Jun Zhan, *Ending the Chinese Civil War: Power, Commerce, and Conciliation Between Beijing and Taipei*, (New York: St. Martin's Press, 1993), 112-116.

52. Ricky Tung, "Economic Integration Between Taiwan and South China's Fukian and Kwangtung Provinces, " *Issues & Studies* 29 (July 1993): 28-30.

53. "Economic Development ROC/Taiwan," 28.

54. Myers, "Two Societies in Opposition, " 141-142, 154-155.

55. John Chang, "Current Political Developments in the ROC and Its Relations with Mainland China," Lecture, Asian Center, St. John's University, New York, 29 June 1993.

56. Zhan, "Ending the Chinese Civil War, " 59.

57. Ibid, 35, 131.

58. "Introduction to the Mainland Affairs Council," MAC/Executive Yuan, the Republic of China, 2011.

59. *China Post*, 27 and 29 April 1993.

60. Chang, Lecture.

61. Author Interview/Dr. Chiang Pin-kung SEF Taipei June 2011 and "Chinese Investment in Taiwan: Will Things Go the Way of Hong Kong?" *China Post* 12 November 2012, 3.

62. Zhan "Ending the Chinese Civil War," 23.

63. Robert Murphy, *Diplomat Among Warriors*, (Garden City, NY: Doubleday, 1964), 352.

64. U.N. General Assembly (UNGA)/Records 18 September 1958, 9.

65. Young, "Negotiating with the Chinese Communists," 186-198.

66. Zhan, "Ending the Chinese Civil War, " 27.

67. *ROC Yearbook 1972*, 763.

68. *ROC Reference Book,* 1983, 425.

69. *ROC Yearbook 1993*, 150, 728-729.

70. Chomg-pin Lin, "Beijing and Taipei: Dialectics in Post-Tiananmen Interaction, " *The China Quarterly* 136 (December 1993, 784.

71. Maria Hsia Chang, "Taiwan's Mainland Policy and the Reunification of China, " Asian Studies Center/The Claremont Institute (Claremont, CA: 1990), 8-11.

72. *China Yearbook 1994*, 148-149.

73. Guidelines for National Unification (Taipei: Mainland Affairs Council, 1991) 17-19.

74. Linda Chao and Ramon H. Myers, "The Divided China Problem: Conflict Avoidance and Resolution," Hoover Institution/ Essays in Public Policy, Stanford University, 2000, 47-48.

75. Author Interview/Dr. Su Chi, Taipei January 2006.

76. Mignonne Man-jung Chan, "Taiwan in APEC: Litmus Test for Regional Peace and Prosperity, " *Prospects and Perspectives 2010,* (Taipei: Prospect Foundation, 2011), 26-27.

77. Comments at "U.S.-Taiwan Relations, Cross-Strait Relations and Implications for U.S.-China Relations," Panel sponsored by the Foreign Policy Research Institute (FPRI): 17 April 2013.

China

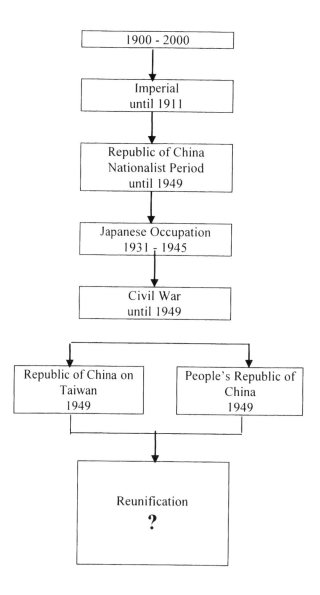

1900 - 2000

Imperial
until 1911

Republic of China
Nationalist Period
until 1949

Japanese Occupation
1931 - 1945

Civil War
until 1949

Republic of China on
Taiwan
1949

People's Republic of
China
1949

Reunification
?

Chapter 9

Chinese Unification/Prospects and Portents

The sage Confucius opined that the longest journey begins with the first step. Clearly a philosopher viewing the tumultuous era of disunity in the Spring and Autumn Period, could well apply this wisdom to the current climate of Chinese unification contacts. While the first hesitant steps have been taken towards some form of ROC/PRC coexistence, one may question whether a metered and logical step-by-step approach will withstand the strain of multifaceted gyrations of political realities.

China's unification in 221 BC under Ch'in Shih Huang-Ti, the First Emperor, lasted with some notable interruptions for 2,133 years. But this unity was constantly challenged by militant usurper dynasties who were often able to conquer and divide the country.[1]

Historians view China's cohesion in a rather poetically amorphous sense although notable periods reflected clear division such as the Three Kingdoms, the North/South division prior to Sui Dynasty reunification, as well as the hated Mongol rule of the Yuan Dynasty. In its present political/geographic form, China has been a single entity since the 1700's when the splendid rule of Emperor Qianlong unified the present reaches of the Kingdom. Yet, the impingement of Chinese sovereignty through the Treaty Ports or the Japanese annexation of Formosa in 1895 illustrates that this huge geographical entity was far from intact.

Dr. Sun Yat-sen, founder of the Republic in 1912 was keenly aware of the limitations of nationalism in China; while the Chinese people had shown the greatest loyalty to the *family and the clan*, there was no real nationalism. Dr. Sun added, "The family and the clan have been powerful unifying forces in China...the unity of the Chinese people had not extended to the Nation." In another missive Sun advised, "Reunification is the hope of all nationals in China. If reunification can be achieved, the people of the whole country will enjoy a happy life; if it cannot be achieved, the people will suffer."[2]

The early Republic was plagued by disunity. Only Chiang Kai-shek's subjugation of the regional warlords brought the nation a period of unity and prosperity in the decade 1927-1937. Nonetheless, the winds of war and the invasion and devastation of China by Imperial Japan tragically set the stage for national chaos and subsequent civil war ending with the division in 1949.

For the first thirty years, the PRC/ROC divide exhibited high levels of political hostility. Only later with a growing economic interaction did the divide exhibit limited socio/economic coexistence in spite of a continuing philosophical/ideological contraposition. Over time a national political convergence could be achieved most likely through *confederal* structures.

Greater China Economic Zones

Economics remains paramount among the factors prompting the thaw in the once glacial ROC/PRC relations. Both the promise of Taiwan trade/investment possibilities on the Mainland and the PRC's willingness to allow economic reforms to resuscitate a land still suffering from the socialist stagnation of the Maoist era indicate that the invisible hand of the market may pull the players together. Although cross straits commerce serves as an inducement to forms of coexistence between the estranged parts of the Chinese family, the political evolution remains volatile and subject to problematic jolts among the antagonists.

Taipei's growing economic dependence on the Mainland market has reached sizable proportions. According to official statistics, ROC trade with the PRC in 1994 accounted for $16.5 billion, a growing dependency comprising 9 percent of Taiwan's total trade. By 2010 an estimated 41 percent of Taiwan's exports were going to the Mainland and only 11 percent to the United States. Equally more than 40,000 Taiwan firms had invested in excess of $100 billion in the Mainland market.[3]

Trade and investment has grown exponentially. In 1999, two-way trade reached $26 billion. By 2000, according to the Ministry of Economic Affairs in Taipei, bilateral trade exceeded $32 billion, buoyed by a huge surplus with Beijing. By 2009 the two-way trade with the PRC stood at $109 billion with an amazing $58 billion trade surplus in Taipei's coffers. Significantly, Taiwan companies are increasingly engaged in producing computer-related products in the PRC.[4]

Taiwan's information technology products have achieved global standing. The island produces 95 percent of the motherboards, 95 percent of the Notebook PC's, 63 percent of Optical Discs and 59 percent of the monitors. Importantly, many *Made in Taiwan* computer products have components made by ROC firms produced on the Mainland.[5]

However Mainland located factories accounted for much of Taiwan's information technology development. Enthusiastic investment by Taiwan firms causes great concern with the Taipei government, a common worry is that it will drain Taiwan's IT industry which currently accounts for 50 percent of the island's annual economic growth. Presently IT products are marketed under brand names of international firms as Compaq, Dell, and IBM. Total Research and Development spending rose from one percent of GDP in 1985 to 2.77 percent in 2008. Taiwan's ranking in the *Science Citation Index* stands at number 17 internationally.[6]

Beyond this there's the security concern of producing a computer IT nerve system in a potentially hostile country. Rationalizations aside, such business moves can have long-term national security consequences.

Former President Richard Nixon advised, "Like a couple who have gone through a bitter divorce, China and Taiwan publicly have irreconcilable differences. The separation is permanent politically but they are in bed together economically; they need each other."[7]

The ROC Ministry of Economic Affairs concedes that nearly 70 percent of Taiwan companies planning to invest overseas choose China. The U.S., Hong Kong, Malaysia, and Vietnam remain other favorite destinations.

A powerful *de facto* South China Economic Zone (SCEZ), Taiwan, Hong Kong, Kwantung, Fukien, Shanghai, offers a particularly seductive commercial logic which thrives in boardrooms but languishes in a political limbo. The region contains substantial capital, technology and manufacturing capacity (Taiwan), outstanding marketing and services acumen (Hong Kong), and a huge endowment of land, resources and labor (Mainland).

Of the world's top ten container shipping ports, seven are in the region ; Shanghai (#2) Hong Kong (#3), Shenzhen (#4) . Taiwan's exceedingly modern and efficient port of Kaohsiung stands as (#12). Singapore remains the world's leading container port. Significantly Shanghai has seen extraordinary growth with container handling rising 30 percent a year since 1991. Shanghai's meteoric growth has surpassed Hamburg in container cargo by a factor of three and the Port of New York by a factor of five.[8]

Add this to the Merchant Marine figures of the PRC, ROC, and Hong Kong and one sees the amazing commercial potential of the South China Economic Zone. China ranks in the top five of maritime states with 3,500 vessels/93 million dw tons. Hong Kong has 680 vessels/34 million dw tons, and Taiwan 631 vessels with 30 million dw tons.

If combined China/HK tonnage ranks third globally; add Taiwan and the SCEZ fleet would be number first globally in vessels and second in dead weight tonnage. Going a step further, Taiwan's Evergreen Line ranks fourth globally in terms of vessels and tonnage, while China's COSCO is number six, Hong Kong's OOCL is number eleven and Taiwan's Yangming is number thirteen. In combined container carry capability, the SCEZ stands as a world-class player.[9]

Cross-strait shipping, with some very specific exceptions, routes through Hong Kong. Still Taiwan's ports of Kaohsiung, Keelung, and Taichung, despite modernization, face stiff competition from Mainland cargo facilities.

The South China Economic Zone evokes and draws historic comparisons with the Hanseatic League. Though lacking a clear political plan and reflecting long-standing political suspicion, the region is bound by commerce. Indeed in the late Middle Ages, the League united together the merchants and cities of north Germany and the Baltic. The Hanse cities did not form a unified government. Rather, their business and governmental leaders cooperated on *mutual economic interests*. Unlike today's European Union,, the Hanseatic League was not a compact among sovereign states, as Murray Weidenbaum asserts, rather the members owed allegiance to various regional powers. The League was an amorphous organization lacking legal status.[10]

Such a model reflecting the *de facto* economic integration already taking place, should bypass the predictable political pitfalls.

In the meantime, necessary consular functions needed to protect and facilitate commerce can be provided by the SEF and ARATS, respectively. The organizations should establish a Joint Secretariat in coastal Xiamen/Amoy for bilateral meetings and practical problem solving sessions. Given the proximity of ROC controlled Quemoy, this region is best suited for such a venue.

Gulangyu Island alongside Xiamen/Amoy would be a propitious location, imbibed in Chinese history and set in Fukien. Should the parties wish to use a mid-point location, Makung in the Pescadores/Penghu in mid-Taiwan Straits offers an equidistant geographical choice with easy access to both capitals.

Given the direct transportation and trade ties between both sides of the Straits, Taiwan/PRC commerce no longer has to route through the *entrepot* of Hong Kong. For Taiwan businessmen, interface with the Mainland market becomes a *sine qua non* for success. Still the PRC offers an overheated high-risk exposure, the lure of a low cost production base, but poses the undeniably dangerous economic dependence for Taiwan.

Former ROC Vice President Lien Chan has called for a wide range of cross-straits exchanges based on *Chinese Confederation* plan. Both Taiwan and the Mainland would work within the "one China" concept.

Naturally a focus on values integration between the two separate Chinese states remains in its infant stages. Stressing *shared cultural values* rather than highlighting *political differences*, would be a prudent first step.

Presently Taiwan movies and some publications are permitted on the Mainland despite cumbersome bureaucratic hurdles. PRC publications now legally enter Taiwan. Taiwan journalists regularly visit the PRC while Mainland journalists can visit the ROC. The state run-Xinhua News Agency plans a Taipei bureau.

Viewing burgeoning but loosely defined "Greater China," Sinologist Harry Harding related that the concept subsumes three distinct themes—economic integration, cultural interaction, and political reunification among the international Chinese community. While commerce underscores a common theme for the three Chinese economies (PRC, ROC, Hong Kong), more than economic forces are at work.[11]

Reflecting the need to formalize burgeoning cross straits commerce, the SEF and ARATS signed the Cross Straits Economic Cooperation Framework Agreement (ECFA) in June 2010. "In terms of Cross-Straits relations, the ECFA will serve as a framework for future economic cooperation between the two sides," states Prof. Wu-ueh Chang. He adds, "How ECFA helps the Cross Straits economic ties to progress will depend on the mutual political trust between Taipei and Beijing and economic reciprocity between the two economies." [12]

Realistically neither Beijing nor Taipei can come to a settlement within the confines defined by the traditional *Nation/State*. Yet the commonalities of Chinese culture, language and commerce can narrow the otherwise widening political gap. Economic relationships alone however will not bridge the divide. Both Chinese states must be creative and be willing to explore with *Commonwealth* or *Confederation, or Common Market* concepts. The PRC could show good will by renouncing the option to *use force* against the island; Taiwan could likewise renounce the provocative *independence* option.

Yet, the seemingly logical argument that China's commerce will temper its political emotions towards Taiwan or the USA for that matter, may hold surprises.

China has emerged as a major recipient of foreign direct investments (FDI). Despite setbacks from the 2008 recession, China gained $106 billion in 2010, while Hong Kong saw a $66 billion inflow. Traditionally FDI focused on export industries; now China's foreign trade has grown from almost nothing in the late 1970's to $475 billion in 2000 to $2.2 trillion in 2007. Foreign firms account for half the exports. [13]

Reform in China has led to increasing regionalism of the economy and to some extent to the nation's politics. Growth and prosperity across China remains uneven thus creating the very conditions which have long haunted the Chinese Communist Party. Such fault lines have historically plagued the Middle Kingdom.

Poignant contradictions between Beijing's stated goals of market socialism and political dictatorship become sharper in the age of the mobile phones, the Internet, and virtual communication.

PRC Premier Wen Jiabao told the United Nations, "People may ask: How does China achieve its development? The answer is through reform and opening up. This year marks the 30th anniversary of China's reform and opening-up policy, a policy that fundamentally changed the closed, backward and ossified situation which had existed in China for years." In surprisingly candid comments he added, "It is a policy that has freed people's minds and aroused their initiative, liberated productive forces, generated great economic and social progress, and installed vigor and vitality into the country." The Premier stated, "The Chinese people have learned from 30 years of reform and opening up that only continued economic and political restructuring and reform in other fields can lead to sustained economic growth and social progress, and only continued opening-up in an all round way can lead the country to greater national strength and prosperity." [14]

The Premier's generally overlooked UN speech, indirectly chastised the first thirty years of the People's Republic and the ossified rule by the very same CCP political party which continues to control the PRC.

PRC membership in the World Trade Organization (WTO) presented Beijing with a double edged sword—on the one hand *open markets* permit Chinese firms new global access; on the other hand, the traditional and inefficient *iron rice bowl* industries cannot withstand global competition that genuinely *open markets* will bring. Here's the dilemma. While social and economic prosperity has improved the lives of a significant minority of Chinese, one ponders whether the proverbial young executive driving his BMW on the *Bund* in Shanghai, juggling cell phones, and doing business deals with foreigners, is content to be ruled by an un-elected political class whose pedigree rests in production quotas, ideological mobilizations, and rigid conformity? Moreover how will China's rising middle-class balance the revolution of rising expectations?

The 80th anniversary of the Communist Party of China illuminated such a contradiction. When Jiang Zemin made a pilgrimage to the little Shanghai house where the party was clandestinely founded in 1921, he was escorted by a Hong Kong real estate developer who had transformed the district into an upscale neighborhood. The area around the socialist museum is surrounded by a Starbucks Cafe, fashionable restaurants, and pricey shops.

The CCP which seized power in 1949, now has 78 million members, more than double the 37 million the 1978 number when the Deng Xiaoping reform process began. When the CCP came to power fewer than one percent of Chinese were members, today the figure stands at 5.7 percent. Almost half are under 45, and 38 percent of new recruits are university students and another 21 percent professionals, have applied to join. Chinese join the Party these days to promote their careers rather than communism. College students are among the most eager to join and much of the interest is career oriented. So too are many people in business, even though the Party does not accept in theory entrepreneurs as members.[15]

"The CCP still holds on to the old ideals of a Leninist party, attempting the same kind of control over the economy and the society through its grass-roots organizations as in the planned economy era," writes Prof. Gore. While the CCP always worked through "organized dependence" he adds, "Size is no guarantee for the perpetuation of the Party's rule. ...Party members views, values, identities and incentives are now shaped more by the market than by Party indoctrination, and Party organizations at the grass-roots level increasingly stand on shifting sand."[16]

The party's hold on power is not guaranteed. Former CCP Chairman and PRC President Hu Jintao, was part of the Shanghai circle. The revival of Shanghai—the city evoking China's best and worst images and memories has been a metaphor for the PRC. Given that the CCP leadership are Shanghai natives, the city has been a particular focus of development and has emerged as a commercial rival to Hong Kong especially since 1997. Shanghai has resumed its historic place as a business and entrepreneurial dynamo, a particular irony since the metropolis had been the epicenter of the *Red Guard* in the 1960's. Shanghai has re-emerged as China's cosmopolitan epicentre where a *bling-bling* standard often defines status. But what are the political confines of China's increasingly *Corporate State*?

Unpredictable socio/economic winds may be triggered by unforeseen events such as a sustained economic recession, a slowing of growth, or rumblings along the Mainland's ethnic faultlines. Equally destabilising may be what many economists fear remains a *statistical sham*, in other words politically padded exaggerations which have been *come to be accepted as unquestioned financial facts*. Such an economic "shock" appears likely with frightening ramifications.

Richard Nixon viewed Beijing's ideological eclipse, "While the Chinese leadership may worship in a communist church, they believe in capitalist scripture. They are committed to free market economic policies, to capitalism with a Chinese face."[17]

New Political Winds Across the Straits

Chinese researchers caution that the PRC, viewing the post-Soviet system in political reform and economic shock treatment, fears the Russian scenario. The age old fear of *chaos* affecting both political equilibrium and economic prosperity is a regular theme of officials. "If you begin political reforms, the results can be the chaos of Russia," opined a leading scholar.

The pace of development is based on political stability. Still, dynamic socio/economic pressures will inexorably clash with the staid political system until very likely the Beijing political center implodes, and the regional economic power units assert themselves politically. Ominously, a PRC political pendulum swing caused by a misjudged power struggle or a bungled military gambit to "liberate a secessionist minded Taiwan," could speed up the process. So too could the jolt of economic recession. The dynamic offers a volatile mix of both promise and peril.

Despite rural protests, the drumbeat of corruption, and a roving force of unemployed, disorders don't yet challenge CCP rule. Rather protests seek to redress particular grievances. Following the fractious Party Congress in November 2012, the new President Xi Jinping has put forth a new doctrine; the Chinese Dream. The mantra mixes nationalism, nostalgia, and themed propaganda to propel a righteous China to its proper place in the world. "The great revival of the Chinese nation," as Xi extols is more about prideful nationalism than moribund Marxism. Part of this nationalist revival seeks both redressing past historic injustices, perceived or otherwise, as much as to seek an almost cosmic reinforcement of China's place in the world, with or without the CCP.

Growth is destabilizing. While there are huge differences, China shares with turn of the 19th century Germany a sense of wounded pride, the annoyance of a giant that has been cheated by the rest of the world. Nicholas Kristof writing in *Foreign Affairs* opined, "China is now undergoing an arms build-up which will allow it to *avenge these wrongs*. Deng is in many respects like Bismarck seeking strength and modernization but trying not to overturn the entire balance of power. The risk remains that Deng's successor will be less talented and more aggressive, a Chinese version of Wilhelm II. Such a ruler may be tempted to promote Chinese nationalism as a unifying force and ideology."[18]

Interestingly in a long forgotten 1979 visit to Bonn by Hua Guo-feng, the PRC Premier "supported the German people's legitimate aspiration for the reunification of their country." He added, "It is abnormal that Germany has been artificially divided into two parts. The Chinese people fully understand how the German people feel."[19]

ROC reunification formulas have seen new recalibration. Aware of its *de facto* engagement on the Mainland, Taipei has increasingly spoken of the need not to *reconquer or regain*, the Mainland but *to reconstruct* it. Such a plan allows for expanding economic ties which naturally help coastal China as well as Taiwan's restive businessmen while also narrowing the economic gap between the estranged Chinese family.

While surmounting political hostility remains the most formidable issue to bridge the Taiwan Straits, the widening ROC/PRC economic divide looms as its greatest long-term challenge. Given Taiwan's per capita GNP of $14,700 and the PRC's $790 in 2000, the gap to be closed stands at a ratio of 19/1. Optimistically viewing the provinces of the emerging SCEZ, we find the GNP of Kwangtung Fukien/Shanghai, would still average a 8/1 PRC vs. Taiwan gap.

A haunting issue remains how much of PRC growth, as that of former East Germany, is based on *falsified or fanciful figures?* Grafting Taiwan's growth-oriented 23 million populace into a supra-state of 1.2 billion people poses a daunting socio/political challenge for any government.

Emerging from Taiwan's economic miracle has been a commensurate desire by the island's 23 million people to achieve political recognition. Whether the ROC follows the traditional "One China, two entities" or a provocative "Taiwan independence" path, there remains a desire to be a player on the world stage.

Taiwan's "pragmatic diplomacy" is aimed at survival. Former Foreign Minister Frederick Chien advised, "pragmatic diplomacy is part and parcel to the ROC's democratic transformation...just as Taiwan is part of China, so is the Mainland. Neither should seek to lord over the other or to claim superiority by size, population or past performance. Both should recognize the fact that two different systems exist in these separate parts of China. While unification is the ultimate goal of the Chinese on both sides of the Taiwan Straits, it should not be pursued simply for its own sake." He added, the process must narrow the "political and economic gaps" and be "peaceful and voluntary."[20]

Beijing has offered stern rebukes to ROC attempts to break the diplomatic deadlock and develop relations with a wider circle of states. The seemingly innocuous visit of ROC President Lee Tung-hui to the United States to accept an honorary degree from Cornell University triggered a shrill series of attacks on both the personage of Lee as well as Washington for allowing the unofficial trip. The PRC's overreaction to the journey reflected a hyper-sensitivity over a "political hallucination for Taiwan independence."[21]

Beijing's political pressures in the aftermath of Taiwan's democratic Presidential elections in 1996 and especially in 2000, posed the ROC with increased levels of PRC intimidation and bellicosity. So too did the drumbeat against Taiwan's diplomacy at the United Nations.

Responding to ROC moves to regain its U.N. seat, PRC Foreign Minister Qian Qichen warned, "Dual recognition is impossible. There is no precedent nor will there be one in the future."[22]

The issue of the ROC rejoining the U.N., while seemingly logical in an era of rapid growth in the membership in the world organization, is shadowed by the fundamental political reality of the PRC Security Council veto which can, and likely would, block Taipei's admission.

While the ROC unquestionably meets the qualifications for U.N. membership, the stark reality remains that the *diplomatic Great Wall* of Beijing's veto is near insurmountable.[23]

In 1993, seven Central American states in a letter to Secretary General Boutros-Ghali, requested consideration of the ROC/Taiwan membership in the 48th General Assembly. While the bid fizzled without vote in committee, a dozen states publicly called for ROC membership during the Assembly session.[24]

At the 49th Assembly, fifteen states unsuccessfully petitioned that Taiwan's status be discussed. During that session twenty speakers, among them Nicaragua's President Violetta Chamorro called for ROC readmission to the U.N. To state the not so obvious: Taiwan's population exceeds that of 140 U.N. members; its gross national product is higher than all but 18 of the 185 members. Taipei meets all the classical criteria for recognition under the Montevideo Convention.[25]

The U.N. debate has triggered a political typhoon on both sides of the Taiwan Straits. Initial ROC trial balloons hinting at the dual recognition model as in the cases of Germany or Korea were punctured by Beijing's sharp ideological barbs. The ROC's decision to participate in the U.N. is not intended to create a permanent split between the two sides of the Taiwan Straits. On the contrary, Taipei believes that participation in the U.N., as did the German states or the Koreas, would increase possibilities for both the ROC and PRC to work together in a common forum.

The PRC Foreign Ministry issued a vitriolic *White Paper* opposing the ROC's bid for U.N. admission and disputing the ROC's legitimacy as a legally constituted nation-state deserving to play a role in international organizations. Likewise the PRC made a strong case against any manifestations of Taiwan separatism.[26]

The China issue returned during the U.N's 50th General Assembly when twenty states petitioned that Taiwan's participation be included as an agenda item, "Consideration of the exceptional situation of the Republic of China on Taiwan in the international context, based on the principle of universality and in accordance with the established model of parallel representation of divided countries in the United Nations." Though the bid was again killed in committee and the item not considered, over twenty Foreign Ministers supported Taipei's U.N. bid during the General Assembly proceedings.

PRC Foreign Minister Qian bluntly told the General Assembly, "There is but one China in the world. The Government of the People's Republic of China is the sole legal government of China. It is the sole representative of China in the United Nations. Taiwan is an inalienable part of China." He warned "any attempt to obstruct peaceful reunification and split Taiwan from China is doomed to failure." President Jiang, addressing the U.N.'s Fiftieth anniversary commemorations repeated the message reiterating, "The peaceful re-unification of the two sides of the Taiwan Straits is the unshakable will and determination of the entire Chinese people, including the Taiwan compatriots."[27]

Significantly, the opposition Democratic Progressive Party (DPP) pushed the U.N. bid onto a wary KMT government agenda. The nuance posed whether Taipei applies as the "ROC" or "Taiwan" hardly amuses the Foreign Ministry in Beijing. One of the few points of agreement between Taipei and Beijing is that they are indisputably China, albeit in their own vision. Any tampering with this fragile formula could trigger a geopolitical jolt in the *status quo* across the Taiwan Straits.

Subsequent annual moves by Taipei to raise the issue of United Nations *participation, membership*, or even *discussion* have met with the PRC's icy rebuke. Each Assembly, though the ROC has marshalled just over a score of countries to raise the issue of Taipei's U.N. participation, formal discussion of the topic is relegated to diplomatic limbo.

Viewing these realities, Taiwan could opt for the non-voting Observer Status, as did the Koreas and Germanies, thus bypassing the Security Council. Such a scenario would allow Taipei participation in the U.N., but as importantly, would offer Beijing the face-saving measure of claiming its delegation still represents and votes for *all China*. A more complex "One nation; two seats," formula insures, while *not* promoting two Chinas, that at unification a successor government is already a U.N. member. In such a case the PRC would retain its Security Council and General Assembly seats; Taiwan would enter the Assembly as "China- Taipei."

After tireless attempts, Taiwan was admitted into the UN's World Health Organization (WHO) as an Observer in 2009. Equally in 2013 Taiwan was allowed to participate in the International Civil Aviation Organization's (ICAO) meeting in Montreal. President Ma Ying-jeou restored equilibrium in cross straits relations. Taipei has likewise observed a "diplomatic truce" with Beijing; neither side will go after or try to "poach" the other side's diplomatic allies. Taiwan seeks international space. Though Taipei's allies have continued to mention the case in the General Assembly the government has toned down the annual appeal for UN "participation."

Scenarios

Logical-Mode/unlikely

A protracted series of often desultory discussions may yield tactical results but no strategic political breakthrough given the personalities of the players in both Beijing and Taipei. Observers must be prepared for a non-traditional scenario which will emerge from major unforeseen political events not at all connected to unity policy but which will put such policy in a different more amenable mode. Thus a phased in and step-by-step approach, while plausibly logical, is probably least likely given the propensity for stunning political shifts on both sides of the Straits, notwithstanding the pragmatic aftermath of the 1997 Hong Kong handover.

Greater Economic Zone/ *de facto*

Economic empowerment serves as the engine of socio/economic modernization and embryonic political democratization. Yet, the development is regional and may lead to regional solutions, not unknown in Chinese history.

Such a plan could bring about a *Chinese Commonwealth* with loose central organization but a common desire for economic gain; the Hanseatic League formula in which commercial interests bound together a loose regional political commonwealth. Conversely a federal system allowing regional rights but reflecting economic provincial power of South China and Taiwan may form. This would have a Beijing political center but socio/economic power spheres in Hong Kong and Taiwan. *Commonwealth, Confederation,* or *Economic Union* offer clear options for solving the impasse. On the practical side, China and Taiwan signed the Economic Cooperation Framework Agreement (ECFA) in 2010 which paves the way to closer cross straits commerce and investment.

Leadership in both Chinese capitals has been less than creative in considering political formulae allowing political autonomy. For the PRC, the ruling communists arrogantly view power as their *imperious right*. In Taipei policy tends to be *reactive and nervously cautious.*

Taiwan independence/wild cards

Resulting both from a desire to seemingly solve the "China question" and in impatient reaction to the *political atrophy* of the Chinese communists, separatist sentiments have grown, forming a strong undercurrent in the DPP. Such feelings not only hold some sympathy among native Taiwanese but are also expressions of frustration with the seemingly endless cross-straits politics. There's understandable resignation which has led to an unexpected backlash.

Polls measuring cross-straits opinions saw growing support for reunification under the PRC's longstanding "one country two systems" scheme. A survey conducted by the Mainland Affairs Council found 33% of respondents supported "status quo indefinitely" another 27 percent status quo now/independence later, 19 percent status quo now/unification later, independence 9 percent and , 6.6 percent independence "asap" while fewer than one percent support "unification with Beijing "asap." Political infighting and economic prospects have caused a malaise which ironically favors the Mainland. Basically half of respondents say the pace of cross-straits exchange is "just right" while another 33 percent say it is "too fast."[28]

"Taiwanese people acknowledge Chinese history, custom and language, but they are simultaneously aware of Taiwan's distinct region and custom" stresses Prof. Frank Liu, adding, "Hence Taiwan's identification crisis is attributable to Taiwan having been identified in China's history as a province of China, and the identification problem on the island seems to be associated with Taiwan's willingness, or lack thereof, to seek 'independence.'"[29]

The lightning rod concept of *Taiwan independence*, though never scoring significantly in surveys, still lurks on the landscape. As the concept confronts the core question of *national sovereignty* and shatters the *status quo*, one must expect Beijing's proportionate military response. Any move towards this option, perceived or real, could trigger a PRC attack. Contrary to the FRG and ROK cases, the ROC no longer benefits from a formal U.S. security pact.

PRC invasion/ response to Taiwan independence

The PRC's oft-stated vow to attack Taiwan should the island declare its independence would likely spark a *wider regional upheaval*. Though an invasion may likely fail, it would almost certainly stoke the fires of separatism in coastal China and perhaps among restive non-Han Chinese peoples in Tibet and Moslems in Xinjiang. Regionalism once ignited, may ultimately bring China a revival of its tumultuous history and lead to a period of East Asian instability.

Fearing the role model of the ROC's democracy, the PRC militarily threatened Taiwan during the island's 1996 Presidential election. The timely and judicious dispatch of a U.S. Navy Carrier battle group to the region stabilized the *status quo*. In 2000 Taiwan's three way Presidential elections with the KMT, the separatist inclined DPP, and the maverick People First Party, posed the PRC with a more complicated challenge. Taiwan's democracy, fractious as it may be, nonetheless confronts the rigid PRC system with profound political uncertainties.

PRC disintegration/possible

Following the death of Deng Xiaoping in 1997, the PRC faced possible political disintegration. A Pentagon study opined that no paramount leader would likely follow Deng and that for a few years the country would be kept on course by a collective leadership. Deng's choice of *dauphin* designate Jiang Zemin, Chief of State and/CCP indeed preserved *order and stability*. Yet factions within the CCP leadership, and especially in the anxious countdown to the 18th Party Congress in 2012, saw the system challenged from within by CCP factions.

The security *apparat*, regional military commands, and many economic reformers are waiting in the wings in the post-Hu Jintao era. The sweeping leadership changes following the CCP's 18th Party Congress, will test how the "new generation" rulers, Xi Jinping and Premier Li Keqiang, will balance China's conflicting forces of social and economic change within an ossified political system. Sparks of unexpected social protest can pose unexpected political reverberations.

The challenges include: rampant corruption inside the ruling CCP, the widening fault lines of economic inequity, and the undetermined influence of the internet, which despite the suffocating Great Firewall protecting the CCP, could be circumvented to offer political outcomes not part of the PRC mantra. The spark of socio/economic uncertainty, and the CCP's misjudged reactions, could produce unforeseen results.

Should Beijing's regime collapse, the ROC ironically becomes heir to a restive and profoundly underdeveloped land. Except for the freewheeling coastal provinces and Shanghai, the ROC will have to pick up the pieces of national unity and enter a period of serious socio/economic instability and political uncertainty. As inheritor of a moribund Marxist China, the ROC government would in an effort to equalize, be challenged with the Herculean task of narrowing the economic gap.

The National Unification Council viewing the meaning of "One China" states, "both sides of the Taiwan Straits agree there is only one China." However, they have different opinions as to its meaning. To Beijing, "One China" means "The People's Republic of China" of which Taiwan is to become a "Special Administrative Region" after unity. Taipei considers "One China" to mean "The Republic of China" founded in 1912 with legal sovereignty over all China.[30]

The Presidency of Chen Shui-bian brought a new tenor to Taipei and its relations with the Mainland. Chen put aside Lee's "two states theory" which enraged Beijing. This has raised hopes in the PRC that Chen, despite has former activism for Taiwan's independence, may be willing to put incendiary rhetoric behind for the wider goal of unified China, albeit it in a yet to be determined formula.

The election of KMT candidate Ma Ying-jeou in 2008 calmed the roiling waters of the Taiwan Straits. Ma's re-election in 2012 continued the calm.

The Nationalists after all remain politically and philosophically wedded to eventual Chinese reunification but are equally realistic to encourage a downshift in tensions with the Mainland. Central to the philosophy remain the crucial "1992 Consensus" what President Ma described as "a critical anchoring point for Taiwan and mainland China to find common ground on the otherwise intractable issue of 'one China.' The consensus reached between the two sides in 1992, established a common understanding of 'one China with respective interpretations.' With this understanding as the foundation, my administration designed a number of *modus operandi* that broadly defined how Taiwan would pursue peace and prosperity with mainland China. These included the 'Three No's; 'No Unification, No Independence, and No Use of Force."[31]

Political semantics can play so far with the PRC given the inherent instability of the regime. Beijing has unresolved disputes regarding land and sea borders, such as *territorial claims on* the Spratly Islands or Taiwan. *What the world may view as aggression, China sees as self-defense.*

Situated in the South China Sea basin, the Spratly islands comprise mostly uninhabited small atolls. There are claims and counter-claims by six regional states including both Chinese governments, Vietnam, the Philippines, Indonesia and

Malaysia. The PRC has described the Spratly's as historically Chinese territory. China's growing military might and political assertiveness has been focused on the South China Sea basin and Spratly group as a kind of *Mare Nostrum* which would allow Beijing a tremendous geopolitical advantage not only of potential mineral and fishing resources but the very sea lanes of communication to Japan, Korea and Taiwan. Despite strong protests from neighbouring states most especially Vietnam and the Philippines, the American Secretary of State Hillary Clinton clearly stated that "the U.S. has a national interest in ensuring the freedom of navigation in the South China Sea."

The long-forgotten Diaoyutai/Senkaku islands lit a nationalistic fuse between Beijing and Tokyo concerning the disputed sovereignty of the uninhabited atolls. The territorial dispute in the East Asia Sea unfolded in the months prior to both the 18th CCP Party Congress as well as parliamentary elections in Japan.

The Diaoyutai Islands consist of five uninhabited islands and three rocky reefs. While the islands first appeared in Chinese historical records during the Ming and Ching Dynasties, the islands fell under Japanese control following 1895 until the end of WWII. Indeed between 1945 and 1972 while the nearby Ryukyu Islands were put under U.S. trusteeship, the Daioyutai were merely subject to U.S. Administrative control. "Regarding the reversion of the Daioyutai Islands to Japan along with the Ryukyu Islands, the U.S. government sent an official note to the Republic of China on May 26th, 1971, stating that Washington's transferring of administrative eights over these islands does not affect the ROC's claim of sovereignty over the Daioyutai Islands. " Later that year, U.S. Secretary of State William Rogers stated that "the U./S. took no position on the sovereignty issue over the Diaoyutai and the "dispute should be resolved through negotiations between the ROC and Japan."[32]

Though Japan exercises administrative rights over the islands, Tokyo does not exercise sovereignty. In August 2012, ROC President Ma proposed a two-stage East China Sea Peace Initiative based on the concept that while sovereignty is indivisible, resources can be shared. The Plan calls on all parties to replace confrontation with dialogue, shelve territorial disputes through negotiations and formulate a Code of Conduct to engage in joint resource development among the three parties Mainland China, Taiwan and Japan. After diligent negotiations between Taipei and Tokyo, a fisheries agreement was signed which safeguards fishing boats from both countries in the disputed waters.[33]

Reflecting the CCP's doctrinal politics-in-command line over all other considerations, the PRC may resort to military options rationalized in the rhetoric of nationalism. The Mainland's meteoric military spending and commensurate desire to project power in disputed borders such as Taiwan and the South China Sea has raised serious geopolitical concerns for regional states and the U.S.

Importantly, as communism has fallen out of favor as an official creed, the Communist Party is trying to use nationalism as a new glue. This high-octane nationalism, really a form of fascism, has redefined the PRC state. Self-righteous nationalism has replaced internationalist communism. Thus the Spratly and the

Diaoyutai Islands naturally offer Beijing both the political rallying/propaganda platform to sustain nationalism as well as justify the growing military budget. Both issues equally deal with core issues in the PRC security lexicon; Taiwan, lingering animosity towards Japan and the PRC's security stance over the *Mare Nostrum* of the South China Sea.

The People's Liberation Army Navy (PLAN) fleet has capabilities beyond traditional coastal defence. "With the PRC aggressively asserting territorial claims in the South China Sea and East China Sea, its ability to enforce maritime claims in a situation short of open hostilities is directly related to its naval influence," opines Dr. Milan Vego of the Naval War College. He adds however, "Although the PLAN is clearly inferior to the U.S. Navy in terms of aggregate tonnage and combat potential,, this does not necessarily mean the latter would exert greater influence in a crisis over Taiwan or Korea, or in a dispute over the South China Sea islands."[34]

Given the hyper-sensitivities concerning the status of Taiwan, there was serious alarm during the summer of 1995 when the PRC conducted *quaintly titled* missile tests just eighty miles north of Taiwan. While the PRC's unarmed M-9 missiles landed harmlessly in the East China Sea, the tests battered both the Taipei *bourse* which fell precipitously and local perceptions about PRC's threat to use force. By 2012, military plans by the Obama Administration to make a strategic "pivot to the Pacific" have unsettled and emboldened Beijing policy planners.

PRC military budgets have been increasing exponentially. Between 2002 and 2011 PRC spending has surged 170 percent. By 2011 Beijing boasted the world's second largest defence spending, $143 billion, behind the USA but double that of Russia.[35]

Such statistics do not reflect the large number of "black programs" which Beijing manages often financed through its huge foreign exchange reserves. China's military capabilities continue to advance. Without question should there be a military confrontation between Beijing and Taipei, the PRC can seriously disrupt Taiwan's economy by targeting/interdicting the shipping lanes and firing missiles at the island itself. PRC cyber warfare capacity is viewed as a way to alter the military balance short of formal hostilities.

The PRC's first operational aircraft carrier, the *Liaoning*, was commissioned in 2012. "Navy Sails into New Era," trumpeted the *China Daily* and boasted, "Aircraft Carrier set to enhance China's maritime combat capability."[36]

The Liaoning offers the People's Liberation Navy enhanced prestige, standing, and force projection capabilities in the regional sphere. This new naval asset, while clearly outclassed in the context of U.S. Navy capabilities, offers Beijing a platform for power projection in the waters east of Taiwan, in the South China Sea among the disputed Spratly Islands, and equally off the disputed Diaoyutai/ Senkaku islands. The *Liaoning* puts the PRC into a small and select group of global naval powers even though coordinating and honing carrier operations capacity will not come overnight.

Deployment of CSS-6, M-9, CS-7 and M-11, and modernized CSS-5 ballistic missiles in the coastal area opposite Taiwan has increased. This is most likely an underestimate of missile numbers. Equally force modernization of the PRC air force and the corresponding age of the ROC air force, has begun to alter Taiwan's traditional technological air superiority advantage. Taiwan's qualitative military advantages, akin to Israel's, has begun to shrink *vis a vis* the Mainland.

Ominously, PRC advances in *cyber-warfare* may in fact pose a wider danger to Taiwan than the traditional D-Day style amphibious invasion. Should PRC cyber-warfare target Taiwan's very vulnerable communications, information industry, electric power grid, and military/ civilian air traffic control, the Mainland can create chaos without firing the proverbial shot nor resorting to even passive naval blockade tactics.

Developing greater expertise in information warfare would give the Mainland a potentially potent weapon which could be used to target weak points not only on Taiwan but also the U.S. Such military/security cyber programs again can be financed in parallel through the PRC's huge foreign currency reserves.

Naturally Taiwan's sovereignty and freedom are based on her defensive capabilities. "For cross-strait relations to continue advancing, the U.S. must help Taiwan level the playing field. Negotiating with a giant like Mainland China is not without the risks. The right leverage must be in place," advised Taiwan Minister Philip Yang. In an address to the Asia Society he stressed, "Ongoing Chinese military modernization efforts, defence concept developments, force structure changes and deployment preparations under way are reasons for Taiwan to firmly continue seeking to acquire F-16 C/D jet fighters and diesel powered electric submarines from the United States, to keep our aerial and naval integrity intact, which is crucial to maintaining a credible defence." He added, "Taiwan also looks forward to deepening security cooperation with the U.S. based on the sound foundation of mutual trust and common strategic interests."[37]

"Generally speaking, Chinese diplomacy remains remarkably risk-averse and guided by narrow national interests. Chinese diplomacy takes a kind of lowest common denominator approach, usually adopting the safest and non-controversial positions and usually waits to see the position of other governments, before revealing their own," states noted Sinologist David Shambaugh. He adds, "The notable exception to this rule concerns China's own narrow self interests: Taiwan, Tibet, Xinjiang, Human Rights and inter maritime claims: on these issues Beijing is hyper vigilant and diplomatically active."[38]

The central political dogma of PRC/ROC relations remains the *status of Taiwan*; for the PRC, any perception of a changing *status quo* across the Straits could trigger cataclysmic events affecting East Asia's equilibrium. ROC elections reflect both a working multiparty democracy as a well as serious political anxieties among the voters not to tamper with the fragile *status quo* in relations with the Mainland. Taiwan's Presidential elections, successfully concluded to the backdrop of Beijing's bluster and bullying, now have entered calmer waters as the PRC can be expected to play by more polite rules, should Taiwan refrain from, at least rhetorically, calling for independence. Taiwan and Tibet after all are viewed by Beijing's rulers as *Core Interests*.

Thus for Taiwan the ultimate political insurance policy becomes a stated and transparent willingness to work within a *Chinese formula* rather than trying to *redefine Taiwan's Chinese identity*. Leading KMT Party officials have made high profile visits to the Mainland; the KMT views relations with the politically divided Chinese family within a *Chinese identity*. The *double entendre* remains that the traditionally anti-communist KMT looks to communist China as a partner in the eventual reunification of China.

On the practical side the ties are booming. Once banned, direct air transport between Taiwan and the Mainland has risen meteorically. Originally the direct flights were only for the Lunar New Year and special holidays. Since 2008, flights expanded from 36 per week, to 108, then 370 flights weekly. Thirty-seven Chinese airports offer direct flights to Taiwan, mostly on Mainland carriers. By 2011 the number of flights per week had reached 558. By 2013 the number had risen to 616, an amazing and once unimaginable Cross-Straits transportation web.

Equally Cross-Straits tourism has blossomed both for sightseeing, shopping and family visits. Chinese tourists surged from 274,000 in 2008 to 1.6 million in 2010 to 2.5 million in 2012.[39]

While high end shopping in Taipei 101 is one undeniable facet, so too are visits to the historic sites of such as Taipei's iconic National Palace Museum, the Chiang Kai-shek Memorial and the National Martyrs Shrine. A rare experience for many Chinese visitors is watching Taiwan's vibrant and effervescent TV talk shows and often socially and politically edgy programming. The Grand Hotel, the jewel of Nationalist China in the 1960's and 1970's, today is a popular accommodation for visiting Mainland provincial dignitaries.

Significantly President Ma Ying-jeou stressed, "Preserving the Republic of China has immense importance that goes far beyond the borders of Taiwan. For the first time in Chinese history, we in Taiwan have proved that democracy can thrive in a Chinese society. It presents a shining ray of hope to the 1.3 billion Chinese people on the mainland."[40]

Reunification sentiment after a period of division, relates Prof. Harry Harding, has deep historical roots. In traditional times, the boundaries of the Chinese states were never static. The size of the empire shrank when the vitality of the central government declined. Peripheral territories became autonomous or independent. The Qing's last days provide an example of the process of territorial disintegration during a period of political decay. Thus by 1949, what had been a single Empire under the Qing had been divided into five separate entities, The People's Republic, the ROC on Taiwan, the Mongolian People's Republic, Hong Kong, and Macao. Since then both Communist and Nationalist governments have been committed to the reunification of China, but what should the boundaries be?[41]

Happily, the thread of common culture and economic interests among the Chinese states offers a genuine opportunity for political cooperation. As Samuel Huntington stressed in his seminal article "The Clash of Civilizations," with the Cold War over, "cultural commonalities increasingly overcome ideological differences, and Mainland China and Taiwan move closer together. If cultural commonality is a prerequisite for economic integration, the principal East Asian economic bloc of the future is likely to be centered in China."[42]

Both Chinese states should stress values integration. Formal political structures can evolve from closer cultural, commercial, and social links. Does Xi Jinping's vision of a "Chinese Dream" hold new options for the divided nation?

That China will eventually reunify is certain, but the formula remains an enigma. Confucian wisdom reveals the dilemma. The philosopher Mencius (372-289 BC), a disciple of Confucius wrote, "When a ruler was not governing in harmony with human feeling for others, Confucius condemned him and all who worked for him...If a ruler really oppresses the common people, he will be killed and the nation will be destroyed. If he oppresses them, but not so badly, he will live in constant danger, and the nation will get chipped away."

ENDNOTES

1. Rene Grousset, *The Rise and Splendor of the Chinese Empire*, (Berkeley, CA: University of California, 1970), 42-43.

2. Yat-sen Sun, *San Min Chu I*, Editor, L.T. Chen, Translation Frank W. Price, (Chungking: Ministry of Information/ROC, 1943), 5-6, and PRC Press/UN 16 February 1995, 7.

3. Author Interview, *Bureau of Foreign Trade*/Ministry of Economic Affairs, Taipei June 2011.

4. *The Development of International Trade in the Republic of China* (Taiwan) 2011, Bureau of Foreign Trade, Ministry of Economic Affairs/Taipei 2011, 11.

5. Economic Development ROC (Taiwan) Council for Economic Planning and Development/Executive Yuan, Taipei, ROC, 2010, 7.

6. Ibid, 38.

7. Richard M. Nixon, *Beyond Peace*, (New York: Random House, 1994), 134.

8. *Review of Maritime Transport 2009*, (Geneva: United Nations, 2009), 113.

9. Ibid, 53, 100.

10. *Christian Science Monitor*, 10 November 1992.

11. Harry Harding, "The Concept of Greater China: Themes, Variations and Reservations, " *The China Quarterly* no. 136, (December 1993), 661-666.

12. Wu-euh Chang, "ECFA's Effects on the Interplay between Taiwan's Political Parties and Cross-Straits Relations," *Prospects and Perspectives 2010*, (Taipei: Prospect Foundation, 2011), 53-54.

13. *Asia-Pacific Trade and Investment Report 2011*, (New York: United Nations, 2011), 47 and *International Trade Statistics Yearbook 2008* (New York: United Nations, 2009), 124.

14. PRC Press/UN 24 September 2008, 2-3.

15. Lance Gore, "Impact of the Market on the Grass Roots Organizations of the Chinese Communist Party, " *East Asian Policy* 3 (Jan/Mar 2011), 53, 62-63.

16. Ibid, 64-65.

17. *Nixon*, 12.

18. Nicholas Kristof, "The Rise of China, " *Foreign Affairs* 72 (November/December 1993), 71-72.

19. PRC Press/UN October 1979.

20. Frederick Chien, "A View from Taipei, " *Foreign Affairs* 70 (Winter 1991-1992), 93-103.

21. *Beijing Review* August 1995, 38, 12-13.

22. *Beijing Review* January 1994, 37, 10.

23. John J. Metzler, "Observer Status Reviewed: A Formula for the ROC to Rejoin the United Nations, " *Issues & Studies* 28 (May 1992), 73-74.

24. UNGA/191 9 August 1993, 1-2.

25. *Washington Times*, 20 December 1994.

26. John Copper, *Words Across the Taiwan Strait; A Critique of Beijing's "White Paper" on China's Reunification,* (Lanham, MD: University Press of America, 1995), 2.

27. PRC Press/UN 27 September 1995, 7-8 and PRC Press/UN 24 October 1995, 11.

28. Public Opinion on Cross Strait Relations/Mainland Affairs Council (MAC) Executive Yuan, Taipei, ROC, May 2011.

29. Frank Liu, "When Taiwan Identifiers Embrace the ROC: The Complexity of State

Identification in Taiwan," *Issues & Studies* 48 (June 2012), 6.

30. "Relations Across the Taiwan Straits/Abstract," Mainland Affairs Council (MAC) Taipei: Executive Yuan, ROC, 1994, 5-7.

31. "Steering Through a Sea of Change" Speech by President Ma Ying-jeou video conference with Center on Democracy, Development and the Rule of Law" Stanford University, California 16 April 2013, 3.

32. *The Diaoyutai Islands: An Inherent Part of the Republic of China (Taiwan),* (Taipei: Ministry of Foreign Affairs/ROC, 2012).

33. *East China Sea Peace Initiative,* (Taipei: Ministry of Foreign Affairs/ROC, 2012).

34. Milan Vego. "China's Naval Challenge," *Proceedings* U.S. Naval Institute April 2011, 37.

35. *SIPRI Yearbook 2012.* (London: Oxford University Press, 2012), 152.

36. "Navy Sails into New Era," *China Daily,* 26 September 2012, 1.

37. "Taiwan's Smart Strategy for Cross-Strait Relations, " Speech by Minister Philip Yang, Government Information Office, ROC, Asia Society/New York 12 July 2011, 8-9.

38. David Shambaugh, *China Goes Global: The Partial Power,* (New York: Oxford University Press, 2013), 9.

39. Author Interview/Dr. Chiang Pin-Kung, Chairman Straits Exchange Foundation, Taipei June 2011 and "Steering Through A Sea of Change," 4.

40. "Steering Through a Sea of Change," 9-10.

41. Harding, 677-678.

42. Samuel Huntington, "The Clash of Civilizations," *Foreign Affairs,* 72 (Summer 1993), 28.

ANNEX

The following tables reflect mutual links within the divided nations, in the *Political, Economic, Security and Social* sectors.

Yes* connotes a *de facto* but *unofficial* relationship; such as Taiwan's trade to Mainland China via Hong Kong

GERMANY

	1954	1974	1990
Political Basket			
Cross-Recognition	No	Yes	Yes
Permanent Representatives	No	Yes	Yes
High Level Contacts	No	Yes	Yes
United Nations Membership	No	Yes	Yes
Economic Basket			
Trade Ties	Yes	Yes	Yes
Cross Investments	No	No	Yes
Direct Transport	Flux	Yes	Yes
Bank Loans	No	No	Yes
Security Basket			
Foreign Defense Treaty	No	Yes	Yes
Foreign Troop Presence	Yes	Yes	Yes
Nuclear Weapons	No	No	No
Non Aggression Pact	Flux	Yes	Yes
Socio/Humanitarian Basket			
Telephone Ties	Flux	Yes	Yes
Postal Links	Yes	Yes	Yes
Monetary Convertibility	No	Yes*	Yes*
Family/Tourist Visits	Flux	Yes	Yes

KOREA

	1954	1974	2000	2012
Political Basket				
Cross-Recognition	No	No	Flux	Flux
Permanent Representatives	No	No	No	No
High Level Contacts	No	Yes*	Yes	Yes
United Nations Membership	No	No	Yes	Yes
Economic Basket				
Trade Ties	No	No	Yes*	Yes*
Cross Investments	No	No	Yes*	Yes*
Direct Transport	No	No	Flux	Flux
Bank Loans	No	No	Yes*	Yes*
Security Basket				
Foreign Defense Treaty	Yes	Yes	Yes	Yes
Foreign Troop Presence	Yes	Yes	Yes	Yes
Nuclear Weapons	No	No	Yes*^{DPRK}	Yes*^{DPRK}
Non Aggression Pact	No	No	Flux	Flux
Socio/Humanitarian Basket				
Telephone Ties	No	No	Yes*	Yes*
Postal Links	No	No	Yes*	Yes*
Monetary Convertibility	No	No	Yes*	Yes*
Family/Tourist Visits	No	No	Yes*	Yes*

Divided Dynamism

CHINA

	1954	1974	2000	2012
Political Basket				
Cross-Recognition	No	No	No	No
Permanent Representatives	No	No	No	No
High Level Contacts	No	No	Flux	Flux
United Nations Membership	Yes^{ROC}	Yes^{PRC}	Yes^{PRC}	Yes^{PRC}
Economic Basket				
Trade Ties	No	No	Yes*	Yes*
Cross Investments	No	No	Yes*	Yes*
Direct Transport	No	No	Flux	Yes*
Bank Loans	No	No	No	Flux
Security Basket				
Foreign Defense Treaty	Yes	Yes	No	No
Foreign Troop Presence	Yes	Yes	No	No
Nuclear Weapons	No	Yes^{PRC}	Yes^{PRC}	Yes^{PRC}
Non Aggression Pact	No	No	No	No
Socio/Humanitarian Basket				
Telephone Ties	No	No	Yes*	Yes*
Postal Links	No	Yes*	Yes*	Yes*
Monetary Convertibility	No	No	Yes*	Yes*
Family/Tourist Visits	No	No	Yes*	Yes*

BIBLIOGRAPHY

GERMANY

Government Documents & Official Sources

Basic Law of the Federal Republic of Germany. Bonn: Press and Information Office/BPA, 1981.

British and Foreign State Papers; 1943-1945, Vol. 145, London: Her Majesty's Stationary Office, 1953.

Charter of the United Nations and Statute of the International Court of Justice, New York: United Nations, 1991.

Constitutions of the GDR; 1949, 1968, 1974; Dresden: Staatsverlag der DDR.

Deutsche Entwicklungspolitik/Memorandum der Bundesregierung zur DAC/Jahresprufung 1991/1992. Bonn: 1991.

Dokumente zur Aussenpolitik der Deutschen Demokratische Republik. Berlin: Staatsverlag der DDR, annual 2 volume reports.

Documents on International Affairs. London: Royal Institute of International Affairs; Annual Series.

Foreign Affairs Bulletin, Berlin: GDR Ministry of Foreign Affairs.

Jahresbericht der Bundesregierung 1988. Bonn: Presse and Informationdienst der Bundesregierung, 1988.

Mandate for Democracy: Three Decades of the Federal Republic of Germany. Bonn: Press and Information Office/BPA, 1980.

Statisisches Bundesamt/DDR 1990 Zahlen and Fakten. Stuttgart:Metzler- Poeschel, 1990.

The Unity of Germany and Peace in Europe/FRG and GDR Monetary Treaty. Bonn: Press and Information Office/BPA, 1990.

U.S. Department of State, *Documents on Germany 1944-1985.* Washington D.C.: GPO, 1985.

————. *American Foreign Policy 1950-1955 Basic Documents*; Volume 2. Washington, D.C.: GPO, 1957.

U.S. Department of State Bulletin, Washington, D.C.

United Nations Development Programme/*Donor Profiles 1994.* New York.

United Nations. *General Assembly*/Official Records. New York.

————. *Security Council*/Official Records. New York.

Verfassung der Deutschen Demokratischen Republik/Dokumente. Berlin, Staatsverlag der DDR, 1969.

White Paper 1979/Security of the Federal Republic of Germany and the Development of the Federal Armed Forces. Bonn: Ministry of Defense, 1979.

White Paper/The German Democratic Republic: Member of the United Nations. Berlin: Ministry of Foreign Affairs, 1974.

Books

Adenauer, Konrad. *Memoirs 1945-53.* Translated by Beate Ruhm von Oppen. Chicago: Henry Regnery, 1966.

Applebaum, Anne. *Iron Curtain: The Crushing of Eastern Europe 1944-1956*. New York: Random House, 2012.

Ash, Timothy Garton. *In Europe's Name; Germany and the Divided Continent*. New York: Random House, 1993.

Blumenwitz, Dieter. *What is Germany? Exploring Germany's Status After World War II*. Bonn: Kulturstiftung Der Deutschen Vertribenen, 1989.

Brandt, Willy. *A Peace Policy for Europe*. New York: Holt, Rinehart, and Winston, 1969.

Campbell, Edwina S. *Germany's Past and Europe's Future: The Challenge of West German Foreign Policy*. New York: Pergamon-Brassey, 1989.

Childs, David. *The GDR; Moscow's German Ally*. London: Allen & Unwin, 1983.

Churchill, Winston. *Triumph and Tragedy*. Boston: Houghton Mifflin, 1953.

Dornberg, John. *The Other Germany:Europe's Emerging Nation Behind the Berlin Wall*. Garden City, NY: Doubleday, 1968.

Fischer, Peter. *Kirche and Christen in der DDR*. Berlin: Verlag Gebr Holzapfel, 1978.

Gann, L.H. and Peter Duignan. *Germany: Key to a Continent*. Stanford: Hoover Institute, 1992.

Grosser, Alfred. *Germany in Our Time: A Political History of the Postwar Years*. Translated by Paul Stevenson. New York: Praeger, 1971.

Haftendorn, Helga. *Coming of Age; German Foreign Policy Since 1945*. Lanham, MD: Rowman and Littlefield, 2006.

Hull, Cordell. *Memoirs of Cordell Hull*. New York: Macmillian, 1948.

Kaiser, Karl. *German Foreign Policy in Transition: Bonn Between East and West*. London: Oxford University Press, 1968.

Kempe, Frederick. *Berlin 1961*. New York: G.P. Putnam's Sons, 2011.

Kramer, Alan. *The West German Economy 1945-1955*. New York: Berg, 1991.

Lange, Thomas and Geoffrey Pugh. *The Economics of German Unification*. Cheltenham, UK and Northampton, MA, Edward Elgar, 1998.

Large, David Clay. *Munich 1972: Tragedy, Terror and Triumph at the Olympic Games*. Lanham, MD: Rowman and Littlefield, 2012.

Livingstone, Robert/Editor. *West German Political Parties: CDU, CSU, FDP, SPD, The Greens*. Washington D.C.: Johns Hopkins, 1986.

Maillard, Pierre. *De Gaulle et L'Allemagne; Le Reve Inacheve*. Paris: Plon, 1990.

Marks, Frederick W. *Power and Peace: The Diplomacy of John Foster Dulles*. Westport, CT: Praeger, 1993.

Mayer, Herbert. *German Recovery and the Marshall Plan*. Bonn: Editions Atlantic Forum, 1969.

Murphy, David and Sergei Kondrashev and George Bailey. *Battleground Berlin; CIA vs KGB in the Cold War*. New Haven: Yale University Press, 1997.

Nawrocki, Joachim. *Relations Between the Two States in Germany: Trends, Prospects and Limitations*. Bonn: Press and Information Office/BPA, 1988.

Schnitzer, Martin. *East and West Germany: A Comparative Economic Analysis*. New York: Praeger, 1972.

Smith, Jean Edward. *Germany Beyond the Wall: People, Politics, Prosperity*. Boston: Little Brown, 1967.

Smith, Eric Owen. *The German Economy*. London: Routeledge, 1994.

Stern, Fritz. *Five Germanys I Have Known*. New York: Farrar, Straus, Giroux, 2006.

Sybesma-Knol, R.G. *Status of Observers in the United Nations*. Brussels: Free University, 1981.

Thatcher, Margaret. *The Downing Street Years*. New York: Harper Collins, 1993.

Whetten, Lawrence. *Germany's Ostpolitik: Relations Between the Federal Republic and the Warsaw Pact Countries.* London: Oxford University Press, 1971.

Winkler, Heinrich August. *Germany The Long Road West 1933-1990, Vol. 2.* New York: Oxford University Press, 2007.

Zelikow, Philip and Condoleezza Rice. *Germany Unified and Europe Transformed; A Study in Statecraft.* Cambridge: Harvard University Press, 1995.

Journals

Ash, Timothy Garton. "Germany's Choice." *Foreign Affairs* 73 (July/August 1994): 65-81.

Asmus, Ronald. "The GDR and the German Nation; Sole Heir or Socialist Sibling?" *International Affairs* 60 (Summer 1984): 403-418.

Blackwill, Robert D. "German Unification and American Diplomacy." *Aussenpolitik* 45 (3/1994): 211-225.

Dean, Jonathan. "Directions in Inner-German Relations." *Orbis* 29 (Fall 1985): 609-632.

Duisberg, Claus J. "Germany: The Russians Go." *The World Today* 50 (October 1994): 190-193.

Eisel, Stephen. "The Politics of a United Germany." *Daedalus* 123 (Winter 1994): 149-171.

Hacke, Christian. "The National Interests of the Federal Republic of Germany on the Threshold of the 21st Century." Aussenpolitik 49 (2/1998):5-25.

Hahn, Walter. "NATO and Germany." *Global Affairs* 5 (Winter 1990): 1-18.

Heilbrunn, Jacob. "Tomorrow's Germany." *The National Interest* no. 36 (Summer 1994): 44-52.

Heineck, Guido and Bernd Sussmuth. "A Different Look at Lenin's Legacy: Trust, Risk, Fairness and Cooperativeness in the Two Germanies." CESifo Working Paper No. 3199, September 2010.

Horn, Hannelore. "The Revolution in the GDR in 1989; Prototype or Special Case?" *Aussenpolitik* 44 (1/1993):56-66.

Joffe, Josef. "The New Europe: Yesterday's Ghosts." *Foreign Affairs* 72 (1992-1993): 29-43.

Kaiser, Karl. "Forty Years of German Membership in NATO." *NATO Review* 43 (July 1995): 3-8.

Kinkel, Klaus. "Peacekeeping Missions: Germany Can Now Play Its Part." *NATO Review* 42 (October 1994): 3-7.

Koch, Burkhard. "Post-Totalitarianism in Eastern Germany and German Democracy." *World Affairs* 156 (Summer 1993): 26-29.

Kohl, Helmut. "German Security Policy on the Threshold of the 21st Century." *Aussenpolitik* 49 (1/1998): 5-11.

Konrad Adenauer Foundation. Policy Series. Bonn and Washington D.C.

Kracht, Tiemo. "German Unification Policies Since 1949: Implications for China." *Issues & Studies* 27 (December 1991): 29-59.

Le Gloannec, Anne-Marie. "On German Identity." *Daedalus* 123 (Winter 1994): 129-148.

Longhurst, Kerry and John Roper. "Forward March." *The World Today.* 56 (October 2000): 23-25.

Mardek, Helmut and Renate Wunsche. "Die Beziehungen der DDR mit der Nationalen Befreiungsbewegung und den Staaten Asiens, Afrikas und Latinamerikas." *Deutsche Aussenpolitik* 24 (May 1979): 54-69.

Metzler, John J. "East Germany's Lutheryear." *Freedom at Issue* no. 77 (March/April 1984): 7-8.

Meissner, Boris. "The GDR's Position in the Soviet Alliance System." *Aussenpolitik* 35 (4/1984): 369-389.

Naimark, Norman. "Is It True What They are Saying About East Germany?" *Orbis* 23 (Fall 1979): 549-577.

Schmidt, Helmut. "Germany in the Era of Negotiations." *Foreign Affairs* 49 (October 1970): 40-50.

———. "Deutschlands Rolle im Neuen Europa. » *Europa Archiv* 46 (November 1991): 611-624.

Schulte, Heinz. "The End of the East German People's Army." *Jane's Soviet Intelligence Review* 2 (October 1990): 459-460.

———. "What Happened to the East German Armed Forces?" *Jane's Soviet Intelligence Review* 4 (April 1992): 185-187.

Sebastian, Hendrik. "Aid Under the Banner of Ideology: Development Policy in East Germany." *Development + Cooperation* (3/1990): 7-8.

Shultz, Siegfried. "Trends and Issues of German Aid Policy." *Konjunkturpolitik* 35 (1989): 361-382.

———. Characteristics of East Germany's, Third World Policy: Aid and Trade. *Konjunkturpolitik* 36 (1990): 309-328.

Stern, Fritz. "Freedom and Its Discontents." *Foreign Affairs* 72 (September/October 1993): 108-125.

Trappen, Friedel and Ulrich Weishaupt. "Aktuelle Fragen des Kampfes um Nationale und Soziale Befreiung im Subsaharischen Afrika." *Deutsche Aussenpolitik* 24 (February 1979): 27-39.

von Plate, Bernard. "Scope and Interest in the GDR's Foreign Policy." *Aussenpolitik* 37 (2/1986): 149-162.

Windelen, Heinrich. "The Two States in Germany." *Aussenpolitik* 35 (3/1984): 227-241.

Newspapers & Periodicals

Die Welt (Berlin)

The Economist (London)

Frankfurter Allegemeine Zeitung (FAZ) (Frankfurt)

Le Figaro (Paris)

NATO Review (Brussels)

The New York Times (New York)

The Week in Germany, Germany-Info.org, German Information Center (New York)

Press Releases and Speech transcripts of the GDR and FRG Missions to the United Nations/New York

KOREA

Government Documents & Official Sources

CIA Cold War Records/The CIA Under Harry Truman. Michael Warner, Editor. Washington, D.C.: Central Intelligence Agency, 1994.

Constitutions of the Republic of Korea 1948, 1987; Korea Overseas Information Service, Seoul.

Economic and Social Survey of Asia and the Pacific 2011. (Bangkok: United Nations, 2011).

Handbook of Korea: 1990. Korean Overseas Information Service, Seoul 1990.

Handbook on North Korea. Seoul: Naewoe Press, 1998.

International Monetary Fund Regional Economic Outlook: Asia/Pacific 2013. (Washington, DC: IMF 2013).

International Trade Statistics Yearbook 2008, Vol 1. New York: United Nations, 2009.

Korea: A Nation Transformed, Selected Speeches of President Roh Tae Woo. Seoul: The Presidential Secretariat, 1990.

Korean Economy, 2001. Korean Economic Institute in America/Washington D.C. 2001.

Korean Peninsula Energy Development Organization; KEDO at Five. New York: KEDO, 1999-2000.

The Korean Peninsula in the 21st Century; Prospects for Stability and Cooperation.
Korean Economic Institute in America/Washington D.C. 2001.

Treaties, Conventions, Etc. Between China and Foreign States, Vol. II Second Edition. Shanghai: Inspector General of Customs, 1917.

United Nations/Development Programme, *Human Development Report:* 2013. New York: Oxford University Press, 2013.

————. *Bulletin*

————. *General Assembly,* Official Records

————. *Security Council,* Official Records

U.S. Department of State, *Korea's Independence,* Far East Series no.18, Washington D.C., 1947.

————. *The Record on Korean Unification 1943-60,* Narrative Summary, Far East Series no.101 Washington D.C. 1960.

————. *Bulletin,* Washington D.C.

World Bank. *Trends in Developing Economies: 1993.* Washington D.C.: The World Bank, 1993.

————. *World Development Indicators 2000.* Washington D.C.: The World Bank, 2000.

Books

Allen, Richard C. *Korea's Syngman Rhee: An Unauthorized Portrait.* Rutland, VT: Tuttle, 1960.

Breen, Michael. *Kim Jong-il: North Korea's Dear Leader/Revised.* Singapore: John Wiley & Sons, 2012.

Chung, Chin. *Pyongyang Between Peking and Moscow: North Korea's Involvement in the Sino/Soviet Dispute 1958-75.* University: University of Alabama Press, 1978.

Cummings, Bruce. Korea's Place in the Sun; A Modern History. New York: Norton 1998.

Gibney, Frank. *Korea's Quiet Revolution: From Garrison State to Democracy.* New York: Walker and Company, 1992.

Hull, Cordell. *Memoirs of Cordell Hull*, New York: Macmillian, 1948.

Heo, Uk and Terence Roehrig. *South Korea Since 1980*. New York: Cambridge University Press, 2010.

Kawai, Tatsuo. *The Goal of Japanese Expansion*. Tokyo: Hokuseido Press, 1938.

Kim, Hak-Joon. *The Unification Policy of South and North Korea, A Comparative Study*. Seoul: Seoul National University Press, 1977.

Kim, Il Sung. *For the Independent Peaceful Reunification of Korea*. New York: International Publishers, 1975.

Koo, Bon Hak. *Political Economy of Self-Reliance: Juche and Economic Development in North Korea, 1961-1990*. Seoul: Research Center for Peace and Unification, 1992.

Korea's Future; Vision and Strategy, Korea's Ambition to Become an Advanced Power by 2030. Seoul: Seoul Selection, 2008.

Lankov, Andrei. *The Real North Korea: Life and Politics in the Failed Stalinist Utopia*. (New York: Oxford University Press, 2013).

Moynihan, Daniel P. *A Dangerous Place*. Boston: Little, Brown and Company, 1978.

Myers, B.R. *The Cleanest Race; How North Koreans See Themselves, and Why it Matters*. Brooklyn, NY: Melville House, 2011.

Nam, Koon Woo. *The North Korean Communist Leadership 1945-1965; A Study of Factionalism and Political Consolidation*. University: University of Alabama Press, 1974.

MacDonald, Donald. *The Koreans: Contemporary Politics and Society*. Boulder, Co: Westview, 1990.

Mc Glothlen, Ronald. *Controlling the Waves: Dean Acheson and U.S. Foreign Policy in Asia*. New York: Norton, 1993.

Morgenthau, Hans J. *Politics Among Nations; The Struggle for Power and Peace*. New York: McGraw Hill, 1993.

Park, Chung Hee. *Korea Reborn: A Model for Development*. Englewood Cliffs, NJ: Prentice Hall, 1979.

Simons, William B./Editor. *The Constitutions of the Communist World*. Alphen an den Rijn: Sijthoff & Noordhoff, 1980.

Un, Lim. *The Founding of a Dynasty in North Korea; An Authentic Biography of Kim Il Sung*. Tokyo: Jiyu-sha Press, 1982.

Zoellick, Robert and Philip Zelikow/Editors. *America and the East Asian Crisis: Memos to a President*. New York: Norton, 2000.

Journals

Ahn, Byung-joon. "The Man Who Would Be Kim." *Foreign Affairs* 73 (November/December 1994): 94-108.

Brown, William. "Engaging and Transforming North Korea's Economy." *Joint U.S.–Korea Academic Studies*, 21, 2011: 133-148.

Chaigneau, Pascal and Richard Sola. « La France face a la Subversion Nord-Coreenne en Afrique. » *Defense Nationale* 43 (January 1987): 111-134.

Chung, Joseph S. "North Korea's Economic Development and Capabilities." *Asian Perspective* 11 (Spring/Summer 1987):45-73.

Eberstadt, Nicholas. "Can the Two Koreas Be One?" *Foreign Affairs* 72 (Winter 1992-93): 150-165.

Hwang, Eni Gak. "Inter-Korean Economic Cooperation Under Different Systems: Its Restrictions and Required Measures." *East Asian Review* 5 (Spring 1993): 64-77.

Kang, Du-yong, Lee Sang-ho and Hwang Sun-oong. "Korea's Post-Crisis Economic Reliance on China and Policy Sugestions." *Korea Focus* 19 (Spring 2011): 106-115.

Kim, Geydong. "South Korea's Nordpolitik and Its Impact on Inter-Korean Relations." *East Asian Review* 4 (Spring 1992): 45-70.

Kim, Hong Nack. "The Koreas: In Search of Reunification." *Current History* 91 (December 1992):430-435.

Kim, Seung-young. "Russo-Japanese Rivalry Over Korean Buffer at the Beginning of the 20th Century and Its Implications." Diplomacy and Statecraft 16 (December 2005), 619-650.

Kim, Sungwoo. "Recent Economic Policies of North Korea." *Asian Survey* 33 (September 1993): 864-878.

Lee, Hy Sang. "North Korea's Closed Economy." *Asian Survey* 28 (December 1988): 1264-1279.

Lee, Junkyu. "Korea's Trade Structure and Its Policy Challenges." *Korea's Economy 2012*, 28, 2012: 21-28.

Lee, Kye-woo. "Aid by Korea: Progress and Challenges." *Korea's Economy 2012*, 28, 2012:45-57. ;

Metzler, John J. "The China Connection and North Korea's Emergence from Isolation." *The American Asian Review* 3 (Winter 1985): 114-132.

————. "Korean Diplomacy." *Global Affairs* 5 (Winter 1990): 130-143.

Natsios, Andrew. "The Politics of Famine in North Korea." *United States Institute of Peace/Special Report* (August 1999): 1-16.

"The Secret Success of U.S. aid to South Korea," *Korea's Economy 2012*, 28: 43-45.

Noland, Marcus. "The Current State of the North Korean Economy." *Korea's Economy 2012*, 28, 2012: 103-109.

Paik, Keun-wook. "Energy Cooperation on the Korean Peninsula." *The World Today* 57 (February 2001): 22-24.

Rhee, Kang-suk. "Korea's Unification--The Applicability of the German Experience." *Asian Survey* 33 (April 1993):360-375.

Rozman, Gilbert. "South Korea's National Identity Sensitivity: Evolution, Manifestations, Prospects." *Academic Paper Series on Korea* 3, 2010: 67-80.

Shinn, Chang-min. "Korean Reunification: Costs, Gains and Taxes." *Korea Focus* 19 (Spring 2011): 82-89.

Yoon, Kikwan. "Review of the Prospects for Inter-Korean Economic Exchange." *East Asian Review* 4 (Spring 1992): 71-98.

Newspapers & Periodicals

Far Eastern Economic Review (Hong Kong)
Korea Society Quarterly (New York)
Korea Times (Seoul)
New Times (Moscow)
The New York Times (New York)
North Korea News (Seoul)
People's Korea (Tokyo)
Pyongyang Times (Pyongyang)
Vantage Point (Seoul)
Press Releases and Policy Statements of the ROK and DPRK
Observer Missions and later Permanent Missions to the United Nations/New York

CHINA

Government Documents & Official Sources

Constitutions of the People's Republic of China: 1954, 1978, 1982. Peking: Foreign Languages Press.

Economic Development ROC (Taiwan). Council for Economic Planning and Development/Executive Yuan, Taipei: Council for Economic Planning, 2010.

Development of International Trade in the Republic of China (Taiwan). 2010-2011. Taipei: Ministry of Economic Affairs, 2011.

Green, Marshall. *U.S. China Policy and the East Asian Community*. U.S. Department of State Bulletin, 22 May 1972.

Liu, Shao-chi. *Report on the Draft Constitution of the People's Republic of China/Constitution of the People's Republic of China.* Peking: Foreign Languages Press, 1954.

Ma Ying-jeou, *Steering through a Sea of Change*. Center on Democracy, Development, and the Rule of Law, Stanford University (video conference) 16 April 2013.

Oppose U.S. Occupation of Taiwan and "Two Chinas" Plot. Peking: Foreign Languages Press, 1958.

Parsons, J. Graham. *The American Role in Pacific Asian Affairs*. U.S. Department of State. Washington D.C.:GPO, 1960.

Relations Across the Taiwan Straits/Abstract, Mainland Affairs Council Taipei: Executive Yuan, 1994.

Republic of China Yearbook 1977, 1994, 1999. Taipei: China Publishing.

Rusk, Dean Rusk. *U.S. Policy Towards Communist China*. U.S. Department of State. Washington D.C.: GPO, 1966.

Sino-British Joint Declaration on the Question of Hong Kong. Beijing: Foreign Languages Press, 1984.

Stoessel, Walter J. *Foreign Policy Priorities in* Asia. U.S. Department of State, Current Policy Series no.274, April 1981.

United Nations *Bulletin*.

————. Asia-Pacific Trade and Investment Report 2011. New York: United Nations, 2011.

————. Development Programme, *Human Development Report*: 2013. New York: Oxford University Press, 2013.

————. *Foreign Direct Investment in the People's Republic of China*. New York: Transnational Centre, United Nations, 1988.

————. *General Assembly*; Official Documents

————. Review of Maritime Transport; 2009. New York: United Nations, 2009.

————. *Security Council*; Official Documents

U.S. Department of State, *American Foreign Policy 1950-1955: Basic Documents*. Washington D.C.: GPO, 1957.

————. *Far Eastern Series*: Speeches, Pamphlets and Updates, 1950's and 1960's. Washington D.C.

————. *Bulletin*, Washington D.C.

————. *In Quest of Peace and Security: Selected Documents on American* Foreign *Policy 1941-1951.* Washington D.C.: GPO, 1951.

————. *Memorandums, Telegrams and Correspondence*, Formosa File 1950's/National Archives, Washington D.C.

White Paper The Republic of China on Taiwan and the United Nations. Taipei: Ministry of Foreign Affairs, 1995.

Yu Tzong-shian. *The Story of Taiwan/Economy.* Taipei: Government Information Office, 1998.

Books

Bush, Richard C. *Uncharted Strait: The Future of China-Taiwan Relations.* Washington, DC: Brookings Institution Press, 2013.

Chai, Winberg/Editor. *The Foreign Relations of the People's Republic of China.* New York: G.P. Putnam, 1972.

China-United States Exchange Foundation. *U.S.-China Economic Relations in the Next Ten Years; Towards Deeper Engagement and Mutual Benefit.* Hong Kong: China United States Exchange Foundation, 2013.

Copper, John F. *Words Across the Taiwan Strait: A Critique of Beijing's "White Paper" on China's Reunification.* Lanham: University Press of America, 1995.

Frantz, Uli. *Deng Xiaoping.* New York: Harcourt, Brace, Jovanovich, 1988.

Gregor, James A. *Arming the Dragon: U.S. Security Ties with the People's Republic of China.* Washington D.C.: Ethics and Public Policy Center, 1987.

————. The China Connection: U.S. Policy and the People's Republic of China. Stanford: Hoover Institution, 1986.

Grousset, Rene. *The Rise and Splendor of the Chinese Empire.* Berkley, CA: University of California, 1970.

Johnson, U. Alexis. *The Right Hand of Power: Memoirs of an American Diplomat.* Englewood Cliffs, NJ: Prentice Hall, 1984.

Kissinger, Henry. *Diplomacy.* New York: Simon & Schuster, 1994.

Kuo, Shirley, Gustav Ranis, John C.H. Fei/Editors. *The Taiwan Success Story: Rapid Growth with Improved Distribution in the ROC 1952-1979.* Boulder, CO: Westview, 1981.

Larkin, Bruce D. *China and Africa 1949-1970; The Foreign Policy of the People's Republic of China.* Berkley: University of California Press, 1971.

Leys, Simon. *Chinese Shadows.* New York: Viking Press, 1977.

Li, K.T. *Economic Transformation of Taiwan, ROC.* London: Shepheard-Walwyn, 1988.

Mansfield, Mike. *Charting a New Course/Mike Mansfield and U.S. Asian Policy.* Rutland, VT: Tuttle, 1978.

Marks, Frederick W. *Wind Over Sand: The Diplomacy of Franklin Roosevelt.* Athens, GA: University of Georgia Press, 1988.

McGregor, Richard. *The Party; The Secret World of China's Communist Rulers.* New York: Harper/Perennial, 2012.

Mosher, Steven W. *China Misperceived: American Illusions and Chinese Reality.* New York: Basic Books, 1990.

Murphy, Robert. *Diplomat Among Warriors.* Garden City, NY: Doubleday, 1964.

Myers, Ramon H./Editor. *Two Societies in Opposition; The Republic of China and the People's Republic of China After Forty Years.* Stanford: Hoover Institution, 1991.

Nixon, Richard. *Beyond Peace.* New York: Random House, 1994.

Patten, Christopher. *East and West; China, Power, and the Future of Asia.* New York: Times Books, 1998.

Peyrefitte, Alain. *La Tragedie Chinoise.* Paris: Fayard, 1990.

Reischauer, Edwin. *Japan: The Story of a Nation.* New York: McGraw Hill, 1990.

Shambaugh, David. *China Goes Global: The Partial Power*. New York: Oxford University Press, 2013.

Spence, Jonathan. *The Search for Modern China*. New York: W.W. Norton, 1990.

Sun, Yat-sen. *San Min Chu I*. Editor, L.T. Chen. Translation Frank W. Price. Chungking: Ministry of Information/ROC, 1943.

The Military Balance 2012. London: International Institute for Strategic Studies, 2012.

Tucker, Nancy Bernkopf, Editor. *China Confidential: American Diplomats and Sino-American Relations, 1945-1996*. New York: Columbia University Press, 2000.

Wei, Lin and Arnold Chao/Editors. *China's Economic Reforms*. Philadelphia: University of Pennsylvania Press, 1982.

Weinstein, Warren and Thomas Henriksen/Editors. *Soviet and Chinese Aid to African Nations*. New York: Praeger, 1980.

Woodruff, John. *China in Search of Its Future: Reform vs. Repression 1982-1989*. New York: Lyle Stuart, 1990.

Young, Kenneth. *Negotiating with the Chinese Communists; The American Experience 1953-1967*. New York: McGraw Hill, 1968.

Zhan, Jun. *Ending the Chinese Civil War; Power, Commerce and Conciliation Between Beijing and Taipei*. New York: St. Martin's Press, 1993.

Journals

Chang, John. "Current Political Developments in the Republic of China and Its Relations with Mainland China," Lecture, 29 June 1993, Asian Center/ St. John's University, New York.

Chang, Maria Hsia. "Taiwan's Mainland Policy and the Reunification of China." Asian Studies Center/The Claremont Institute, Claremont, CA, 1990, 8-11.

Chao, Linda and Ramon H. Myers. "The Divided China Problem; Conflict Avoidance and Resolution." Hoover Institution/Essays in Public Policy, Stanford University, 2000, 47-50.

Chen, Qimao. "The Taiwan Issue and Sino-U.S. Relations." *Asian Survey* 27 (November 1987): 1161-1175.

———. "New Approaches in China's Foreign Policy." *Asian Survey* 33 (March 1993): 237-251.

Chien, Frederick. "A View From Taipei." *Foreign Affairs* 70 (Winter 1991-92): 93-103.

Copper, John F. "Taiwan's Diplomatic Isolation: How Serious a Problem?" *The Journal of East Asian Affairs* 6 (Winter/Spring 1992):202-215.

Gore. Lance LP. "Impact of the Market on the Gras-Roots Organizations of the Chinese Communist Party." *East Asian Policy* 3 (Jan-Mar 2011): 52-65.

Gregory, Neil and Stoyan Tenev. "The Financing of Private Enterprise in China." *Finance and Development/IMF* 38 (March 2001):14-17.

Harding, Harry. "The Concept of Greater China: Themes, Variations, and Reservations." *The China Quarterly* no. 136 (December 1993): 660-686.

Kao, Charng. "A Greater China Economic Sphere: Reality and Prospects." *Issues & Studies* 28 (November 1992): 49-64.

Kristof, Nicholas. "The Rise of China." *Foreign Affairs* 72 (November/December 1993): 59-74.

Li, K.T. "Sources of Rapid Economic Growth: The Case of Taiwan." *Journal of Economic Growth* 3 (Summer 1989):4-13.

Lin, Chong Pin. "Beijing and Taipei: Dialectics in Post Tiananmen Interaction." *The China Quarterly*, no. 136,(December 1993):770-804.

Liu, Frank C.S. "When Taiwan Identifiers Embrace the ROC: The Complexity of State Identification in Taiwan." *Issues & Studies* 48 (June 2012): 1-34.

Loh, Ping-cheung. "Development Assistance and the International Cooperation an Development Fund." Lecture, 6 September 2000, Asian Center/St. John's University, New York.

London, Miriam. "China: The Romance of *Realpolitik*." *Freedom at Issue* no. 110 (September/October 1989): 9-13.

Metzler, John J. "Observer Status Reviewed: A Formula for the ROC to Rejoin the United Nations." *Issues & Studies* 28 (May 1992):73-87.

Myers, Ramon H. "China's Economic Revolution and Its Implications for Sino-U.S. Relations." Hoover Institution/Essays in Public Policy, Stanford University, 1995, 1-15.

Pan, Stephen. "Legal Aspects of the Yalta Agreement." *American Journal of International Law* 46 (January 1952): 40-59.

Shambaugh, David. "Deng Xiaoping: The Politician," *China Quarterly* Vol. 135, (September 1993): 457-490.

Tung, Ricky. "Economic Integration Between Taiwan and South China's Fukian and Kwangtung Provinces." *Issues & Studies* 29 (July 1993): 26-42.

Vego, Milan. "China's Naval Challenge." *Proceedings* U.S. Naval Institute April 2011.

Wong, John. "China's Economy 2010: Continuing Strong Growth, with Possible Soft Landing for 2011." *East Asian Policy* 3 (January/March 2011): 13-26.

Wu, Harry. "China's Gulag: Suppressing Dissent Through the Laogai." *Harvard International Review* 20 (Winter 1997/98): 20-23.

Zhang, Jialin. "China's Response to the Downfall of Communism in Eastern Europe and the Soviet Union." Hoover Institution/Essays in Public Policy, Stanford University, 1994, 1-26.

Zhang, Junjie. "Delivering Environmentally Sustainable Economic Growth: The Case of China." Asia Society/New York September 2012.

Zheng Yongnian, Lye Liang Fook and Chen Gang. "China's Foreign Policy in an Eventful 2010: Facing Multiple Challenges in a Deteriorating External Environment." *East Asia Policy* 3 (Jan-Mar 2011): 27-36.

Newspapers & Periodicals

Asian Wall Street Journal Weekly (Hong Kong/New York)
China Daily (Beijing)
China Post/International Edition (Taipei)
Far Eastern Economic Review (Hong Kong)
Free China Journal/Taipei Journal (Taipei)
Free China Review /Taipei Review (Taipei)
Freedom at Issue (New York)
International Monetary Fund (IMF) Survey (Washington D.C.)
Le Monde (Paris)
Peking/Beijing Review (Peking)
PRC Press Releases at the United Nations/New York
South China Morning Post (Hong Kong)

INDEX

About the Author

The author teaches International Relations and East Asian comparative government at St. John's University in New York.

Professor Metzler was has written over twenty-five academic articles focused on Far Eastern political and security issues as well as United Nations matters related to Asia.

In parallel to his academic career, John Metzler is likewise a longtime United Nations Correspondent writing a syndicated column on diplomatic, defense, and developmental issues. Covering the U.N. since 1978, he has regularly reported on Security Council meetings, General Assembly proceedings, and often interviews Premiers and Foreign Ministers.

He regularly visits Europe and East Asia for editorial research projects and national elections. He has reported from fifty-five countries.

The author's degrees are in Government/International Relations (BA) and East Asian History/Economics (MA), with additional study in the Far East.